Giuliano Bugialli's
Foods of
ITALY

PHOTOGRAPHS BY JOHN DOMINIS

Giuliano Bugialli's Foods c

Stewart, Tabori, & Chang
PUBLISHERS, NEW YORK

TALY

In memory of my father

Frontispiece: Giuliano Bugialli's Kitchen in Florence.
  (© P. Sclarandis/Black Star)
This page: Succulent peaches, green and purple
  figs, and the yellow squash of Mantua.

Library of Congress Cataloging in Publication Data
Bugialli, Giuliano.
  Giuliano Bugialli's Foods of Italy.
  Includes index.
  1. Cookery, Italian. 2. Diet...Italy. 3. Food.
I. Title. II. Foods of Italy.
TX723.B765   1984   641.5945   84-2543
ISBN 0-941434-52-4 (hardcover)
ISBN 1-55670-370-8 (paperback)

Published and distributed in the United States
by Stewart, Tabori & Chang, 575 Broadway,
New York, New York 10012.

Distributed in the English language elsewhere in the world
(except Canada and Central and South America) by Melia
Publishing Services, P.O. Box 1639, Maidenhead, Berkshire.
SL6 6YZ England.
Canadian and Central and South American accounts
should contact Sales Manager, Stewart, Tabori & Chang.

DESIGNED BY NAI CHANG
Printed and bound in Japan
9HBMC/1P94

Contents

Pere ripiene al cioccolato
(Pears Stuffed with Cream and Chocolate).

List of Recipes

Preface

Top: Serving bresaola *by the shore of Lake Como.*
Center: Selecting fresh produce at the market in Florence.
Bottom: Sniffing the aroma of a lemon. (©P. Sclarandis/
Black Star)

*T*he food of Italy is certainly among the most visually striking in the world, and its appeal is most direct when seen against its own background and landscape. Dishes seem to reflect the sea and sky, the countryside and cityscape, the whole Italian way of looking at things. This is an elusive magic and something I have long wished to capture in a book.

Bringing this dream to life has been a rewarding collaborative effort. For months, photographer John Dominis and I, along with a crew of dedicated assistants, traveled through the different regions of Italy, not only tasting and photographing the food, but breathing in the special atmosphere of this rich and varied peninsula.

In the course of our travels, we had many warm and amusing experiences as we struggled to overcome Italian restrictions against setting up equipment for taking photographs in public places. Yet, in each case, we managed to triumph over bureaucratic rules because of the friendliness and interest of local officials. But while officials could intercede and make locations and architectural treasures available to us, they could offer little help when it came to persuading the local people to break with tradition. Once, while we were attempting to photograph a young woman in the very traditional South, a high window shutter opened as if on cue, and the woman's mother and fiancé waved "no" in unison. There was nothing to be done. We had considerably more luck photographing the little *mugellesi* hens near Florence.

Foods of Italy emphasizes those traditional dishes that embody the feeling and aesthetics of the regions of Italy through which we traveled. And these dishes are all shown in their own ambience. In selecting these recipes, and in presenting the finished dishes where they originated, I have tried to capture a balance between the natural and the sophisticated, a balance Italians have struggled to preserve over the centuries.

Such a book cannot help but have a personal feeling. As I traveled through Italy in the course of working on this project, I was flooded with memories of growing up in Italy, specifically in Tuscany. I was struck by how much of the Italian tradition—food preparations, dining habits—has disappeared; this realization has reinforced my determination to fix some of the color, charm, and beauty of Italy's cuisine on the printed page.

After researching the dishes—often in very old cookbooks—I tested and retested them in their original locale with the guardians of each local tradition. I then tested the recipes in New York and made any necessary substitutions so that each dish could be reproduced as authentically as possible outside of Italy. I have prefaced each recipe with a brief note about the history or folklore of the dish, appropriate accompaniments, and classic presentation.

I hope that this book will inspire you to recreate authentic Italian dishes, and even more, that it will encourage you to taste these dishes in their own Italian settings.

Top: Choosing ingredients in Florence. (©P. Sclarandis Black Star) Center: Picking an armful of broom flowers. Bottom: Preparing the dishes for an al fresco *meal in the Sienese countryside.*

Vegetables

V

egetables, even more than pasta, are the cornerstone of Italian cooking. They appear as appetizers, in soups, and mixed with pasta; as elaborate main dishes and *piatti di mezzo*, or in-between courses; as accompaniments to meat, poultry, and fish. In Italian cooking vegetables are always treated with respect and served on their own separate plate.

In summer, many Italians live almost entirely on fresh vegetables, prepared in a variety of ways, but usually in the simplest way possible to retain their flavor, shape, and texture. In fact, one summer day, while I was searching through the ancient town of Cremona and its countryside for the special regional dishes of the area, such as the stuffed pasta *Marubini* or the *Budino* made with slices of veal and *prosciutto*, all the local people I asked told me that one couldn't find Cremona's characteristic dishes at that time of year because of the Italian's passion for fresh vegetables in season.

Many of the vegetables popular in Italian cooking today were developed in Italy centuries ago and exported all over the world. Both broccoli and cauliflower were developed from the cabbage and were eventually adopted as far away as China. The artichoke probably originated wild in Sicily, made its way to Florence, and then traveled to France via the gastronomically ubiquitous Caterina de' Medici. The traffic seems to have been both ways, however; carrots reached Italy from Afghanistan, and spinach came from Persia.

The colonization of the Americas was a boon to Mediterranean cooking unprecedented since Roman times. All capsicum family peppers, both sweet and hot, most common beans and squash, corn and cornmeal, tomatoes, and many other basics of

Preceding overleaf: Shoppers select produce inside the huge iron-and-glass San Lorenzo market in Florence, where today's menus are determined by the quality and abundance of Tuscany's fruits and vegetables.

Opposite: On the steps of the Rialto wholesale market, a Venetian shop-keeper loads purchases onto his boat.

Below: Young, tender string beans, long zucchini, delicate zucchini blossoms, and fresh porcini *mushrooms on proud display in the Florence market.*

Italian cooking arrived from the Americas in the sixteenth century—fortunately a period of great curiosity and inventiveness in cooking in Italy. This was also the period of greatest Italian influence on the cooking of other European countries. The notable exception was in the area of vegetable cookery, as many vegetables could not be as easily grown in northern Europe. In addition, some other countries with great courts and culinary traditions did not place vegetables in the important position that the Mediterranean countries did. Perhaps this is changing in our own time, with the emphasis on freshness and healthfulness in food. Italy has not adopted the Japanese and Chinese practice of cooking vegetables as briefly as possible as have other Western countries, primarily because its own cooking times, until recently the briefest in European cuisine, are traditional in relation to the *cucina* as a whole. In Italy vegetables are fully cooked, but they retain their shape and all their flavor.

OLIVES AND THE OILS OF ITALY

Sunflowers are the main ingredient in the best mixed-seed vegetable oil, *olio di semi,* used in Italy for cooking and frying when the dish does not require the taste of olive oil, butter, or lard; cooking with it leaves no aftertaste. This light oil is basic to present-day Italian *cucina.*

The sunflower seeds from which oil is extracted are the same ones that are so often eaten roasted. Until recently in Italy, you could buy a piece of a huge sunflower in the market if you wished to roast the seeds yourself, or you could buy the seeds from carts on the street corners where they were roasted in the open and sold, salted, in paper cones. Today they are sold, already roasted, in shops.

The oil used when flavor is most important is olive oil. In addition to its many uses in cooking, even more often it is added uncooked to salads and to many cooked dishes just before serving.

Olio santo! Sacred oil. Olive oil itself was sacred to the Etruscans and to the Romans who succeeded them. It was not only food, but a healing balm for illness, the chief fuel to light the lamps of homes and of the temples of the gods, and a restorer of youth for the old; it was also used to massage and soothe the bodies of the athletes before and after their games.

The tradition of the sacred oil is now far from its origins, but the name is retained—a half-remembered echo of ancient times—for a simple and wonderful preparation of the Tuscan farms. The oil, made very spicy by the addition of whole hot red peppers, is most often seen floating as a large drop in a bowl of clear broth. In ancient times, spicy recipes probably used only this hot oil (much like the hot oil that the Chinese still use) rather than the dried hot red pepper flakes that we use today.

Olio santo exists under other names in southern Italy, where traditionally it is added at the last moment to sauced pasta. (It is never used this way in central Italy.)

Three jars of first-pressing Tuscan virgin olive oil, each taken from a different grove, showing varying shades of green. A drop of Olio santo *is being ladled into the bowl of broth.*

Olio santo
"HOLY" OIL

2	cups olive oil	5	whole dried small hot red peppers
15	fresh basil leaves		

Pour the olive oil into a mason jar. Add the whole basil leaves and the peppers. Close the jar tightly and let the oil sit in a dark place for 15 days before using it.

MAKES 2 CUPS.

*A*n average family-sized olive vineyard in which the olives are grown and pressed using the old artisan method is usually restricted to a single hill. Because the position on the hill and the sunlight varies from hill to hill, the olives of one vineyard may be more mature than those of another when all the fruit are pressed to produce the oil in December or January. The hills that receive stronger sunlight yield riper olives, which produce darker oil. Unfortunately, however, the darkness of the green color does not absolutely guarantee that the oil will be the best virgin olive oil. There is the possibility that some less scrupulous farmers may put leaves into the oil for a short time to intensify the green color. Therefore, because color alone is not a reliable indicator of quality, each year's oil is tested by tasting.

For an Italian to add anything other than wine vinegar and salt to this oil would be as unthinkable as adding spices or other flavors to a great wine. The taste and bouquet of the oil are complex enough to bring out the flavor of a simple boiled vegetable or combination of salad greens.

Each vineyard grows a variety of olive types, such as *frantoio, correggiolo* (small olives with large pits), *moraiolo* (round black olives), and *leccino*. While the mature ripened olives are pressed for their oil, unripe green, as well as black, olives may be used whole in cooking. Green and black olives may be preserved in a salt-water solution called brine or in oil, pitted or unpitted, stuffed or not. Black olives may also be preserved by baking them with spices. The olives most often used in traditional Italian cooking are unpitted and uncooked.

Left: The avenue, or viale, *of cypresses leads up to the villa of Calcinaia, the residence of Count Neri Capponi. Cypresses have been cultivated in Italy since Etruscan times, and the Romans extracted a perfume from the bark and leaves of the tree.*

Overleaf: The ancient olive trees of Puglia have been described as resembling prehistoric monoliths. The cloths wrapped around the trees are used to catch and gather the olives during the harvest.

Above: During the harvest season, fresh olives are increasingly available for purchase even in markets far from the olive groves.

Opposite: Fresh olives sautéed in olive oil sparkle with coarse-grained salt.

Many cooked and uncooked sauces contain preserved olives of some type as an ingredient. Among examples that blend the different tastes of green and black olives together are the cooked sauce of *Ossobuco alla novese* and the uncooked one for *Cappon magro*, the cold fish and vegetable dish. *Coniglio alla genovese*, Rabbit Stew Genoese Style, contains an abundance of whole olives, which blend beautifully with the flavor of rosemary in the sauce.

The picking of the olives, in the fall in the South and later in central Italy, varies from one region to another. In Tuscany, each olive is generally hand-picked by workers standing on tall, flexible stepladders placed close to the branches. When harvest time comes, the entire family works long hours each day until the precious crop is safely gathered.

In another celebrated olive area, Puglia, the methods are different. Huge cloths are wrapped around the tree trunk and spread out around the entire tree, so that it resembles an ancient Roman in a long toga. While some workers shake the trees, others beat them with sticks to make the olives fall onto the cloths, to be gathered up in them.

When I was a child, my brothers and I were allowed to join the farmers in the olive gathering on the grounds of the villa. Our job was to collect the fruit that fell by accident from the baskets held by those picking from the branches up high. How we looked forward to the day when we might be allowed to climb those trees ourselves. We almost didn't mind the first cold weather, because we could anticipate the roaring fire in the room with the huge stone press and the warm oil in which we would dip pieces of bread lightly rubbed with garlic and toasted over a wood fire. Father would probably have been upset if he had known that we also joined the farmers in washing the *fettunta* down with the young wine pressed only two or three months before.

It's a great treat to be present when the ripe olives are gathered and to eat them in some special, simple preparation that highlights their freshness. A favorite preparation is Sautéed Fresh Olives.

Olive fritte
SAUTÉED FRESH OLIVES

2   tablespoons olive oil

1   pound fresh black olives

½   tablespoon coarse-grained salt

Pinch of freshly ground black pepper

Put the oil in a frying pan over medium heat and, when the oil is lukewarm, add the olives. Sprinkle them with salt and pepper. Sauté gently for 15 minutes, stirring occasionally so the olives do not stick to the pan. Remove the pan from the heat and transfer the olives to a serving dish. Serve immediately.

SERVES 6 AS AN APPETIZER.

CAPERS AND PEPPERS

One of the most picturesque sights all over Italy is the beautiful caper plant with its pink and white flowers growing out of the crumbling stone of the thousand-year-old castles, churches, and monasteries. Caper plants grow spontaneously when the seeds lodge in arid or subarid soil, such as crumbling rocks or very dry volcanic soil. The seeds are unique in that they become more fecund as they age and dry. Many capers grow wild, but they can be cultivated by inserting the dry seeds, at least one year old, in the loose stones of a wall or in the dry volcanic soil of Lipari or Puglia, or Pantelleria, Sicily.

The seeds are contained in the berry, which is in a pod, while the edible caper is the unopened bud of the flower. Once the bud flowers, it is no longer useful gastronomically. The flowers can carry a heavy bouquet, but are not commonly utilized as edible flowers. The Greeks and Romans seem to have eaten the bud, but not preserved in brine or salt as we do.

When Panonto, in the mid-sixteenth century, made up a menu that included a salad of mint, lettuce, flowers, and capers, did he mean that the capers were eaten fresh along with

Opposite: A flowering caper bush grows from the wall of a fourteenth-century monastery above a plate of Insalata di peperoni e capperi *(Pepper Salad with Capers).*

Below: It is the unopened bud of the caper plant that is a gourmet's delicacy; once the bud flowers it has no role in cooking.

25

some opened caper flowers? If so, it may indicate that the Greco-Roman practice of eating the bud fresh continued until the Renaissance and that the flowers were eaten as well. Perhaps with the shift to preserving the capers, the flowers simply were not preservable and fell into disuse.

Sweet peppers that are bell shaped or long have slightly different flavors, but they are generally used interchangeably. The exception is in the many variations of stuffed peppers, for which the bell shape is more suitable.

Roasted peppers, which are used for cold salads and *antipasti*, are also eaten in hot dishes, such as the Roman version of *peperonata*, peppers stewed in tomato. In Rome, the peppers are generally roasted before being lightly stewed, and capers are added at the end. In other versions of *peperonata*, the peppers, with the skins left on, are simply stewed in tomatoes.

The most usual way of roasting peppers in Italy, next to a pot of steaming water—either on top of the stove or as described in the following recipe, in the oven—is really a combination of roasting and steaming.

Insalata di peperoni e capperi
PEPPER SALAD WITH CAPERS

1	large ripe tomato	¼	cup olive oil
1	medium-sized clove garlic, peeled		Salt and freshly ground black pepper
5	fresh basil leaves, torn into thirds	4	large sweet green or yellow bell peppers, or a combination of both
15	whole fresh mint leaves	2	tablespoons capers in wine vinegar, drained

Cut the tomato into pieces and pass the pieces through a food mill, using the disc with the small holes, into a small crockery or glass bowl.

Finely chop the garlic and add it to the bowl along with the basil and 5 of the mint leaves. Pour the oil over the herbs and add salt and pepper. Mix very well with a wooden spoon. Cover the bowl with aluminum foil and refrigerate for 1 hour.

Preheat the oven to 375 degrees. Place a baking dish with 4 cups of cold water on a lower shelf of the oven. After 5 minutes, put the whole peppers on the shelf above the steaming water. Roast the peppers for about 40 minutes, turning them over three or four times.

Remove the peppers from the oven and put them into a plastic bag. Let them stand for 15 minutes.

Put the peppers in a large bowl of cold water and peel them, removing the stems and seeds.

Cut the peppers into thin strips. Arrange the strips on a serving dish and pour the prepared sauce over them. Mix very well and cover the dish with aluminum foil. Refrigerate for at least 1 hour. Serve, sprinkling the remaining mint leaves and the capers over the peppers.

SERVES 6.

BROWSING IN THE MARKETS
OF FLORENCE AND VENICE

Each market in Italy reflects its own town's traditions: the immense, irregularly shaped Prato della Valle of Padova, the Piazza Mercanzia of Prato, or even the Piazza of little Greve in Chianti was each once a great cattle market for the farmers of the surrounding area. The ancient Roman forums of Italian towns, now arcaded piazzas in Roman or Romanesque style, often had become markets as early as the Middle Ages. In the Renaissance, the Mercato Vecchio of Florence included the important gourmet "take out" shops and caterers, as the rich but cost-conscious merchant families kept only a small staff, preferring to have their glorious entertainments catered.

The district of San Lorenzo has also housed important markets of Florence since the third century, when the bazaars of the Oriental merchants were located here in order to supply the Roman army. When the church of San Lorenzo was built in the fifteenth century, stores and produce stands were built next to it; some were even built into the church itself. The indoor market that stands in the district today was built only a hundred years ago.

The huge two-story iron and glass art-nouveau structure across from the church of San Lorenzo is one of the greatest indoor markets in Italy, reflecting the variety of agriculture around Florence. The many fruit and vegetable stands have different specialties, one stressing the widest variety of wild mushrooms, another the greatest selection of wild field salads, another the many varieties of tomatoes, still another only *produzione nostrale*, vegetables and fruit from the farms within the city limits of Florence.

The stand keepers vie with one another to arrange their produce in the most aesthetic way possible in the early morning. This is also the time when the chefs of all the best restaurants will be there to select their produce, haggling over prices, joking with the suppliers, and trying to avoid each other, as rivals.

Frugal home cooks still go to the market every day, purchasing the food they need at different stands. Once-a-week shopping in supermarkets is just beginning to make its impression in Italy.

Because of their intimate connection with the water, the markets of Venice have a different character from those of Florence. Produce is transported by boat through the canals, first to the wholesale market at the foot of the Rialto bridge and then by boat to the retail stores.

Though Venice itself is built on hundreds of little islands, precluding agriculture, it has always had farms on the mainland. The city once ruled a very large area that bordered on Milan in the west and Greece in the east, and its produce came in great variety from all these areas.

Overleaf: A greengrocer from Venice prepares to catch a box of red radicchio, which grows in nearby Treviso and Chioggia. The large bargelike boat is always accompanied by a smaller one just in case the cargo of fruits and vegetables proves too heavy and threatens to sink the larger boat.

WILD MUSHROOMS

Porcini are the most popular wild mushrooms in Italian cooking, but other types are also used: delicate chanterelles, or *gallinacci*; fan-shaped, ridged *pineroli*; *prataioli* (found in the fields, but also cultivated); large, meaty *spugnole*; and orange-skinned *ovoli*, generally eaten raw in a salad.

When checking *porcini* for freshness, both the stem and cap should be firm. The stem should be full and stocky and the top skin of the cap uniformly golden brown. The underside of the cap should not be soft, greenish, or grayish. The inside meat should be white.

The dried mushrooms used in Italian cooking are almost always *porcini*, because their flavor intensifies in a unique way when they are dried. They are not considered an inferior substitute for fresh mushrooms because they have their own distinct role, perhaps even more important in Italian *cucina* than that of fresh mushrooms.

It is not unusual for Italian families who spend time in the country to be familiar with wild mushrooms and the special areas where their favorite types grow. They gather them for a wonderful meal of different dishes based on as many as three or four kinds of mushrooms. When they gather mushrooms in the same places year after year, they are always careful to replace the soil so that the growing conditions will remain the same, increasing the probability that the same mushrooms will reappear.

Freshly picked porcini *mushrooms in a market in Florence.*

Nepitella, called *menluccia* in many dialects, is the ideal herb to combine with fresh *porcini*. Though it is a kind of wild mint, its flavor is not minty, but rather aromatic and game like, close to a sage-rosemary combination. *Nepitella* grows wild along the roadsides and in the fields. Although most references say it favors wooded areas, I have always found it in open fields and along roadsides rather than in the woods. I have also had some luck in growing it from seeds in a pot.

When driving through the hills of Italy, I still cannot resist jumping out to pick the *nepitella* along the roads; it imparts a special flavor to potatoes and young June peas.

Gallinacci, lighter in flavor than *porcini*, combine best with other herbs, such as marjoram or thyme. They lend themselves well to the delicate mousse-like *sformatini*. Just as there is no adequate English translation for the French *mousse*, neither is there a way to translate the name for the particular kind of molded dish that the Italians call *sformato*, which literally means "unmolded."

The small, individual mushroom *sformatini* are made with a combination of fresh *gallinacci* and dried *porcini*, which yields a balanced flavor in which neither mushroom dominates. Dishes based on a combination of mushrooms are actually quite rare in traditional Italian cooking, but lately cooks have begun combining the intensely flavored dried *porcini* with the easily dominated commercial white champignon mushrooms, used fresh, to give the texture of fresh mushrooms with the taste of *porcini*—a useful substitute for fresh *porcini* when they are not available.

The wild herb nepitella, *which is seen here in flower, is frequently added to complement* porcini *mushrooms in Italian dishes.*

31

Sformatini di funghi
PORCINI MUSHROOM SFORMATINI

FOR THE SAUCE

3 ounces dried *porcini* mushrooms

1 pound fresh chanterelles (*gallinacci*) or champignon mushrooms

Juice of 1 lemon

1 small red onion, peeled

15 sprigs Italian parsley, leaves only

1 medium-sized clove garlic, peeled

1 small piece lemon peel

4 tablespoons (2 ounces) sweet butter

3 tablespoons olive oil

1 cup dry white wine

Salt and freshly ground black pepper

Pinch of dried thyme

1 tablespoon tomato paste

1 cup lukewarm homemade beef broth

FOR THE MOLDS

6 tablespoons (3 ounces) sweet butter

1½ cups unbleached all-purpose flour

Salt and freshly gound black pepper

Pinch of freshly grated nutmeg

PLUS

2 extra large eggs, separated

2 extra large eggs

TO SERVE

15 sprigs Italian parsley, leaves only

Soak the *porcini* mushrooms in 5 cups of lukewarm water for ½ hour. Clean the chanterelles and put them in a bowl of cold water with the lemon juice until needed.

Finely chop the onion, parsley, garlic, and lemon peel together on a board.

Heat the butter and oil in a large heavy casserole over medium heat and, when the butter is completely melted, add the chopped ingredients. Sauté for 5 minutes.

Meanwhile, drain the chanterelles and put them in a bowl. Drain the *porcini* mushrooms, saving 2 cups of the soaking water. Be sure no sand is still attached to the mushrooms. Add the chanterelles and *porcini* to the casserole and stir very well. Cook, uncovered, for 20 minutes, stirring occasionally.

Put 2 pieces of paper towel in a strainer and strain the mushroom soaking water through the toweling to catch all the sand.

Add the wine to the casserole and let it evaporate for 15 minutes. Taste for salt and pepper and add the thyme.

Dissolve the tomato paste in the broth and add the mixture to the casserole. Mix very well and cook for 30 minutes longer. By that time the mushrooms should be completely cooked and the sauce should be thick.

Remove the casserole from the heat and transfer 2 cups of the sauce to a blender or food processor and grind moderately fine. Reserve remaining sauce.

Prepare the molds: Melt the butter in a heavy saucepan over medium heat and, when the butter is completely melted, add the flour and mix very well. Then add the ground sauce. Stir very well to incorporate all the flour with the other ingredients. Cook for 4 minutes. Remove the pan from the heat and let stand until needed.

Put the strained mushroom soaking water into a small saucepan and bring to a boil over medium heat. Return the saucepan with the mushroom mixture to very low heat and add all of the hot water at once. Stir until the sauce is smooth. When the sauce reaches the boiling point, add salt, pepper, and nutmeg and continue to stir gently while it cooks for 5 minutes longer. Remove the pan from the heat and transfer the sauce to a crockery or glass bowl, pressing a piece of buttered wax paper down over the sauce

to prevent a skin from forming. Let the sauce cool completely (about ½ hour).

Preheat the oven to 375 degrees. Prepare a baking dish with lukewarm water to make a *bagnomaria* (*bain-marie* or water bath) for the molds.

Remove the wax paper from the sauce and add the egg yolks and the whole eggs. Mix very well with a wooden spoon and taste for salt and pepper.

Butter and lightly flour 8 ½-cup molds.

Use a wire whisk to beat the egg whites until stiff in an unlined copper bowl. Gently fold the whites into the sauce, always incorporating them in a rotating motion.

Ladle ⅜ cup of the sauce into each mold. Tap each mold on the counter to flatten the contents and to make sure that there are no air bubbles. Place the molds in the prepared *bagnomaria* and bake for 40 minutes.

Remove the baking dish from the oven and let it stand for 5 minutes.

Reheat the reserved unground mushroom sauce.

Remove the molds from the baking dish and unmold each *sformatino* onto its plate. Ladle some of the reheated sauce all around each *sformatino* and serve with some parsley leaves on the side.

SERVES 8.

*T*he mushroom tart in the following recipe must be prepared with dried *porcini*, not fresh ones. First the dried mushrooms are reconstituted by soaking them in a bowl of lukewarm water. The concentrated flavor of the mushrooms perfumes the soaking water (which may be strained through paper towels or a coffee filter and saved to flavor a variety of other dishes in which the mushrooms themselves are not prominent).

The tart crust must be recently baked, fresh and not refrigerated, so that it remains flaky. In typical Italian usage, the crust is as important as the filling and, in this way, differs from tarts that are served cold, in which the crust invariably assumes a secondary role.

Opposite: Still in their molds, a trio of Sformatini di funghi (Porcini Mushroom Sformatini), fresh from the oven. Above: Unmolded, an individual serving of the dish is surrounded by a porcini *and chanterelle mushroom sauce.*

Torta di funghi
WILD MUSHROOM TART

FOR THE CRUST

8	ounces (1 cup) unbleached all-purpose flour	
4	ounces (1 stick) sweet butter at room temperature	

Pinch of salt

5 tablespoons cold water

FOR THE STUFFING

2 ounces dried *porcini* mushrooms

1 medium-sized red onion, peeled

15 sprigs Italian parsley, leaves only

¼ cup olive oil

2 tablespoons (1 ounce) sweet butter

1 tablespoon tomato paste

1 cup lukewarm homemade beef broth

Salt and freshly ground black pepper

PLUS

3 extra large eggs

½ cup freshly grated *Parmigiano*

Prepare the crust first: Sift the flour onto a board and arrange it in a mound. Cut the butter into pieces and place them over the mound. Let stand for ½ hour, or until the butter softens. Start mixing the flour into the butter with your fingers; then rub the flour and butter between your palms. Make a well and put in the salt and water. Start mixing with a fork, absorbing the flour-butter mixture. Form a ball of dough with your hands. Knead gently until the dough becomes very smooth (about 2 minutes).

Slightly dampen a cotton dish towel and wrap the ball of dough in it. Let the dough rest in a cool place or on the bottom shelf of the refrigerator for at least 1 hour.

Meanwhile, prepare the stuffing: Soak the dried mushrooms in a bowl of lukewarm water for about ½ hour.

Finely chop the onion and parsley together on a board.

Heat the oil and butter in a heavy saucepan and, when the butter is completely melted, add the chopped ingredients. Sauté gently for 10 minutes.

Drain the mushrooms and be careful that no sand remains attached to them. Add the mushrooms to the pan and then add the tomato paste. Sauté for 5 minutes, stirring occasionally. Add the broth and season the mixture with salt and pepper. Cook slowly until almost all the broth has evaporated and the stuffing is thick and homogeneous (about 35 minutes). Remove the pan from the heat and transfer the stuffing to a crockery or glass bowl to cool completely (about 1 hour).

Butter a 9½-inch tart pan with a removable bottom.

Flour a pastry board. Unwrap the dough and knead it for about 1 minute on the board. Then use a rolling pin to roll out the dough to a round shape with a diameter of about 14 inches. Roll up the dough on the rolling pin and unroll it over the buttered pan. Gently press the dough into the bottom of the pan. Cut off the dough around the rim of the pan by moving the rolling pin over it. Using a fork, make several punctures in the pastry to keep the pastry from puffing up. Fit a sheet of wax paper or aluminum foil loosely over the pastry; then put weights or dried beans in the pan. Refrigerate the pastry for ½ hour.

Preheat the oven to 375 degrees.

Put the tart pan in the oven and bake for 40 minutes. Remove the pan from the oven, lift out the paper containing the weights and return the pan to the oven until the pastry is golden brown (10 to 15 minutes longer).

Meanwhile, finish the stuffing: Add the eggs and *Parmigiano* to the cooled ingredients. Taste for salt and pepper and mix very well with a wooden spoon.

Remove the tart pan from the oven and let the pastry cool in the pan on a rack for 10 minutes. Pour the stuffing into the baked shell and return it to the oven for 20 minutes longer.

Remove the pan from the oven and let the tart cool for 15 minutes. Then transfer the tart from the pan to a serving platter. Slice it like a pie to serve. The tart may be eaten warm as a main dish or it may be served warm or at room temperature as an appetizer.

SERVES 8.

Opposite: Torta di funghi (*Wild Mushroom Tart*) *on an antique serving plate.*

Overleaf: A delicious snack of tender raw vegetables to be eaten in pinzimonio, *dipped in olive oil, salt, and pepper, along with* focaccine, *little salted pizzas, is served with a light, white Tuscan wine on the beach in Forte dei Marmi in Tuscany.*

Buffet-style summer parties are a recent trend in Italian dining. This menu consists mostly of vegetable dishes served at room temperature. Clockwise from top, the

dishes are: Carciofi ripieni *(Stuffed Artichokes)*, Insalata di gamberi alla menta *(Shrimp Salad with Mint Leaves)*, Zucchini "a scapece" *(Marinated Zucchini)*, Pecorino marinato *(Marinated Pecorino Cheese)*, Pomodori al riso verde *(Tomatoes Stuffed with Green Rice and Fish)*, Pasta con tonno fresco *(Pasta with Marinated Tuna)*, and, *in the center,* Broccoli in insalata *(Broccoli Salad); left:* Crema di fagioli *(Bean Cream with Bay Leaves)*.

TOMATOES

The name tomato comes from the Aztec word *tomatl,* and although the sixteenth-century Sienese physician Matthioli gave the fruit its Italian name, *pomi d'oro* (in modern Italian, *pomodori*), or golden apples, when it first reached Italy, many Italian dialects call it *tomato* from the Spanish-Aztec. Some authorities think that the fruit arrived in Europe with a golden color and that the Mediterranean sun, milder than that of Mexico, brought out the reddish rather than the golden pigment in the skin.

Most varieties of tomatoes were developed in America, but were quickly adopted in Italy. The famous plum-shaped San Marzano variety was developed in southern Italy, then planted in the Naples area where it flourished as nowhere else. (Most plum tomatoes are really a smoother variety, the *lampadina,* but are marketed as the more famous San Marzano.) The plum shape of the San Marzano is celebrated because it ripens equally all over and is useful for preserving, as it peels easily and the removed stem leaves no hole.

The round tomato, ridged or unridged, is the one used for stuffing. *Pomodori al riso verde* has an unusual filling of rice enriched with chopped spinach and fish. A versatile dish, it may be eaten as an appetizer, *primo piatto,* or main course.

Pomodori al riso verde
TOMATOES STUFFED WITH GREEN RICE AND FISH

FOR THE FISH

1   sole fillet, about ½ pound

Coarse-grained salt

2   cups dry white wine

3   cups cold water

1   medium-sized carrot, scraped

1   bay leaf

1   whole clove

Pinch of dried thyme

1   teaspoon coarse-grained salt

5   whole black peppercorns

FOR THE TOMATOES

6   large ripe but not overripe tomatoes

6   tablespoons raw rice, preferably Italian Arborio

Coarse-grained salt

⅓   cup boiled spinach, finely chopped (from ½ pound fresh spinach, stems removed)

10   sprigs Italian parsley, leaves only

1   medium-sized clove garlic, peeled

½   cup olive oil

Salt and freshly ground black pepper

TO SERVE

6   fresh basil leaves

Prepare the fish: Wash the fish in cold water and put it in a small bowl of cold water with coarse-grained salt.

Pour the wine and the 3 cups of water into a saucepan or small fish poacher. Bring to a boil over medium heat and add the whole carrot, bay leaf, clove, thyme, the 1 teaspoon of coarse-grained salt, and the whole peppercorns. Simmer for 20 minutes; then add the sole fillet and cook for 3 minutes. Remove the pan from the heat and let the fish cool in the poaching liquid for 1 hour.

Meanwhile, soak the whole tomatoes in a bowl of cold water for ½ hour. Then drain the tomatoes and dry them with paper towels. Slice off the tops of the tomatoes and save them. Using a melon-ball cutter, remove the seeds, pulp, and the fleshy separations of the tomatoes, putting them in a bowl. Arrange the tomatoes in a 13½- x 8¾-inch baking dish.

Pass the reserved tomato seeds and flesh through a food mill, using the disc with the small holes, into a small saucepan. Add enough water to the pan to make 3 cups of liquid. Bring to a boil over medium heat and add coarse-grained salt to taste. Then add the rice and boil for 5 minutes. Remove the pan from the heat and let stand until needed.

When the fish is cool, drain the rice, reserving the broth. Put the rice in a crockery or glass bowl. Then add the spinach to the bowl.

Coarsely chop the parsley and finely chop the garlic and add them to the bowl along with 6 tablespoons of the oil. Use a strainer-skimmer to transfer the fish to the bowl with the rice. Season the stuffing with salt and pepper and use a wooden spoon to break up the fish and to mix it through the rice. Fill each tomato two-thirds full with the stuffing. Cover each tomato with its reserved top.

Preheat the oven to 375 degrees.

Add the remaining 2 tablespoons of oil to the reserved rice liquid and taste for salt and pepper. Pour the liquid into the dish with the tomatoes. If the liquid does not reach to one third the height of the tomatoes, add enough cold water to make it do so. Bake for about 50 minutes.

Transfer the tomatoes to a serving dish, pour some of the liquid from the baking pan over each tomato, and serve immediately or at room temperature with a fresh basil leaf on top of each tomato.

SERVES 6.

SQUASH AND EGGPLANTS

The name *"a scapece"* is a fascinating one which in the Neapolitan dialect means "from Apicius" (*Esca Apicii*, in Latin). There exists a whole category of these dishes, also called *"scabeccio"* (all over Italy) and *"scaveccio"* (in the Ligurian area), which derive from *De Re Coquinaria*, the ancient Roman cookbook of Apicius. Though the dishes themselves have been known since the time of ancient Rome, the recognition of their connection with Apicius probably occurred in the Renaissance with the revival of interest in the ancient Latin texts. The continuity of many traditions from the world of antiquity to our own is one of Italy's greatest delights.

Zucchini "a scapece"
MARINATED ZUCCHINI

6	medium-sized zucchini	2	medium-sized cloves garlic, peeled
2	cups corn oil		
1	cup sunflower oil	5	tablespoons red wine vinegar
¼	cup olive oil	20	fresh mint leaves
	Salt and freshly ground black pepper		

Soak the zucchini in a bowl of cold water for ½ hour. Then remove the zucchini from the water and cut off both ends.

Preheat the oven to 375 degrees.

Cut the zucchini lengthwise into ¼-inch-thick slices. Cut each slice in half. Arrange the zucchini on 2 baking sheets and bake for 25 minutes. Remove the baking sheets from the oven and transfer the zucchini to paper towels to drain for ½ hour.

Heat the oils together in a deep-fat fryer. Line a baking sheet with paper towels. When the oil is hot, add some of the zucchini slices and cook for 2 minutes on each side, or until they are light golden brown. With a strainer-skimmer transfer the cooked zucchini to the prepared baking sheet to drain. When all the zucchini are cooked and drained, transfer them to a serving dish and sprinkle them with salt and pepper.

Finely chop the garlic on a board and sprinkle it over the zucchini. Pour the wine vinegar over all. Wrap the dish in aluminum foil and place it on the bottom shelf of the refrigerator for at least 2 hours. Remove the dish from the refrigerator ½ hour before serving, mix, and distribute the mint leaves over the zucchini.

SERVES 8 AS AN APPETIZER.

The people of Mantua are very chauvinistic about their large yellow squash (*zucca gialla*), whose orange pulp they use to stuff *tortelli* and to make the characteristic squash soup, among other dishes.

In attempting to duplicate the taste of the squash away from Mantua, cooks have devised recipes that substitute pumpkin, sweet potatoes, and so on. However, after using pumpkin myself for a while, it occurred to me that all true squash reached Europe from the New World and that I should be able to find a similar-tasting squash in America. After trying every squash I saw in the United States, I found that the butternut squash is really the *zucca gialla*, only smaller, and that the taste is identical.

The squash soup so famous in Mantua is made in other nearby places, with variations. Although in Mantua they generally make it with milk, I prefer the version with broth made in some nearby towns. The spices vary from place to place, too, with some versions being quite aromatic. One recipe even adds saffron.

Opposite: Soups, such as this Mantua-style squash soup, were traditionally served as first courses before the triumph of dried pasta dishes in the nineteenth century.

Minestra o passato di zucca alla mantovana
SQUASH SOUP MANTUA STYLE

1	butternut squash, about 2 pounds	3	cups cold homemade beef broth
8	tablespoons (4 ounces) sweet butter		Salt and freshly gound black pepper
4	ounces *prosciutto* in one piece		TO SERVE
		6	basil leaves, fresh or preserved in salt (see Note)

Cut the squash into thirds; then remove the skin and seeds. Cut the squash into small pieces and soak them in a bowl of cold water for ½ hour.

Melt the butter in a heavy casserole over low heat and, when the butter is completely melted, add the whole piece of *prosciutto*. Sauté for 5 minutes over low heat.

Drain the squash and add it to the casserole. Cover and cook for 15 minutes. Add the broth, cover again, and simmer for 15 minutes longer.

Discard the *prosciutto* and pass the soup through a food mill, using the disc with the small holes, into a second casserole. Put the casserole over medium heat. Taste the soup for salt and pepper and cook, covered, for 10 minutes, stirring occasionally with a wooden spoon. Serve hot with the basil leaves floating on top of each serving.

SERVES 6.

NOTE: *To preserve fresh basil, rosemary, sage, etc., in salt, put a layer of coarse salt in the bottom of a mason jar with a tight-fitting lid. Then make a layer of the fresh herbs on top of the salt. (Do not wash the herbs, but wipe them with a towel before layering them.) Alternate layers of salt and herbs until the jar is full. Cover the top layer of herbs completely with a layer of salt and cover the jar with the lid. Store in the refrigerator.*

When using dried rosemary it is best to blanch the leaves for a few seconds in boiling water to soften them before using. When blanched, use the same quantity of leaves as you would fresh.

$\mathcal{E}$ggplants are particularly versatile gastronomically because they so easily absorb the different flavors of the other ingredients in a dish. The meaty texture of eggplant also makes it, along with the larger mushrooms, the most familiar vegetable substitute for meat or fish.

Although the vegetable was known in Europe in the Middle Ages, it was not trusted. Indeed, the Latin name *melum insanum* means "unhealthy apple," and fourteenth- and fifteenth-century Italian cookbooks do not use it, although they feature many other vegetables.

Southern Italy grows the greatest variety of eggplant types: long purple, round purple, and light purple with white areas and thinner skin; they are interchangeable in recipes. Northern Italy grows mainly the long type.

The famous Eggplant *"alla parmigiana,"* "Parma style," originated in the Parma area in northern Italy. Although the dish has *Parmigiano* cheese, the name does not refer to that. People mistakenly think that *"alla parmigiana"* always means with *Parmigiano* and tomato sauce, but there is scarcely another dish in "Parma style" that has that combination. I have seen fennel prepared with tomatoes labeled *"alla parmigiana"* on restaurant menus; this is misleading because there is a dish called fennel *"alla parmigiana"* that is made with butter and cheese.

Melanzane carpionate *(Eggplant Neapolitan Style). (©Franco Pasti)*

Eggplant adapts very well to the following wine vinegar-garlic sauce. This is one of the few Italian dishes that uses the vegetable peeled. It is fried, as in other dishes *in carpione* (see page 154), but it differs in that it is eaten hot.

Melanzane carpionate
EGGPLANT NEAPOLITAN STYLE

6 medium-sized thin eggplants

  About ½ cup coarse-grained salt

  About 1½ cups unbleached all-purpose flour

PLUS

2 cups vegetable oil, or 1 pound solid vegetable shortening

¼ cup olive oil

FOR THE SAUCE

½ cup olive oil

3 whole anchovies in salt, or 6 anchovy fillets in oil, drained

15 sprigs Italian parsley, leaves only

2 medium-sized cloves garlic, peeled

2 tablespoons red wine vinegar

  Salt and freshly ground black pepper

Peel the eggplants and cut them into 1½-inch cubes. Spread the cubes over a large platter and sprinkle the coarse-grained salt over them. Let stand for ½ hour. Then rinse the eggplant cubes under cold running water and dry them with paper towels.

    Heat the vegetable oil and olive oil together in a deep-fat fryer. Line a serving dish with paper towels.

    Lightly flour the eggplant by shaking some of the pieces together with ¼ cup of the flour in a colander, so the excess flour will fall through. Continue flouring the eggplant until all of it is done.

    When the oil is warm (about 375 degrees), fry about 15 pieces at a time, turning them until they are golden brown all over. Transfer the cooked eggplant to the prepared serving dish to drain.

    While the eggplant cubes are cooking, prepare the sauce: Put the oil in a small heavy saucepan over low heat. If using anchovies in salt, fillet them under cold running water.

    Finely chop the parsley and garlic together on a board.

    When the oil is warm, add the anchovy fillets and mash them with a fork, incorporating the oil. Add the wine vinegar and salt and pepper and let the vinegar evaporate for 2 minutes. By that time the eggplant cubes should all be cooked. Transfer the eggplant to another serving platter, pour the anchovy sauce over it and sprinkle it with the chopped parsley and garlic. Mix together very well and serve immediately.

SERVES 8.

*S*liced eggplant, very simply seasoned with garlic, parsley, and olive oil and baked, is one of the many dishes from southern Italy without tomato sauce. The beautiful purple skin is left on the eggplant and adds to the visual appeal and flavor of this simple and delicious dish.

Melanzane al forno
BAKED EGGPLANT

2   very large, round Sicilian-type eggplants

4   tablespoons olive oil

4   cloves garlic, peeled and cut into 6 slivers each

    Salt and freshly ground black pepper

5   sprigs Italian parsley, leaves only

Carefully wash the eggplants and remove the stems. Cut the eggplants horizontally into 1-inch-thick slices.

Preheat the oven to 375 degrees. Oil two 13½- x 8¾-inch baking dishes with 1 tablespoon of the oil each.

Arrange the eggplant slices in each baking dish in a single layer. Insert 2 slivers of garlic into each slice. Season the slices with salt and pepper. Pour the remaining oil over the slices. Bake for 25 minutes.

Remove the baking dishes from the oven and transfer the eggplant slices to a serving platter. Sprinkle them with the parsley leaves and serve immediately.

SERVES 6.

Melanzane al forno (*Baked Eggplant*).

BROCCOLI AND CAULIFLOWER

Until very recently, Italians ate only the vegetables grown locally. In my Florentine childhood, broccoli was an exotic vegetable from other "countries," Lazio (Rome) and Campania (Naples). The local traditions are so strong that modern transportation does not modify this practice. After all, broccoli could easily have been shipped to Florence from southern Italy for the last hundred years, but it wasn't. It was an exciting local dish you ate when you visited Rome or Naples. Although this attitude is changing slightly, many broccoli dishes are still unobtainable in central Italy.

The unusual combination of boiled broccoli and curled, shredded carrots in this cold salad has an interesting texture. Even for a salad, broccoli and cauliflower are always cooked.

Broccoli in insalata
BROCCOLI SALAD

2	bunches broccoli		Juice of 4 lemons
	Coarse grained salt	½	teaspoon hot red pepper flakes
4	small carrots		Salt and freshly ground black pepper
½	cup olive oil		

Soak the broccoli in a large bowl of cold water for ½ hour.

Bring a large pot of cold water to a boil; then add coarse-grained salt to taste.

Remove the woody ends of the broccoli. Cut the flowerets from the large stems and keep them separate. Then cut the stems into strips about 2 inches long and ½ inch thick and immediately put them into the boiling water. Cook for 5 minutes and add the flowerets. Cook for about 4 minutes longer. Drain the broccoli and put it in a bowl of cold water for 10 minutes.

Meanwhile, scrape the carrots and, using a vegetable peeler, shred them. Put the carrot shreds in a bowl of cold water with ice cubes. Let them soak for 5 minutes.

Put the oil, lemon juice, hot red pepper flakes, and salt and pepper to taste in a small crockery or glass bowl. Mix together with a wooden spoon. Drain the broccoli and put it on a serving dish.

Pour half of the sauce over the broccoli and mix very well.

Drain the carrots and put them in a bowl. Mix them with the remaining sauce. Combine the carrots with the broccoli, mix well, and serve.

SERVES 6.

*P*urple cauliflower, which resembles both cauliflower and broccoli, has its own distinct, delicate flavor. The beautiful purple tints of the plant turn light green when it is cooked. Modern-day Romans are the greatest champions of purple cauliflower, but it is becoming better known outside Italy.

The most usual preparation is as a cold *antipasto*, with the same anchovy sauce that is often used with white cauliflower. Another preparation, Purple Cauliflower Roman Style, is a substantial dish in which the sautéed vegetable is served warm over sautéed bread with butter sauce. It should be a separate vegetable course or appetizer, but not a vegetable accompaniment.

Broccoli romani con prosciutto
PURPLE CAULIFLOWER ROMAN STYLE

2   heads purple cauliflower

     Coarse-grained salt

3   tablespoons (1½ ounces) sweet butter or lard

2   tablespoons olive oil

2   cloves garlic, peeled but left whole

4   ounces *prosciutto*, cut into thin strips

     Salt and freshly ground black pepper

PLUS

4   ounces (1 stick) sweet butter

12   2-inch squares crusty Italian bread (Tuscan type, see page 75), ½ inch thick

     Salt and freshly ground black pepper

Wash the cauliflower and cut off the large stems. Soak the cauliflower in a bowl of cold water for ½ hour.

Bring a large pot of cold water to a boil. Add coarse-grained salt to taste; then add the cauliflower. Boil for 5 minutes.

Transfer the cauliflower to a bowl of cold water to cool for 2 minutes. Put the cauliflower on paper towels to drain, covering them with a dampened cotton dish towel. Let stand until needed.

Heat the butter and oil in a large heavy casserole over medium heat. When the butter is completely melted, add the garlic and sauté until it is golden brown (about 4 mintues).

Cut the whole flowerets off the heads of cauliflower, leaving a short piece of stem attached to each floweret. Cut the remaining small stems into 2-inch pieces.

Discard the garlic and add the *prosciutto* to the casserole. Sauté for 3 minutes; then add the cauliflower. Taste for salt and pepper and gently mix all the ingredients together. Lower the heat and cook for about 2 minutes.

Meanwhile, melt the 4 ounces of butter in a frying pan over medium heat. When the butter is completely melted, sauté the bread squares for less than a minute on each side, or until they are lightly golden brown. Season them with salt and pepper. Transfer the bread to a large serving platter and arrange the pieces in a ring around the edge of the platter. When the cauliflower is ready, spoon it inside the ring of bread. Serve hot.

SERVES 6.

Left: The finished dish, Broccoli romani con prosciutto *(Purple Cauliflower Roman Style), and some of the fresh ingredients gathered for its preparation.*

Opposite, clockwise from top right: Shoppers negotiate prices and aisles in a Florence market; birds for sale in Bari; discriminating shoppers check for quality in a Venetian market; a Florentine grocer shoulders his crates of produce; a fruitseller catches a quiet moment at his market stand in Florence; and shoppers discuss prices at a Venice fruit and vegetable stand.

ARTICHOKES AND SWISS CHARD

Riding through Puglia from October through March, you see miles of flat fields with green and silver artichoke plants waving in the breeze. These thistles, which grow like weeds, bear a mysterious vegetable to which many strange properties have been attributed. In the Renaissance, it was considered one of the more efficacious aphrodisiacs. Artichokes, which are actually tight flowers, were first cultivated in Italy in the fifteenth century by a Florentine, Filippo Strozzi, who succeeded in growing them in the Naples area, then in Tuscany.

In Italy artichokes are always cleaned so that everything served can be eaten, either whole, cut into quarters—each having both leaves and bottom—or cut into pieces. They are never eaten leaf by leaf.

Each region has its own stuffings for artichokes. The piquant vegetarian stuffing in the following recipe comes from the South, and the unique feature is that the whole artichokes are baked upside down, with the stems still attached. The stuffing is bound together by the bread and bread crumbs and does not fall out.

Artichokes are rarely cooked with tomato sauce, the main exception being in Liguria, where the combination of artichokes and wild mushrooms is often joined by tomatoes. In general, the flavor of the vegetable is best enhanced by olive oil and herbs.

Carciofi ripieni (*Stuffed Artichokes*).

Carciofi ripieni
STUFFED ARTICHOKES

Soak the artichokes for ½ hour in a large bowl of cold water to which the lemon halves have been added.

Clean the artichokes: Cut off the ends of the stems. Trim off all of the darker outer ring of the stems. Remove as many rows of the outer leaves as necessary until you arrive at those leaves in which you can see the separation between the green at the top and the light yellow at the bottom. Remove the top green part by pressing your thumb on the bottom yellow part of each leaf and, with your other hand, tearing off the top green part. When you reach the rows in which only the very top of the leaves are green, cut off these tips completely with a knife.

To remove the hair and the choke, first cut all around the choke with a knife; then scoop out the choke and the attached hair, using a long-handled teaspoon. As each artichoke is cleaned, return it to the bowl with the acidulated water until it is needed.

Prepare the stuffing: Soak the bread in a small bowl of cold water for 5 minutes.

Coarsely chop the pepper and capers together on a board. Finely chop the parsley and garlic together on a board. Combine the coarsely and finely chopped ingredients in a bowl.

Squeeze the water out of the soaked bread and add the bread to the bowl along with the bread crumbs and the oil. Mix very well with a wooden spoon and season with salt and pepper. Be sure that all the ingredients are well amalgamated.

Preheat the oven to 375 degrees.

To cook the artichokes, coarsely chop the clove of garlic and sprinkle it in a 13½- x 8¾-inch baking dish. Then add the parsley, mint, and water to the dish.

Stuff each artichoke with the prepared filling and place them in the baking dish upside down, with the stems pointing up. Pour the oil over the artichokes and sprinkle them with salt and pepper. Wrap the dish with aluminum foil and bake for 40 to 60 minutes, depending on the size and toughness of the artichokes.

Remove the dish from the oven and transfer the artichokes and the pan juices to a platter. Serve hot or at room temperature.

SERVES 6.

6   large artichokes

2   lemons, cut in half

FOR THE STUFFING

2   slices white bread, crusts removed

1   sweet red bell pepper in wine vinegar, drained

2   tablespoons capers in wine vinegar, drained

15 sprigs Italian parsley, leaves only

1   medium-sized clove garlic, peeled

¼   cup unseasoned bread crumbs, preferably homemade

½   cup olive oil

    Salt and freshly ground black pepper

TO COOK THE ARTICHOKES

1   clove garlic, peeled

15 sprigs Italian parsley, leaves only

5   fresh mint leaves

1   cup cold water

¼   cup olive oil

    Salt and freshly ground black pepper

*S*wiss chard originated in Europe and very early on was taken to Asia Minor and India, where it now belongs to the cooking of those countries as well as to that of many European countries. Waverley Root says that he cannot understand why the name "Swiss" is attached to this vegetable in America, as it has no special connection to Switzerland. Perhaps Americans first encountered it in the Swiss resorts, which were the most popular ones for wealthy Americans in the nineteenth century.

The ancient Romans ate mainly the leaves, but in modern times a whole repertory of dishes has grown up in Italy around the stems as well. Sometimes the stems and leaves are boiled together, then sautéed. When the large white stems of the chard are used for a dish, the leaves may be reserved for soup or another preparation. Stuffed Swiss Chard Stems is really a type of "sandwich," with two pieces of stem on the outside and a filling in between, which is then dipped in batter and deep-fried.

Gambi di bietola ripieni
STUFFED SWISS CHARD STEMS

Opposite: Stuffing preparations for Gambi di bietola ripieni *(Stuffed Swiss Chard Stems).*

FOR THE BATTER

1   cup unbleached all-purpose flour

    Pinch of salt

    Pinch of freshly grated nutmeg

1   tablespoon olive oil

2   tablespoons dry white wine

¾   cup cold water

3   extra large egg whites

TO COOK

4   pounds Swiss chard with large white stems

    Coarse-grained salt

FOR THE STUFFING

2   slices white bread, crusts removed

2   heaping tablespoons capers in wine vinegar, drained

2   hard-boiled extra large eggs

    Salt and freshly ground black pepper

PLUS

2   cups vegetable oil, or 1 pound solid vegetable shortening

    Salt

1   lemon, cut into wedges

Prepare the batter: Sift the flour and put it in a large crockery or glass bowl. Add a pinch of salt and nutmeg to the flour and mix with a wooden spoon. Make a well in the flour and add the oil and the wine. Start mixing with a wooden spoon, incorporating some of the flour. Then add the water a little at a time to prevent lumps from forming. When all the water is incorporated, let the batter rest for at least 1 hour in a cool place.

Cut off the large white stems from the chard and cut the stems into about 24 3½-inch-long pieces. (You may reserve the leaves for another dish.) Soak the stem pieces in a large bowl of cold water for ½ hour.

Bring a large pot of cold water to a boil; then add coarse-grained salt to taste. Add the chard stem pieces and boil for about 10 minutes. Drain and cool them under cold running water. Lay out the stem pieces on paper towels and let them stand until needed.

Prepare the stuffing: Soak the bread in a small bowl of cold water for 10 minutes. Finely chop the capers on a board. Shell the hard-boiled eggs and discard the whites. Squeeze out the water from the bread and put the bread in a crockery or glass bowl. Add the chopped capers and egg yolks to the bowl. Season with salt and pepper to taste and mix all the ingredients together very well with a wooden spoon.

Spread about ½ tablespoon of the stuffing on each of 12 chard stem pieces. Cover each stuffed stem with an unstuffed one, pressing them together so they adhere to each other.

Line a serving dish with paper towels. Heat the oil in a deep-fat fryer.

Use a wire whisk to beat the egg whites until stiff in an unlined copper bowl. Use a wooden spoon to gently fold the beaten egg whites into the batter, always incorporating them in a rotating motion.

When the oil is hot, dip each "sandwich" in the batter; then put it in the fryer and cook for ½ minute on each side, or until golden brown. Remove the deep-fried "sandwiches" from the pan and put them on the prepared serving dish. When all the stuffed stems are cooked, remove the paper towels, sprinkle the stems with a little salt, and serve hot with the lemon wedges.

MAKES ABOUT 12; SERVES 6.

BEETS AND PEAS

Opposite: Sliced beets sprinkled with salt and ready to be dipped in batter as other Barbabietole fritte *(Batter-Fried Beets) fry in bubbling oil.*

Beets, with their beautiful red coloring, have not inspired many unusual types of preparations. An exception is a wonderful dish that is not as well known as it ought to be, in which beet slices are fried in a light and fluffy batter. The skins should be left on when the beets are preboiled to keep the color from bleeding. They are then peeled for frying, and the batter coating seals in the deep color.

Barbabietole fritte
BATTER-FRIED BEETS

4	medium-sized beets	¾	cup cold water
	Coarse-grained salt		Pinch of freshly grated nutmeg
	Salt and freshly ground black pepper	3	extra large egg whites

FOR THE BATTER

PLUS

1	cup unbleached all-purpose flour	4	cups vegetable oil, or 2 pounds solid vegetable shortening
	Pinch of salt and a twist of freshly ground black pepper		Salt
3	tablespoons olive oil	1	lemon, cut into wedges

Wash the beets carefully and cut off the leaves. Do not cut off the stems completely or the color will bleed out.

Place a pot of cold water over medium heat and, when the water comes to a boil, add coarse-grained salt to taste and then the whole beets. Boil for about 1 hour. By then the beets should be cooked but still firm. Drain the beets and cool them under cold running water. Peel the beets, removing the stems, and let them stand until needed.

Prepare the batter: Sift the flour into a large bowl. Add the salt and pepper and mix them in with a wooden spoon. Make a well in the flour and add the oil. Start mixing with the wooden spoon, incorporating some of the flour. Then add the water a little at a time to prevent lumps from forming while incorporating the rest of the flour. When all the water has been incorporated, sprinkle the nutmeg over the batter and mix very well. Let the batter rest in a cool place for at least 1 hour.

Cut the beets into ¼-inch-thick slices and arrange them in 1 layer on a serving dish. Sprinkle the slices with salt and abundant pepper.

Heat the oil in a deep-fat fryer. Line a serving dish with paper towels.

Beat the egg whites until stiff with a wire whisk in an unlined copper bowl. Use a wooden spoon to gently fold the beaten egg whites into the batter, incorporating them in a rotating motion.

When the oil is hot, dip the beet slices in the batter one by one and put them in the fryer to cook for 30 seconds on each side. Use a strainer-skimmer to transfer them from the fryer to the prepared serving dish.

When all the beets are cooked, remove the paper towels, sprinkle the beets with a little salt, and serve hot with the lemon wedges.

SERVES 6.

Below: The simple but elegant Piselli e Paternostri, *served with some local white wine, is just ready on the terrace of this* masseria, *or villa, in the south of Italy. Designed to be self-sufficient, this representative* masseria *in Puglia includes a family chapel and a round tower for storage and defence.*

*I*n the traditional Puglia dish, fresh peas with small dried tubular pasta *(Paternostri)*, the vegetable rather than the pasta dominates in a fixed two-to-one proportion of peas to pasta. The tradition of the pasta type is fixed, too. The two types of short tubular pasta originally were called *Avemarie* (Hail, Mary) and *Paternostri* (Our Father) after the two sizes of beads on a rosary, the *Avemarie* being the smaller of the two. In our more secularized society, new names have been invented for these two traditional shapes of pasta *(ditalini,* etc.), but in the highly traditional area of Puglia, the old religious names survive.

Piselli e Paternostri
PEAS AND PATERNOSTRI

3   pounds fresh peas, unshelled

1   tablespoon unbleached all-purpose flour

    Coarse-grained salt

25 sprigs Italian parsley, leaves only

1   small clove garlic, peeled

½   cup olive oil

1   cup warm homemade beef broth

    Salt and freshly ground black pepper

½   pound very short tubular dried pasta, such as *Paternostri*, *Avemarie*, or *ditalini*

TO SERVE

15 sprigs Italian parsley, leaves only

Wash the unshelled peas very well in cold running water. Then shell them and save both the peas and the pods. Put the peas in a bowl of cold water. Mix the flour into the water and let the peas soak for ½ hour to tenderize them.

Put the pea pods in a large quantity of cold water over medium heat. When the water begins to boil, add coarse-grained salt. Cook the pods for 20 minutes. Drain, reserving the cooking water and discarding the pods.

Drain and rinse the peas.

Coarsely chop the parsley and finely chop the garlic on a board.

Heat the oil in a heavy saucepan over medium heat. When the oil is warm, add the chopped ingredients and sauté for 1 minute. Add the peas, cover the pan, and cook for 5 minutes. Add ½ cup of the broth and taste for salt and pepper. Cover the pan again and cook over low heat, adding more broth as needed, until the peas are cooked but still firm (about 15 to 25 minutes, depending on the size of the peas).

Return the water in which the pea pods were cooked to a boil. Add the pasta and stir with a wooden spoon. Cover the pot to bring the water back to a boil as quickly as possible. Uncover the pot and cook the pasta until it is *al dente* (from 9 to 12 minutes, depending on the brand). Drain the pasta and transfer it to the pan with the peas. Stir very well and cook for 1 minute longer. Taste again for salt and pepper. Serve immediately, sprinkled with the parsley.

SERVES 4 TO 6.

MIXED VEGETABLES

Zabaione, made with dry white wine, is an old specialty from Piedmont. In other parts of Italy, people are often taken aback at the idea of *zabaione* being used as a sauce for vegetables—but only until they taste it. The mixed vegetables should not include those from the cabbage family, with the exception of cauliflower, as they do not blend with this sauce.

Traditionally, *zabaione* was mixed with a *frullino* in a pot with a curved bottom that fit over a pot of boiling water. Holding the handle of the *frullino* between the palms, it was made to twirl back and forth in an action much like the modern blender or electric mixer. The end of the round wooden spoon was ridged with some holes cut between the rows of wood. This implement was also used for making *maionese*.

In earlier generations, the *frullino* was an important member of each family, as the older members of the family used it to make their own tonics, composed of eggs, sugar, and a liqueur; this cordial was then added to the morning coffee. Perhaps the idea of the sweet, warm dessert *Zabaione*, which is better known in Italian restaurants abroad than in Italy, derives from these old cordials.

The frullino *and copper pot.*

Verdure con zabaione secco
VEGETABLE COMPOTE WITH DRY ZABAIONE

2   pounds of 1 boiled vegetable or a compote of different boiled vegetables, such as asparagus, string beans, zucchini, fennel bulbs, cauliflower, small pearl onions, potatoes, and artichokes

Salt and freshly ground black pepper

FOR THE *ZABAIONE SECCO*

5   extra large egg yolks

Abundant salt and freshly ground black pepper

¾   cup dry white wine

Arrange the vegetable or the compote of vegetables on a large platter. Cover the vegetables with a cotton dish towel that has been dampened in cold water. Let stand until needed.

Prepare the sauce: Put water in the bottom of a double boiler and place it over medium heat.

Put the egg yolks in a crockery or glass bowl and add salt and pepper. Stir with a wooden spoon, always in the same direction, until the eggs and seasonings are well amalgamated and the egg yolks turn a lighter color. Add the wine slowly, mixing continuously.

The top part of the double boiler should not be placed over the boiling water until the ingredients have been well mixed together. When all is ready and the water is boiling, transfer the contents of the bowl to the top part of the double boiler and insert it over the boiling water. Stir constantly with a wooden spoon, always in the same direction. At the moment just before it comes to a boil, the *zabaione* should be thick enough to coat the wooden spoon. Absolutely do not let the *zabaione* come to a boil. Remove the top part of the double boiler from the heat, stir the contents, and transfer the sauce to a crockery or glass bowl. The sauce may be used hot or at room temperature. If using the sauce at room temperature, let it cool a little and then pour it into an empty wine bottle. Cork the bottle until ready to use the sauce. The boiled vegetables should also remain at room temperature.

SERVES 6.

The word *carabaze*, old Catalan for squash, was introduced to Italian cooking no later than the early fifteenth century; it was the word for a squash soup almost identical to *Minestra di zucca alla mantovana* (see page 45). By the sixteenth century, *carabazada*, made of finely chopped vegetables—squash or melon, zucchini, eggplant, onion or cucumber, hearts of lettuce—had become a major category of first course. The meatless dish, when made today, may have oil, lemon juice, water, and spices. If made with meat, a rich meat broth and often *prosciutto* with its fat and egg yolks are used.

Later versions are called *carabacce*. The word became Italianized and, in fact, entered the Italian language outside of its food origins, to mean a combination of many inexpensive things. Our *carabaccia* is just that: It includes many vegetables (some not so inexpensive), served around a slice of good bread topped with a poached egg and flavored with wild fennel.

Wild fennel is the most common type found in Italy. It does not have the swollen stem base, or bulb, of sweet fennel, and it is the leaves and seeds that are used most. Sweet fennel may have been developed from the wild, possibly in the famous Renaissance garden maintained by the Medici, *Giardino dei Semplici,* where botanical experiments were encouraged. Hence, it is often known as Florence fennel.

Dill is related to wild fennel and is widely used throughout the Mediterranean. It is not favored in Italy, however, where it is known as "smelly fennel," "fetid fennel," and "bastard fennel." Despite these unpleasant names, its leaves are closer to the taste of wild fennel than are those of sweet fennel and should be substituted in the following recipe if wild fennel is unavailable.

Decorative fountain putti *overlook* Verdure con zabaione secco *(Vegetable Compote with Dry Zabaione).*

59

Carabaccia alla luna piena
CARABACCIA OF THE FULL MOON

1   pound fresh peas, shelled

1   tablespoon unbleached all-purpose flour

2   medium-sized red onions, peeled

6   celery stalks, leaves removed

6   medium-sized carrots, scraped

10 sprigs Italian parsley, leaves only

5   basil leaves, fresh or preserved
    in salt (see Note on page 43)

5   sprigs wild fennel, or 10 sprigs
    dill, fresh or preserved in salt
    (see Note on page 43)

¾   cup olive oil

    Salt and freshly ground black
    pepper

    Juice of 1 lemon

6   pieces crusty
    Italian bread,
    (Tuscan type,
    see page 75)
    1-inch thick

1   cup lukewarm homemade
    chicken broth

1   tablespoon red wine vinegar

    Coarse-grained salt

6   extra large eggs

6   tablespoons freshly grated
    Parmigiano

Put the peas in a bowl of cold water. Mix the flour into the water and let the peas soak for ½ hour to tenderize them.

Coarsely chop the onions, celery, and carrots together on a board. Finely chop the parsley, basil, and fennel together on a board.

Put the oil in a heavy casserole and heat it over medium heat. When the oil is lukewarm, add both the coarsely and finely chopped ingredients. Sauté for 5 minutes; then lower the heat and cover the casserole.

Cook for 10 minutes. Taste for salt and pepper and add the lemon juice. Cover the casserole again and cook for 15 minutes longer.

Drain the peas, wash them in cold running water, and add them to the casserole. Cover the casserole again and cook for ½ hour longer, stirring occasionally with a wooden spoon.

Preheat the oven to 375 degrees. Toast the bread in the oven for 15 minutes on each side, or until it is golden brown.

Meanwhile, bring a casserole of cold water to a boil. Add coarse-grained salt to taste and then the wine vinegar. At that time the vegetables should be cooked and the bread toasted. Put the bread slices in individual soup bowls or small individual terra cotta terrines. Pour some of the chicken broth over each slice.

Crack the eggs into the boiling water, cover the casserole, and simmer the eggs for 4 minutes.

When the eggs are almost cooked, arrange the vegetables so that they surround the bread slices. With a slotted spoon place 1 poached egg on top of each slice of bread. Sprinkle each serving with 1 tablespoon of the grated *Parmigiano* and serve immediately.

SERVES 6.

Left: **Carabaccia alla luna piena** (*Carabaccia of the Full Moon*) encircle a feathery centerpoint of wild fennel sprigs, also shown below.

DRIED BEANS

Most dried beans used in Italian cooking arrived in Europe from Mexico and Central America. Only lentils and chick-peas are indigenous to Europe, both going back to the Sumerians and Egyptians. Although Greek physicians, with the exception of Hippocrites, felt that lentils and chick-peas were unhealthy, they remained a staple of the Greek and Roman diet, undoubtedly providing the calories and protein of the meat many could not afford.

How many of us have actually seen fresh lentils or eaten them? They do grow in pods with a small number of seeds, usually two, and, to my knowledge, they have always been eaten dried. Lentils are especially typical of New Year's feasts, for they signify good luck.

In Italy, lentils are not usually used puréed as they are in India and the Middle East. There are regional dishes for pasta and lentils, rice and lentils, and lentil soups. Most commonly, they are used in a sauce to accompany *cotechino* or *zampone* (cooked sausages).

Ceci, or chick-peas, are always used dried in Italy, puréed in soups and in a batter for baking, and whole in *pasta e ceci* and as a vegetable accompaniment.

Borlotti (called Roman beans or red beans in English) appear in many far northern and southern regions in dishes similar to those in which the white kidney-shaped *cannellini* are used in

central Italy. For example, *borlotti* appear in spicy appetizers, *minestroni*, *pasta e fagioli*, and in vegetable dishes meant to accompany main courses.

Fagioli in stufa
CANNELLINI BEANS WITH ROSEMARY

2   cups dried *cannellini* beans (see Note)

3   ounces *pancetta* in one piece

4   tablespoons olive oil

3   medium-sized cloves garlic, peeled

3   tablespoons rosemary leaves, fresh or preserved in salt or dried and blanched (see Note on page 43)

Salt and freshly ground black pepper

Soak the beans overnight in a bowl of cold water. The next morning drain the beans and rinse them under cold running water. Put them in a terra cotta or enamel casserole.

Preheat the oven to 375 degrees.

Cut the *pancetta* into ½-inch cubes. Finely chop the garlic. Add the *pancetta*, oil, garlic, and rosemary to the casserole. Pour in enough cold water to come 1 inch above the beans.

Cover the casserole and bake for about 1½ hours, stirring two or three times. Season with salt and pepper.

Remove the casserole from the oven and let the beans cool for 10 minutes before serving.

SERVES 6.

NOTE: *In recent years, the process for drying beans in Italy seems to have changed, so that the cooking times are now sometimes as much as an hour shorter. It is best to taste the beans after the minimum time given in the recipe to see if further cooking is necessary.*

C rema di fagioli, a soup of puréed *cannellini* and aromatic herbs, is served with drops of rich green Tuscan olive oil added at the last moment and with fresh bay leaves floating on top. The word *crema* in the name of the soup refers to a purée, not to cream.

Fresh bay is so common as a hedge in Italy that it is never necessary to buy bay leaves. In addition, because it is an evergreen, it is available fresh the entire year. A non-Italian friend, on his first visit to Italy and unaware of this fact, was cooking a fish dish that called for bay leaves. He searched in many greengroceries without finding them and complained to me of his difficulty. Laughing, I led him to a neighboring public garden where we picked some off the bushes surrounding the park.

An antique Florentine copper soup tureen.

Crema di fagioli
BEAN CREMA WITH BAY LEAVES

1	cup dried *cannellini* beans (see Note on page 63)		Salt and freshly ground black pepper
¼	pound *prosciutto,* sliced	4	cups homemade chicken broth
2	medium-sized celery stalks		PLUS
2	medium-sized carrots	6	to 8 bay leaves
½	medium-sized red onion, peeled	6	to 8 teaspoons olive oil
2	tablespoons olive oil		Freshly ground black pepper

Soak the beans overnight in a bowl of cold water. The next morning drain the beans and rinse them under cold running water.

Coarsely cut the *prosciutto.* Cut the celery into ½-inch pieces. Scrape the carrots and cut them in the same way as the celery. Coarsely chop the onion.

Heat the oil in a terra cotta or enamel casserole over medium heat. Add the *prosciutto* and sauté lightly for 2 minutes.

Add the beans to the casserole; then add the celery, carrots, onion, and enough water to cover all the ingredients completely. Season with salt and pepper. Cover the casserole and simmer over medium heat for about 1½ hours. By that time the beans should be completely cooked and the water almost absorbed by the beans.

Pass the contents of the casserole through a food mill, using the disc with the small holes, into a second casserole. Add the chicken broth. Simmer, uncovered, over medium heat for about 1 hour. By that time the texture of the *crema* should be thick and smooth. Taste for salt and pepper.

Meanwhile, soak the bay leaves in a bowl of lukewarm water for about 5 minutes. Drain them and add them to the *crema.* Simmer for 5 minutes longer.

Serve the soup hot in individual warm soup bowls, floating 1 bay leaf on top of each serving. Add 1 teaspoon of olive oil and a twist of black pepper to each serving.

SERVES 6 TO 8.

*P*uglia is a region that values rough beauty. This is evident in its rough-hewn terra cotta vessels, which show the tear-marks made when the bowls are torn apart after being fired together, one on top of the other. The concept of "finish" does not exist with these bowls and would clash with their natural beauty.

One of Puglia's most characteristic regional dishes, the wild green *cicoriella* of the dandelion family, is served in the rough terra cotta bowls with a white purée of fava beans. In this area, the dark skins of the dried *fave* are removed after soaking them, so you do not get the dark purée sometimes made with this bean. The concept of this dish is original to the area; the combination must be tasted to understand how special it is.

The greens and the bean purée, both dressed with the strong southern olive oil, are eaten alternately, never mixed together. When *cicoriella* is not available, the dish may be made with dandelion greens or Swiss chard.

The finished Purea di fave con cicoria *(Fava Bean Purée with Dandelion Greens) is shown behind both the unsoaked dark beans and the light-skinned soaked ones. Fava beans are usually served with l'ecorino cheese, in the foreground, and Altamura bread, which comes from the medieval town of Altamura in the Murge hills.*

Purea di fave con cicoria
FAVA BEAN PURÉE WITH DANDELION GREENS

FOR THE FAVA BEAN PURÉE

2   cups dried fava beans, about 12 ounces (see Note on page 63)

2½ quarts cold water

1   tablespoon coarse-grained salt

Pinch of freshly ground black pepper

1   tablespoon olive oil

1   red onion, peeled but left whole

1   large clove garlic, peeled but left whole

FOR THE DANDELION GREENS

1½ pounds dandelion greens, large stems removed, or Swiss chard

Coarse-grained salt

1   large clove garlic, peeled and finely chopped

TO SERVE

Abundant olive oil, preferably southern Italian

Freshly ground black pepper

Soak the fava beans in a bowl of cold water for about 5 hours. Drain the beans and remove the dark skins.

Put the water in a large stockpot with the salt, pepper, olive oil, onion, and garlic. Bring to a boil; then add the fava beans. Simmer, uncovered, for 1½ hours.

Discard the onion and pass the contents of the pot through a food mill, using the disc with the small holes. Return the puréed fava beans and their broth to the pot. Simmer, uncovered, for 1½ hours, stirring occasionally to be sure the purée does not stick to the bottom of the pot. Taste for salt and pepper and mix very well. Transfer the purée to a crockery or glass bowl and cool for about 1 hour.

Soak the dandelion greens in a large bowl of cold water for ½ hour.

Bring a pot of cold water to a boil. Add coarse-grained salt to taste and the chopped garlic. Add the dandelion greens and cook for 3 to 6 minutes, depending on the toughness of the leaves.

Meanwhile, reheat the fava bean purée in a different pan. Transfer the reheated purée to a warm soup tureen and cover.

Drain the dandelion greens, reserving 4 cups of the cooking water. Transfer the dandelion greens and water to a second soup tureen and cover.

To serve, bring both tureens to the table and prepare each serving with a ladleful of purée on one side of the soup bowl and some cooked dandelion greens, served from the tureen with tongs, on the other side of the bowl. Pour some olive oil over all and season with freshly ground black pepper.

SERVES 6.

These mysterious dwellings in Puglia are called trulli; *the name refers to their cone-shaped roofs made of layers of stone without mortar. One local theory explaining why the stones were not set permanently in place is that since taxes were determined by the size of the building, it was advantageous to be able to dismantle most of it quickly before the appearance of the tax collector and put it back together after he left. The rustic stone table in front of the* trulli *is set with a typical Puglia repast—country bread, sheep's milk cheese, a fava bean dish, and a local wine, unlabeled, in an uncorked bottle.*

Above: The ingredients for pesto *are contained in an old stone mortar with its metal pestle. The roughness of the stone helps grind the basil, garlic, walnuts, and pignoli into the classic Italian sauce.*

Opposite: A generous portion of finished pesto *sauce is served on top of* Minestrone alla genovese.

A picturesque feature of old Genoa was the fleet of small boats selling Genoese delicacies, which met travelers at the harbor. These *dispense ambulanti*, "moving shops," were particularly prized for their *minestrone*—the local version made, of course, with *pesto*. The beans most used are *borlotti*, also associated with Rome and Naples, rather than *cannellini*. The *mescia*, Genoa dialect for the combination of beans and cut up vegetables used in the *minestrone*, may also contain cubed eggplant and the yellow squash of Mantua, although they are not used in this version. Either pasta or rice may be added. The Genoese consider that a *minestrone* is successful if it is as good at room temperature as it is hot.

Liguria has a kind of small-leaf basil that is not common even in other parts of Italy. Its flavor is distinctly different from that of the more common larger leaf variety, although, of course, this is merely a subtlety and perfectly good *pesto* can be made outside of Liguria with the large-leaf type.

Ligurian olive oil is lighter in color and less full-bodied than Tuscan. When making Genoese dishes, it is perhaps better to substitute a good French virgin olive oil, if Ligurian oil is not available, rather than to use an oil from central or southern Italy.

68

Minestrone alla genovese
MINESTRONE GENOESE STYLE WITH PESTO SAUCE

½ cup dried *cannellini* beans (see Note on page 63)

Coarse-grained salt

1 leek, or 1 large red onion, peeled

1 medium-sized red onion, peeled

3 medium-sized celery stalks

15 sprigs Italian parsley, leaves only

1 large boiling potato (not a new potato), about 6 ounces

3 medium-sized carrots

½ cup olive oil

1 ripe tomato, peeled and seeded

1 cup homemade beef broth

FOR THE *PESTO* SAUCE

6 walnuts, shelled

1 tablespoon pignoli (pine nuts)

1 tablespoon sweet butter

1½ cups loosely packed fresh basil leaves

2 heaping tablespoons drained boiled spinach

2 medium-sized cloves garlic, peeled

¾ cup olive oil

2 ounces freshly grated *Parmigiano*

2 ounces freshly grated *Sardo* cheese or 2 additional ounces freshly grated *Parmigiano*

Salt and freshly ground black pepper

PLUS

½ pound short tubular dried pasta, such as elbow macaroni

Soak the beans overnight in a bowl of cold water. The next morning bring 10 cups of cold water to a boil in a casserole, then add coarse-grained salt to taste. Drain the beans, rinse them under cold running water, and add them to the casserole. Simmer, half covered, until they are cooked but still firm (45 minutes to 1½ hours, depending on the dryness of the beans). Stir the beans occasionally while they cook.

Clean the leek, removing and discarding the green part. Wash the white part very well. Coarsely chop the leek, onion, celery, and parsley together on a board. Peel the potato and cut it into ½-inch pieces. Scrape the carrots and cut them lengthwise into quarters. Then cut the quarters into ½-inch pieces.

Heat the oil in a stockpot and add the chopped ingredients, potato, and carrots. Sauté for 5 minutes, stirring with a wooden spoon. Add the tomato and sauté for 5 minutes longer.

Meanwhile, heat the broth and then add it to the stockpot with the vegetables and herbs. Cook for 5 minutes. Season with salt and pepper.

Drain the cooked beans, saving their cooking liquid. Put the beans into a crockery or glass bowl and cover the bowl with aluminum foil.

Add the cooking liquid from the beans to the stockpot and simmer, uncovered, for ½ hour.

Prepare the *pesto*: Put the walnuts, pine nuts, butter, basil, spinach, garlic, and ¼ cup of the oil in a blender or food processor and grind until very fine. Add the remaining oil and blend all the ingredients together until very smooth. Transfer the ground ingredients to a crockery or glass bowl. Add the *Parmigiano* and *Sardo* cheese and salt and pepper. Mix all the ingredients together with a wooden spoon. Cover the bowl with aluminum foil and let stand until needed.

Raise the heat under the stockpot until the liquid comes to a boil. Add the pasta and cook until it is *al dente* (9 to 12 minutes, depending on the brand). Remove the stockpot from the heat, add the reserved beans, and mix very well. Let stand for 2 minutes. Add half of the *pesto* to the stockpot, stir very well, and serve, adding some of the remaining *pesto* to each serving.

SERVES 8 TO 10

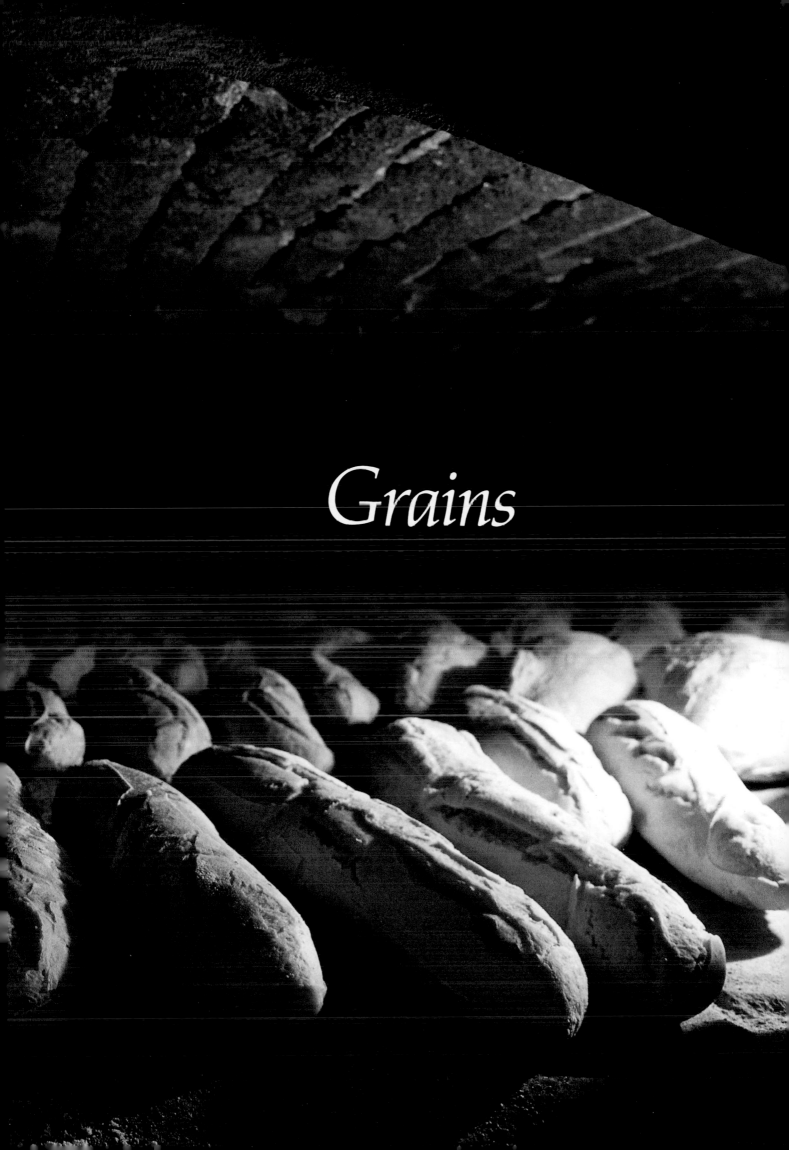

Grains

A WHEAT HARVEST

One of my most vivid childhood memories is of the ceremony and ritual of harvesting the wheat. The farmers from all about the villa gathered to cut and collect the spikes of wheat and spread them over the stone floor of the front courtyard called the *aia*. Each farmer had a simple, homemade thresher made of two thick, rounded wooden sticks tied together with a piece of rope. One stick was held as a handle, while the other was whipped against the grain to break the shells around the wheat berries, thereby separating the kernels from the spikes. All the farmers struck in chorus, as though led by Toscanini himself. Precision was important, as the men could strike one another if they beat out of rhythm.

The liberated wheat berries fell through to the floor of the *aia*. The seedless spikes remained on top. They were already dry when the wheat was picked, and they became the straw that would be used during the winter. This straw was thrown around a central pole, creating a huge, cone-shaped mound called a *pagliao*. We children were encouraged to jump on it to press the straw down so that it would become so tightly packed that the rain water would slide off without penetrating.

These straw stacks were always aesthetically shaped, and many were made to resemble little pitch-roofed houses. The straw was cut from the little "houses" as needed to make beds for the cattle, which stayed indoors all winter. The dirty straw was removed every couple of days and left for six months in a small square building, called the *concimaia*, or fertilizer house, far from the other buildings. An amusing testimony to the value of postwar Italian real estate is that most of these *concimaie* have since been sold as country houses; their rustic appearances have been left intact on the outside, but they have been turned into fancy dwellings inside.

After the straw had been removed, what remained on the stones was the pile of berries mixed with the broken shells. A small pile at a time was placed in the *staccio*, a cradle-shaped wooden object used to separate the kernels from their shells, where it was shaken vigorously up and down. The lighter shells rose to the top and were removed and placed in a pile next to the chicken house, where the chickens would peck away looking for any kernels still left inside the shells. The pile of berries remained in the *staccio* and was stored in the *granaio,* a large, airy granary, to dry.

The berries were ground as needed. A sifter separated the larger pieces of cracked chaff from the finely ground flour. Some chaff was used to make the darker breads, and the rest was fed to the pigs, chickens, and rabbits.

While the men were still threshing, the women prepared the immense ritual outdoor dinner to thank the neighboring farmers who had come to help, just as they would be helped when their moment of harvest came.

Geese, chickens, and rabbits that had been raised just for this feast were cooked. Vegetables considered particularly difficult were coaxed to grow in small quantities for this meal. And the wines served were those that had been designated at the time of corking as special enough for this occasion. The white tablecloth, in one unsewn piece, was long enough to cover a table for fifty people—threshers, guests, family—and it had taken an entire day to iron it. Everyone was as impeccably clean for this meal as for Sunday Mass, having followed the country custom of bathing in the *lavatoi,* the huge stone tubs that were also used for washing the clothes with the pure spring water of the nearby well.

Everyone ate without limit, as tray after tray was passed around the table. Earlier in the harvest, when the wheat had first to be cut, a consensus of organization had existed in the fields, which had grown out of centuries of experience. Each row of men with scythes had been arranged in order, from the fastest to the slowest, so that the scythes always moved in a diagonal line and no one would be cut by his neighbor. At that time, the fastest had been separated from the slowest. But now, at the big feast, no discrimination existed—the slowest workers were encouraged to eat as much as the fastest, for each had worked at the pace that was natural to him.

74

BREADS

In recent years, Prato has grown to be the second largest city of Tuscany. An ancient town, it has its own traditions, separate from those of Florence, even though it is only about 12 miles away. Like the bread of Florence, *Pane di Prato* is virtually without salt, but its technique of preparation is different. Both types of bread are useful for making *crostini*.

Pane di Prato
BREAD FROM PRATO

FOR THE SPONGE

- 2 ounces (4 cakes) fresh compressed yeast, or 4 packages (8 teaspoons) active dry yeast
- 1 cup lukewarm or hot water, depending on the yeast
- 2 cups unbleached all-purpose flour

FOR THE DOUGH

- 2 cups lukewarm water
  Pinch of salt
- 5 cups unbleached all-purpose flour

Prepare the sponge: Dissolve the yeast in the water.

Put the flour in a large bowl and make a well in it. Pour the dissolved yeast into the well and mix with a wooden spoon, incorporating enough of the flour to make a thick batter. Cover the bowl with a cotton dish towel and let rest overnight in a warm place away from drafts.

Prepare the dough: The next morning, start adding the 2 cups of water a little at a time, stirring continuously with a wooden spoon, to dissolve the sponge. Then add the salt and 4 of the 5 cups of flour, a small quantity at a time, while stirring with a wooden spoon. Cover the bowl with a cotton dish towel and let rest for ½ hour.

Line the bottom shelf of the oven with unglazed terra cotta tiles and preheat the oven to 400 degrees.

Spread out the remaining flour on a pasta board and put the risen dough on it. Knead the dough, incorporating more flour. Then divide the dough into 2 pieces and shape them as you wish. Wrap each loaf in a cotton dish towel and let rest for 15 minutes.

Unwrap the loaves and place them directly on the tiles in the oven. Bake for about 1 hour. Remove the loaves from the oven and let them cool on a rack.

MAKES 2 LOAVES.

In this small bakery in Sesto Fiorentino, near Florence, bread baking begins at 2 A.M. Opposite, top left: After bakers form and knead the dough, allowing time for it to rise, they transfer it from the mixer to a large container from which small amounts of dough are taken to form individual loaves by hand. Center left: A baker tosses twigs and branches of oak, cypress, lime, olive, and other woods into the oven's fire. Each type of wood contributes to the flavor of the bread. Bottom left: The blazing fire heats up the bricks. An experienced baker knows just how much wood must burn for the brick oven to reach the necessary temperature. When the fire has burned out, the hot ash is brushed all around the sides of the oven. Top right: A baker places loaves on a coarse cotton cloth where they are left to rise again. Bottom right: The loaves are now ready for the oven. Large loaves are placed on the sides, near the ash, in the hottest part of the oven. Below: Baked loaves are removed with a pala, *or bread shovel.*

Opposite: Crostini di fagioli *(Bean Paste Canapés),* on the left, and Crostini di fegatini *(Rustic Canapés of Chicken Livers),* on the right, are often served together.

*B*read not only accompanies a meal, particularly the main course, but it has also given rise to many dishes—*antipasti,* first courses, main courses, and desserts. Among the popular *antipasti* are the many types of rustic canapés called *crostini.* These are made with the bread either left as it is, toasted over a wood fire, or fried in butter or oil. Often a variety of *crostini* may be served together. An interesting combination is *Crostini di fagioli,* which has a topping of spicy puréed beans, and *Crostini di fegatini,* which is covered with both coarsely chopped and puréed chicken livers that have been seasoned with juniper and sage.

Crostini di fagioli
BEAN PASTE CANAPÉS

1   cup dried *cannellini* beans (see Note on page 63)

½   teaspoon hot red pepper flakes

2   level teaspoons tomato paste

Salt and freshly ground black pepper

1   medium-sized clove garlic, peeled

1   tablespoon rosemary leaves, fresh or preserved in salt or dried and blanched (see Note on page 43)

1   cup homemade chicken broth

2   tablespoons (1 ounce) sweet butter

2   tablespoons olive oil

1   lemon

16   pieces crusty Italian bread (Tuscan type, see page 75), 3 x 3 inches, ½ inch thick

10   sprigs Italian parsley, leaves only, finely chopped

Soak the beans overnight in a bowl of cold water. The next morning, drain the beans and rinse them under cold running water. Put them in a small saucepan with 4½ cups of water, half of the hot red pepper flakes, the tomato paste, and salt and pepper to taste. Put the pan over medium heat and cook, covered, for 2 hours. At that time almost all the water should have been absorbed and the beans cooked and very tender. Pass the beans and any remaining liquid through a food mill, using the disc with the medium-sized holes, into a small bowl.

Finely chop the garlic, rosemary, and the remaining hot red pepper flakes together on a board.

Heat the broth to lukewarm in a small saucepan.

Heat the butter and oil in a second saucepan over medium heat and, when the butter is completely melted, add the chopped ingredients. Sauté for 2 minutes. Then add the bean purée and stir very well with a wooden spoon until all the ingredients are well amalgamated. Pour the heated broth into the bean paste, stir very well to incorporate it, and cook for about 10 minutes longer, stirring every so often, until the texture is very smooth and fairly thick.

Preheat the oven to 400 degrees. Put the bread on a baking sheet and heat it in the oven for 3 minutes.

Squeeze the lemon and put the juice in a small cup.

Remove the bean paste from the heat, add the lemon juice, and stir very well.

To make the canapés, spread 1 heaping tablespoon of the paste on each piece of bread. Arrange the *crostini* on a large serving platter, sprinkle the parsley over them, and serve hot.

SERVES 8 AS AN APPETIZER.

Crostini di fegatini
RUSTIC CANAPÉS OF CHICKEN LIVERS

10 chicken livers, cleaned and fat removed

4 sage leaves, fresh or preserved in salt (see Note on page 43)

4 juniper berries

¼ cup olive oil

1 clove garlic, peeled but left whole

½ cup dry red wine

16 pieces crusty Italian bread (Tuscan type, see page 75), 3 x 3 inches, ½ inch thick

Salt and freshly ground black pepper

TO SERVE

16 fresh sage leaves

Finely chop 5 of the chicken livers together with the 4 sage leaves and the juniper berries on a board.

Heat the oil in a small heavy saucepan over medium heat. When the oil is warm, add the chopped ingredients and the garlic and sauté for 10 minutes. Then add the wine and let it evaporate for 10 minutes.

Preheat the oven to 400 degrees and, when it is hot, put the bread pieces on a baking sheet and heat for 10 minutes.

Meanwhile, cut the remaining chicken livers into quarters and add them to the saucepan. Season with salt and pepper and cook for 4 minutes. Remove from the heat and transfer the contents of the saucepan to a crockery or glass bowl.

To make the canapés, spread 1 tablespoon of the topping on each piece of bread. Arrange the *crostini* on a large serving platter and serve. If fresh sage is available, place 1 leaf on top of each canapé.

SERVES 8 AS AN APPETIZER.

*P*anzanella, or bread salad, is a typical summer dish, served chilled as an appetizer or as the main course in a light lunch. The Umbrians use a greater variety of vegetables in combination for their version of bread salad, called *pan bagnato,* than are used in the *panzanella* of Tuscany.

Pan bagnato o panzanella umbra
UMBRIAN BREAD SALAD

1   large red onion, peeled

3   large ripe tomatoes (about ½ pound each)

3   white celery stalks, leaves removed

1   very small thin cucumber without seeds, peeled

10 fresh basil leaves, torn into thirds

1   pound crusty Italian bread (Tuscan type, see page 75), several days old

2   tablespoons capers in wine vinegar, drained

Salt and freshly ground black pepper

½   cup olive oil

1½ tablespoons red wine vinegar

TO SERVE

5   large fresh basil leaves, torn into thirds

Several red *radicchio* leaves

Soak the onion, tomatoes, celery, cucumber, 10 leaves of basil, and the bread in a bowl of cold water for ½ hour. Squeeze the water from the bread and put the bread in a plastic container.

Dice the onion and put it on top of the bread. Cut each celery stalk lengthwise into three strips; then cut the strips into 1-inch pieces. Sprinkle the celery pieces over the onion.

Cut the cucumber into slices of less than ½ inch thick and place them over the celery. Then add the torn basil leaves, the capers, and, finally, the tomatoes which have been cut into ½-inch squares. Close the plastic container and refrigerate it for at least 2 hours before serving.

Transfer the contents of the container to a large bowl. Add salt and pepper to taste and then the olive oil and wine vinegar. Toss very well and serve with the remaining basil leaves and the *radicchio*.

SERVES 6.

*I*t's called *fettunta* in Tuscany and *bruschetta* in Umbria and some other places, but both names mean a thick slice of country bread toasted over a wood fire (or in the oven) and anointed with good virgin olive oil. Often the bread is rubbed with garlic just after it is toasted.

It is mainly in the areas of central and southern Italy, where full-bodied olive oils are produced, that you will also find country bread. It is interesting to note that in the northern parts of Italy, where no oil is produced, the bread is more "refined" and not as crusty. Liguria is the only olive oil area that shares the northern type of bread; but its oil is light and not full bodied.

Fettunta is usually thought of as a late fall dish—the season when the olives are newly pressed—but it can also be a summer dish when the tomatoes and basil are at their peak. In those areas lucky enough to have fresh black truffles, the *fettunta* is topped with them finely chopped.

Fettunta o bruschetta al pomodoro
FETTUNTA OR BRUSCHETTA WITH TOMATOES

18 pieces crusty Italian bread, (Tuscan type, see page 75), 3 x 2 inches, 1 inch thick

2 cloves garlic, peeled and cut in half

18 fresh basil leaves

½ cup olive oil

Salt and freshly ground black pepper

2 large ripe but not overripe tomatoes (about 1 pound total weight)

Preheat the oven to 375 degrees. Place the pieces of bread on the shiny side of a piece of aluminum foil and toast them for 10 minutes on each side. Then rub both sides of each slice with the cut garlic.

Arrange the basil leaves on a large platter; then put the pieces of bread over them.

Warm the oil in a small saucepan over very low heat for 5 minutes. Immediately pour the warm oil over the bread. Sprinkle with salt and pepper to taste.

Cut the tomatoes horizontally into 1-inch-thick slices; then cut each slice in half. Place 1 half-slice of tomato on top of each slice of bread and serve immediately.

SERVES 6.

A particularly interesting version of *bruschetta* exists in Puglia, where the Altamura type of crusty country bread is used with the local oil. Unexpectedly, garlic, which is so characteristic of southern Italy, is omitted in this dish. The fascinating variant here is *ruchetta* (known abroad as *arugola*), which is added to the tomatoes. It makes a truly delicious *bruschetta*.

Italians make use of country bread and olive oil in another interesting dish called *pappa*, or bread soup. It is best known in its Florentine version, but is made in other parts of Tuscany in a variation flavored with leeks. *Pappa* may be eaten hot or at room temperature.

Bruschetta con ruchetta
BRUSCHETTA WITH ARUGOLA

18 pieces crusty Italian bread
(Tuscan type, see page 75),
3 x 2 inches, 1 inch thick

2 large ripe but not overripe
tomatoes (about 1 pound total
weight)

¼ pound *ruchetta* (*arugola*), with
small stems

½ cup olive oil

Salt and freshly ground black
pepper

Opposite: In the shadow of the Benedictine abbey of San Vito near Bari, Bruschetta con ruchetta (Bruschetta with Arugola) rests on the quay, surrounded by a variety of young field greens, which throughout southern Italy are eaten raw, as a salad, and served with cool white wine.

Preheat the oven to 375 degrees. Place the pieces of bread on the shiny side of a piece of aluminum foil and toast them for about 10 minutes on each side. Arrange the toasted bread on a large platter.

Slice the tomatoes horizontally into 1-inch-thick slices; then cut each slice in half. Arrange the slices to cover the bread on the platter. Distribute the *ruchetta* over everything. Pour the oil over all and sprinkle with salt and pepper. Serve immediately.

SERVES 6.

Pappa al pomodoro con porri
BREAD SOUP WITH LEEKS

Clean the leeks: Slice off the ends with the attached roots. Slice off the green leaves at the point where the white stems turn green. Cut the remaining white stems into rings about ¼ inch thick. Put the leeks in a bowl of cold water and let them soak for ½ hour. Drain the leeks and rinse them very carefully under cold running water.

Heat the oil in a large casserole, preferably of terra cotta, over medium heat. When the oil is warm, add the leeks and sauté for 15 minutes.

Meanwhile, pass the tomatoes through a food mill, using the disc with the small holes. Add the tomatoes to the leeks. Then add salt and pepper to taste and the hot red pepper flakes. Simmer, covered, for about ½ hour.

Cut the bread into small pieces and add it to the casserole. Mix very well and sauté for 5 minutes. Then add the broth, mix very well again, and remove the casserole from the heat. Cover the casserole and let it stand for 1 hour.

When ready to serve, stir the *pappa* very well and taste for salt and pepper. You can reheat the bread soup or eat it as is. Serve the soup in individual soup bowls, adding 1 fresh basil leaf and 2 teaspoons of olive oil to each serving.

SERVES 6.

4 leeks

½ cup olive oil

1½ pounds fresh tomatoes or 1½
pounds canned imported
Italian tomatoes, drained

Salt and freshly ground black
pepper

½ teaspoon hot red pepper flakes

1 pound crusty Italian bread
(Tuscan type, see page 75),
several days old

3 cups hot homemade beef broth

6 basil leaves, fresh or preserved
in salt (see Note on page 43)

12 teaspoons olive oil

*T*aralli are yeast-dough rings eaten throughout southern Italy. They are flavored in a number of different ways and, according to their flavoring, may be used as bread, appetizer, or dessert. The special feature of their preparation is that the risen dough is quickly boiled before it is baked. Both this step in the preparation and the ring shape are shared with the bagel of Eastern European Jewish origin. Perhaps there was some connection centuries ago; at this point only speculation is possible. Yet it seems unlikely that two breads with a common technique and shape would have evolved in two totally unconnected circumstances.

Taralli

TARALLI

FOR THE SPONGE

1	ounce (2 cakes) compressed fresh yeast, or 2 packages (4 teaspoons) active dry yeast
½	cup lukewarm or hot water, depending on the yeast
1	cup unbleached all-purpose flour

FOR THE DOUGH

1¾	cups unbleached all-purpose flour
2	tablespoons olive oil
2	extra large eggs
2	teaspoons fennel seeds
1	teaspoon salt
10	twists black pepper

PLUS

Coarse-grained salt

1   extra large egg

Prepare the sponge: Dissolve the yeast in the water in a small bowl, stirring with a wooden spoon.

Put the cup of flour in a larger bowl and make a well in it. Pour the dissolved yeast into the well. Mix with a wooden spoon, incorporating half of the flour. Cover the bowl with a cotton dish towel and put in a warm place away from drafts. Let the sponge rest until it has doubled in size (about 1 hour).

Prepare the dough: Arrange the 1¾ cups of flour in a mound on a pasta board. Make a well in the flour. Place the sponge in the well with the remaining unincorporated flour. Then add the oil, eggs, fennel seeds, salt, and pepper. Use a wooden spoon to carefully mix together all the ingredients in the well. Then start absorbing some of the flour from the inside rim of the well little by little. Keep mixing until all but about 5 tablespoons of the flour is incorporated. Knead the dough with the palm of your hand in a folding motion until it is homogeneous and smooth (about 5 minutes).

Cut the dough into 4 pieces. Using the four fingers of both hands, lightly roll each piece, moving both hands apart gradually from the center to the sides. Keep repeating the motion until the strip is rounded and about 25 inches long. Divide the strip into 5 pieces (each 5 inches long); then take each individual piece and connect the two ends together to form a round shape. Repeat this technique with all the other pieces of dough.

Let the *taralli* rest, covered with a cotton dish towel, for 15 minutes in a warm place away from drafts.

Preheat the oven to 375 degrees. Lightly oil two baking sheets.

Place a large casserole of cold water over medium heat and, when the water comes to a boil, add coarse-grained salt to taste; then put in 4 or 5 *taralli* at a time and boil them for 30 seconds.

Lay a piece of wax paper on a board. With a slotted spoon, transfer the lightly boiled *taralli* onto the wax paper. When they are all on the wax paper, transfer them to the prepared baking sheet with a metal spatula.

Stir the egg in a small bowl and brush the *taralli* tops with it. Bake for 30 minutes. Remove the *taralli* from the oven and put them on a rack to cool.

MAKES ABOUT 20 *TARALLI.*

*I*n the Puglia area, onions, tomatoes, and olives are used as ingredients in bread dough and to stuff pizza. Sometimes these *pizze* are made with a potato dough rather than a yeast dough. In the following recipe, tomatoes and sliced onions are incorporated into the bread dough, producing a subtle and delicious flavor.

Pane con pomodori e cipolle
TOMATO–ONION BREAD

Slice the onions into thin slices and put them in a large bowl of cold water. Soak for ½ hour.

Bring a small pot of cold water to a boil; then add coarse-grained salt. Blanch the tomatoes in the water for a few minutes; then put them in a bowl of cold water. Remove the skins and seeds. Put the tomato pieces on paper towels to drain.

Heat the oil in a small saucepan over medium heat and, when the oil is warm, add the tomatoes and the drained onion slices. Sauté for 5 minutes; then season with salt, pepper, oregano, and the hot red pepper flakes. Cover the pan and cook for 10 minutes longer. Remove from the heat and transfer the contents of the pan to a crockery or glass bowl. Cover and let cool until needed.

Meanwhile, prepare the sponge: Dissolve the yeast in the water in a small bowl.

Put the 2 cups of flour in a bowl and make a well in it. Pour the dissolved yeast into the well. Mix with a wooden spoon, incorporating half of the flour. Cover the bowl with a cotton dish towel and put it in a warm place away from drafts. Let the sponge rest until it has doubled in size (about 1 hour).

Arrange the 4 cups of flour in a mound on a pasta board. Make a well in the flour. Place the sponge in the well with the remaining unincorporated flour; then add the contents of the crockery bowl and salt. Use a wooden spoon to carefully mix together all the ingredients in the well, little by little. Keep mixing until all but about 5 tablespoons of the flour is incorporated. Gently knead the dough with the palm of your hand in a folding motion for 1 minute. Divide the dough in half.

Flour a cotton dish towel and wrap the dough in it. Let the dough rest until doubled in size (about 1 hour).

Preheat the oven to 375 degrees. Lightly oil a baking sheet. Transfer the risen dough onto the prepared baking sheet and bake for 1 hour. Remove from the oven and transfer the bread to a rack to cool for about 1 hour.

MAKES 2 LOAVES.

2 medium-sized red onions, peeled

Coarse-grained salt

4 medium-sized ripe tomatoes (about 1 pound total weight)

¼ cup olive oil

Salt and freshly ground black pepper

Pinch of dried oregano

¼ teaspoon hot red pepper flakes

FOR THE SPONGE

3 ounces (6 cakes) fresh compressed yeast, or 6 packages (12 teaspoons) active dry yeast

1 cup lukewarm or hot water, depending on the yeast

2 cups unbleached all-purpose flour

FOR THE DOUGH

4 cups unbleached all-purpose flour

Pinch of salt

PASTA

Preceding overleaf: Tagliatelle con dadi di prosciutto *(Tagliatelle with Creamed Prosciutto Sauce) is presented in a hollowed-out wheel of Parmigiano.*

Pasta is made primarily from finely ground wheat flour. Although an understanding of the health benefits of whole wheat flour has spurred some cooks to try to develop whole wheat pasta, generally it is not popular in Italy. The pasta has a slightly sour taste, and the dough is heavier.

More coarsely ground wheat flour, called semolina, is used in some special southern Italian pastas and, in my experience is always made without eggs. The use of semolina for egg pasta is an idea that has occurred to some non-Italian chefs abroad, perhaps as a misconception of the way pasta is made in Italy.

In the Parma area, the sheet of pasta is made with flour, eggs, and salt, but no oil. Cut into *tagliatelle,* it is combined with marvelous *prosciutto,* cut into cubes, and, in this recipe presented as only Parma itself could afford to do it—in a hollowed out wheel of its own local cheese, the world-famous *Parmigiano-Reggiano.* Although this touch cannot be reproduced often, it does make the dish even more special, because the *tagliatelle* and sauce absorb the flavor of the wheel of cheese so completely. This quintessential Parma sauce for the *tagliatelle* is served with its three famous ingredients pure and unadorned: *prosciutto di Parma,* butter, and *Parmigiano.*

Tagliatelle con dadi di prosciutto
TAGLIATELLE WITH CREAMED PROSCIUTTO SAUCE

FOR THE PASTA

4   cups unbleached all-purpose flour

5   extra large eggs

Pinch of salt

FOR THE SAUCE

4   ounces very lean *prosciutto,* in one piece

8   tablespoons (4 ounces) sweet butter

1½ cups heavy cream

Salt and freshly ground black pepper

Pinch of freshly grated nutmeg

¾   cup freshly grated *Parmigiano*

TO COOK THE PASTA

Coarse-grained salt

Make the pasta with the ingredients and quantities listed above. To make pasta by hand or with a manual pasta machine, put the flour in a mound on a pasta board. Use a fork to make a well in the center and put the eggs and salt in the well. (In other pastas using oil, the oil is also placed in the well at this point.) Use a fork to mix together the contents of the well and incorporate the flour from the inner rim of the well.

Start kneading the dough by hand to get an elastic ball of dough; then finish kneading by hand or with the rollers of the pasta machine. Stretch the pasta to the thickness you need with a rolling pin or with the pasta machine. Cut the pasta into the shape you need manually, using a knife or pastry wheel, or with the cutting attachments of the pasta machine. For details of pasta making, see *Giuliano Bugialli's Classic Techniques of Italian Cooking,* pages 118–178.

For *tagliatelle,* stretch the pasta to a thickness of less than $\frac{1}{16}$ inch by hand, or with a pasta machine to the finest setting. Cut it into strips $\frac{1}{4}$ inch wide. Let them rest until needed.

Bring a large pot of cold water to a boil.

Meanwhile, cut the *prosciutto* into cubes a little smaller than $\frac{1}{2}$ inch.

Melt the butter in a large casserole over low heat. Add the *prosciutto* and sauté it lightly for 1 minute.

Add coarse-grained salt to the boiling water; then add the pasta and cook from 30 seconds to 1 minute, depending on the dryness of the pasta, after the water has returned to a boil. Drain the pasta and add it to the casserole with the *prosciutto.*

Immediately pour the cream over the pasta and season with salt, pepper, and nutmeg. Gently mix all the ingredients together; then add the cheese, mix again, transfer to a warm serving dish, and serve immediately.

SERVES 8.

*T*he violet flower *crocus sativus* belongs to the iridaceae family, whose very name means "brightly colored." The pistils of this flower are the precious saffron threads. Originating in Persia, *crocus sativus* spread through the ancient world as a medicinal spice and is mentioned in the Egyptian papyruses, in the Hebrew *Song of Songs,* and in the Greek *Iliad.*

It was in the late Middle Ages and early Renaissance in Europe that it first came to be used in cooking, giving rise to a whole category of *ginestra,* or yellow dishes. Despite its costliness, a pinch of saffron was used in so many dishes that in fourteenth-century Italian cookbooks one can read "and add the usual salt, pepper, and saffron." We must not forget that black pepper was also a luxury at that time.

Although Spanish saffron is the most famous, the flower is not difficult to cultivate in many other places. Much of the saffron used in Italy originates there, and it is of good quality. Especially prized is that which comes from the area of L'Aquila in Abruzzi.

It is not the rarity of the plant as much as the labor involved in gathering the pistils that makes saffron so expensive, for a huge quantity is needed to produce even a small amount of the spice. It is best to buy saffron threads rather than the already ground spice, as the latter can be mixed with inferior saffron.

While the color is a desirable by-product, the taste of the saffron is the main reason for adding it to pasta dough. Veal shank meat combines particularly well with saffron, and that is the meat used in this sauce. (In Italy, pasta and *risotto* are not really considered appropriate as side dishes to any main course. The chief exception is the pairing of saffron *risotto* with *Ossobuco alla milanese.*)

Saffron is traditionally ground into
a powder with a marble mortar and
pestle. The marble has just enough
friction to grind the soft threads of
the saffron without absorbing the
powder. In Pasta allo zafferano
(Saffron pasta) the bright yellow,
freshly made pasta is served with
a veal sauce.

Pasta allo zafferano
SAFFRON PASTA

FOR THE SAUCE

3   medium-sized leeks, or 3 medium-sized red onions, peeled

¼   cup olive oil

2   tablespoons (1 ounce) sweet butter

1   ossobuco (a 1½-inch slice of veal shank, with bone and marrow in the center)

1   tablespoon unbleached all-purpose flour

½   medium-sized red onion, peeled

1   small celery stalk

1   small carrot, scraped

1   small piece lemon rind

1   cup dry white wine

3   cups canned imported Italian tomatoes, drained

1   tablespoon tomato paste

Salt and freshly ground black pepper

PLUS

1   large clove garlic, peeled

15   sprigs Italian parsley, leaves only

4   sage leaves, fresh or preserved in salt (see Note on page 43)

Grated peel of 1 lemon

2   tablespoons (1 ounce) sweet butter

FOR THE PASTA

4   cups unbleached all-purpose flour

5   extra large eggs

Pinch of salt

1   scant teaspoon powdered saffron, or ⅛-gram package saffron threads, finely ground with a marble mortar and pestle

TO COOK THE PASTA

Coarse-grained salt

Cut off the ends of the leeks with the attached roots. Then cut off the green leaves at the point where the white stems turn green. Slice the remaining white stems into rings less than ½ inch wide. Put the rings in a bowl of cold water and let them soak for ½ hour, or until all the sand is removed.

Heat the oil and butter in a casserole over medium heat and, when the butter is completely melted, drain the leeks and add them to the casserole. Sauté for 5 minutes.

Tie the ossobuco with string all around the edge to keep it together while it cooks. Use the tablespoon of flour to lightly flour the ossobuco on both sides. Add the meat to the casserole and sauté until it is golden brown on both sides (about 4 minutes on each side).

Meanwhile, finely chop the onion, celery, carrot, and lemon rind together on a board. Add the chopped ingredients to the casserole and sauté for 2 minutes longer. Add the wine and let it evaporate over low heat for 20 minutes. Add the whole tomatoes and the tomato paste, cover the casserole, and simmer for 40 minutes, stirring occasionally. Taste for salt and pepper. Turn the ossobuco, cover the casserole again, and simmer for 25 minutes longer. Transfer the meat to a board and remove the string and the bone.

Pass the contents of the casserole and the ossobuco meat through a food mill, using the disc with the medium-sized holes, into a second casserole. Simmer the sauce, uncovered, over medium heat for about 15 minutes. Taste for salt and pepper. Once the sauce is ready, remove the casserole from the heat and let it stand, covered, until needed.

Finely chop the garlic, parsley, and sage together on a board. Transfer the chopped ingredients to a small crockery or glass bowl. Add the grated lemon peel and mix all the ingredients together with a wooden spoon. Cover the bowl and let stand until needed.

Prepare the pasta with the ingredients and quantities listed above, following the instructions on pages 86–87. Add the saffron to the well in the flour together with the eggs and salt.

Stretch the pasta to a thickness of less than ¹/₁₆ inch by hand, or with a pasta machine to the finest setting. Cut the pasta into tagliatelle.

Put the cut pasta on cotton dish towels to dry for 15 minutes, or until needed. Cooking time will vary, depending on how dry the pasta is.

Bring a large quantity of cold water to a boil and add coarse-grained salt to taste. Melt the butter on a large serving platter placed over the pot of boiling water. Reheat the sauce.

When the butter is melted, remove the platter and add the pasta to the salted boiling water. Cook for 40 seconds to 1 minute, depending on the dryness of the pasta. Drain the pasta and transfer it to the serving platter with the melted butter. Pour the sauce over and toss very well; then sprinkle with the chopped aromatic herbs in the small bowl and serve immediately.

SERVES 8.

*T*he pale green tints in this homemade spaghetti come from the unripe, uncooked, green tomatoes that have been puréed and then added to the pasta dough. Their special flavor, slightly tart but still with some tomato sweetness, combines magnificently with the full ripeness of the fresh red tomatoes in the sauce. A few leaves of fresh basil complete the taste.

Puréed green tomatoes belong in the very small category of foods that combine well with pasta dough; puréed sweet bell peppers, dried wild mushrooms, the classical spinach of green pasta, beets or tomatoes of red pasta, and cocoa of chocolate pasta* almost exhaust the list.

Spaghetti alla prematura
GREEN TOMATO SPAGHETTI

FOR THE PASTA

1   medium-sized green tomato

2¾ cups unbleached all-purpose flour

2   extra large eggs

2   teaspoons olive oil or vegetable oil

     Pinch of salt

TO COOK THE PASTA

     Coarse-grained salt

PLUS

8   tablespoons (4 ounces) sweet butter

6   fresh basil leaves

FOR THE SAUCE

1½ pounds ripe tomatoes or 1½ pounds canned imported Italian tomatoes, drained

¼   cup olive oil

1   tablespoon (½ ounce) sweet butter

1   medium-sized clove garlic, peeled but left whole

     Salt and freshly ground black pepper

10   sprigs Italian parsley, leaves only

3   basil leaves, fresh or preserved in salt (see Note on page 43)

Make the pasta first: Remove the stem from the tomato; then cut the tomato into quarters and discard the seeds. Finely grind the tomato in a blender or food processor. Weigh out 3 ounces of the ground tomato, discarding the rest.

Prepare the pasta with the ingredients and quantities listed above, placing the 3 ounces of ground tomato in the well in the flour together with the eggs, oil, and salt, and following the directions on pages 86–87.

Stretch the pasta to a thickness of ⅛ inch with the pasta machine and cut it into strips ⅛ inch wide, using the *taglierini* cutter on the pasta machine. Let the prepared spaghetti rest until needed.

Prepare the sauce: Remove the stems from the ripe tomatoes. Then cut the tomatoes into quarters and remove the seeds.

Heat the oil and butter in a heavy saucepan over medium heat and, when the butter is competely melted, add the garlic and sauté for 5 minutes. Discard the garlic and add the tomatoes to the pan. Lower the heat and cover the pan. Cook for 15 minutes, stirring occasionally with a wooden spoon. Taste for salt and pepper.

Finely chop the parsley on a board and tear the basil leaves into thirds. Add the parsley and basil to the sauce, cover the pan again, and simmer for 5 minutes longer.

Bring a large pot of cold water to a boil.

Meanwhile, pass the contents of the saucepan through a food mill, using the disc with the small holes, into a second saucepan. Put the saucepan over low heat to reduce the sauce further (about 3 minutes). Taste for salt and pepper.

Add coarse-grained salt to taste to the boiling water; then add the pasta and cook for 1 to 3 minutes, depending on the dryness of the pasta.

Warm the dinner plates and use a double boiler or *bagnomaria* to melt the butter. Drain the pasta and place it on a large serving dish; then add the melted butter and toss very well.

Prepare each serving of pasta with some sauce on top and a whole basil leaf. Serve hot.

SERVES 6.

I revived this traditional type of pasta, as well as saffron pasta, several years ago. They have since become popular in several variations among Italian, French, and nouvelle cuisine *chefs.*

A few herbs as well as spices may be added to pasta dough. Pasta containing whole fresh parsley leaves is a representative dish from Puglia. Other herbs are chopped very fine before they are added to the dough, but with parsley it is traditional to add the whole leaves, probably because the chopping would discolor them. Besides, the attractive pattern they produce is reason enough to use the leaves whole.

This dough has another special feature: The grated cheese is mixed into the dough itself rather than sprinkled on the cooked pasta. Most pastas in this region are eaten without the addition of grated cheese. When local *Pecorinos*, hard sheep's milk cheeses, were much more available, no doubt they were used as the cheese, but now it is more usual to find *Parmigiano*.

The parsley pasta is usually cut into the square-shaped *quadri* or *quadrucci*, of varying size. They are most commonly eaten in turkey broth or with a lamb sauce or with melted butter and sage leaves.

The shape of *quadrucci* and the use of broth rather than sauce accentuate the beauty of the whole-leaf pattern of the pasta, so that the dish almost resembles an embroidery.

FOR THE BROTH

2	pounds turkey dark meat, with bones
	Coarse-grained salt
1	medium-sized red onion, peeled
1	celery stalk
1	medium-sized carrot, scraped
1	medium-sized clove garlic, peeled but left whole
1	whole cherry tomato
5	sprigs Italian parsley
3	extra large egg whites

FOR THE PASTA

3½	cups unbleached all-purpose flour
½	cup freshly grated *Parmigiano*
5	extra large eggs
	Pinch of salt
6	twists black pepper
30	sprigs Italian parsley, leaves only

Quadrucci in brodo
QUADRUCCI IN BROTH

Prepare the broth: Put the turkey, coarse-grained salt to taste, the whole onion, celery, carrot, garlic, tomato, and parsley sprigs in a large stockpot. Add 4 quarts cold water and put the pot over medium heat, uncovered. Simmer for 2 hours, skimming off the foam as it rises to the top.

Remove the meat from the pot and reserve it for another dish. Pass the rest of the contents of the pot through a fine strainer, to remove the vegetables and impurities, into a large bowl. Let the broth cool; then place the bowl in the refrigerator overnight to allow the fat to rise to the top.

Use a metal spatula to remove the solidified fat; then clarify the broth. Add 8 quarts cold water and put the pot over medium heat, uncovered. In a small bowl, lightly beat 2 tablespoons of broth with the egg whites. Pour the broth–egg-white mixture into the rest of the cold broth and whisk very well. Transfer the broth to a pot and place it on the edge of a burner. Bring to the simmering stage, half covered, and simmer for about 10 minutes, or until the egg whites rise to the top with the impurities and the broth becomes transparent.

Meanwhile, place a wet cotton dish towel in the freezer for 5 minutes. Then stretch the dish towel over a colander and strain the broth through it to clarify it completely. The broth should be absolutely clear.

Prepare the pasta with the ingredients and quantities listed above, placing the grated *Parmigiano*, salt, pepper, and eggs in the well in the flour, and following the directions on pages 86–87.

Stretch the pasta to a thickness of ⅛ inch by hand or with the pasta machine. Place the whole parsley leaves on top of half the length of the layer of pasta. Fold the other half of the layer of pasta over the parsley, and press the layers together. Continue to roll out the layer of pasta until it is ¹/₁₆ inch thick. Using a scalloped pastry cutter, cut the pasta into squares of about 2 inches.

Bring the broth to a boil and add the pasta. Cook for 1 to 3 minutes, depending on the dryness of the pasta. Serve hot without adding cheese.

SERVES 12.

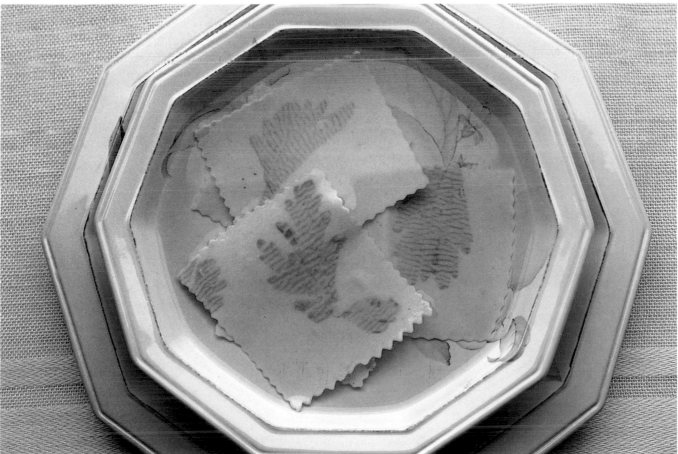

Two representative bean dishes from Puglia—Purea di fave con cicoria (Fava Bean Purée with Dandelion Greens) on the left, and Cavatelli con fagioli *(Pasta and Beans Puglia Style) on the right.*

*C*avatelli are made from the same pasta dough as are *orecchiette*, and the technique for making them begins with the preparation of *orecchiette* (see page 110). But instead of leaving the ear-shaped pasta in its concave form, each one is rolled up by hand. In Puglia *cavatelli* are eaten in a dish together with *cannellini* beans. Sometimes a red-pepper-spiced olive oil, a counterpart to the Tuscan *olio santo*, is sprinkled over the finished dish. Unlike *olio santo*, which is used only with broth, the Puglia hot oil is also used with some pasta, bean, and *minestrone* dishes.

In the past, working-class people all over Italy often ate a delicious meal made with left-over *pasta e fagioli* dishes. They would hollow out a crusty country bread and fill it with the pasta and beans. Eating it involved spooning the pasta and beans out of the loaf, then breaking off and eating pieces of the bread, which were suffused with the flavors of the dish.

Cavatelli con fagioli
PASTA AND BEANS PUGLIA STYLE

1	cup dried *cannellini* beans (see Note on page 63)	5	tablespoons olive oil
1	small red onion, peeled	2	cloves garlic, peeled but left whole
2	medium-sized celery stalks	2	whole bay leaves

94

Salt and freshly ground black pepper	2 cups unbleached all-purpose flour
Pinch of hot red pepper flakes	Pinch of salt
6 cups cold water	1 cup cold water
1 pound dried *cavatelli*, preferably imported Italian, or fresh *cavatelli*, prepared with the following ingredients (see Note)	TO COOK THE PASTA Coarse-grained salt
	TO SERVE
1 cup semolina flour	6 tablespoons olive oil
	Freshly ground black pepper

Soak the beans in a bowl of cold water overnight. The next morning, finely chop the onion and celery together on a board.

Heat the oil in a heavy casserole over medium heat and, when the oil is warm, add the chopped ingredients and the garlic and bay leaves. Sauté gently for 5 minutes; then add salt and pepper to taste and the hot red pepper flakes. Add 1 cup of water, cover the casserole and, when the water comes to a boil, cook for 30 minutes. Discard the garlic and bay leaves.

Pass the contents of the casserole through a food mill, using the disc with the medium-sized holes, into a bowl and return the passed vegetables to the casserole. Add the remaining 5 cups of water; then drain the beans and rinse them under cold running water and add them to the casserole. Put the pan over medium heat and, when the water comes to a boil, lower the heat, cover the pan (but not completely), and simmer for about 1 hour. When the beans are cooked, they should still retain their shape, and the water should be half incorporated.

Bring a large pot of cold water to a boil and add coarse-grained salt to taste. Then add the *cavatelli*. Cook them, whether they are homemade or a dried commercial brand until they are *al dente*. (Cook the homemade pasta 5 to 10 minutes, depending on the dryness of the pasta. Cook the commercial pasta 9 to 12 minutes, depending on the brand.)

Meanwhile, drain the beans into a small bowl and return the cooking broth to the casserole. Reduce it over medium heat (about 2 minutes).

Drain the pasta and transfer it to the casserole. Taste for salt and pepper and mix very well. Cook for 1 minute longer; then add the beans. Stir very well and serve immediately, adding a tablespoon of oil and a twist of black pepper to each serving.

SERVES 6.

NOTE: *To make homemade* cavatelli, *see the instructions for* orecchiette *on page 110 and the introduction to this recipe.*

*S*wiss chard, alone or in combination with spinach, with a touch of some local field herbs found only in Parma, provides the cooked green vegetable basis for the stuffing for *Tortelli di erbette*. The dish is not quite the same if it is made without the particular field herbs found only in the Parma area, but the difference in taste without them is so subtle that perhaps one must be from Parma to miss them. The amounts of Parma butter and of *Parmigiano* used by the natives are prodigious. I have reduced the proportions of these ingredients to amounts that are scarcely frugal, but which the natives of Parma would certainly find insufficient.

Tortelli alla parmigiana o di erbetti
TORTELLI PARMA STYLE

FOR THE STUFFING

2 pounds Swiss chard

1 pound spinach

   Coarse-grained salt

15 ounces whole milk ricotta

4 extra large eggs

6 ounces freshly grated *Parmigiano*

4 tablespoons (2 ounces) sweet butter at room temperature

   Salt and freshly ground black pepper

   Freshly grated nutmeg

FOR THE PASTA

4 cups unbleached all-purpose flour

5 extra large eggs

   Pinch of salt

TO COOK THE PASTA

   Coarse-grained salt

FOR THE SAUCE

16 tablespoons (8 ounces) sweet butter

1 cup freshly grated *Parmigiano*

Prepare the stuffing: Wash the Swiss chard and spinach carefully, removing the large stems.

Bring a large stockpot of cold water to a boil. Add coarse-grained salt and then the vegetables. Cook for 10 minutes; then drain and cool under cold running water. Squeeze and finely chop the cooked greens on a board. Put the ricotta in a large bowl and add the eggs, chopped greens, *Parmigiano,* and butter. Season with salt, pepper, and nutmeg. Mix all the ingredients together with a wooden spoon to obtain a smooth texture. Cover the bowl and refrigerate until needed.

Prepare the pasta with the ingredients and quantities listed above, following the directions on pages 86–87.

Stretch the layer of pasta to a little less than 1/16 of an inch thick or the finest setting of the pasta machine.

To make into *tortelli,* use ½ tablespoon of the filling for each dot. Start 1 inch from the top and side edges of the sheet of pasta and make 2 lengthwise rows of filling dots, each 2 inches apart. Continue the 2 rows halfway down the sheet of pasta. Fold over the other half of the sheet of pasta and quickly press down around the dots of filling. Use a scalloped pastry wheel to cut out 2-inch squares and seal them all around (see Note).

Bring a large stockpot of cold water to a boil.

Melt the butter for the sauce in a double boiler or *bagnomaria.*

When the water comes to a boil, add coarse-grained salt to taste. Then add the *tortelli* and cook for 1 to 2 minutes, depending on the dryness of the pasta.

Pour ¼ cup of the melted butter onto a large serving dish and, with a skimmer-strainer, transfer the *tortelli* from the pot onto the prepared dish, sprinkling some *Parmigiano* and pouring some melted butter over each layer. Serve hot.

SERVES 8.

NOTE: *It is best to stuff the pasta while it is still very fresh. If it has dried a bit, moisten the edges with water or beaten egg white to seal.*

Another stuffed pasta typical of Parma is *anolini*. Unlike the square *tortelli*, they are round with smooth unscalloped edges. Since the name *anolini* is a corruption of the word for *ravioli* in Parma dialect, they were likely made, like the Florentine *ravioli nudi*, without pasta, as dumplings. They were already referred to as *anolini* by the great Renaissance chef Scappi in the mid-sixteenth century, and his illustrations of kitchen implements include an *anolini* cutter.

While *Tortelli alla parmigiana* have only one classic stuffing, *di erbette*, *anolini* are stuffed in many different ways; only grated *Parmigiano* is an ingredient in all of the variations. *Anolini* are usually eaten in broth, and, even when they are sauced, they are first cooked in broth rather than in salted water. This delicate stuffing of veal brains and *prosciutto* is one of my favorites.

The sixteenth-century church of the Madonna della Steccata in Parma is a splendid example of the Classical style. The celebrated pasta dish of Parma, Tortelli alla parmigiana, is served on a terrace overlooking the church.

Anolini al ragù di prosciutto
ANOLINI WITH PROSCIUTTO SAUCE

FOR THE SAUCE

2 ounces dried *porcini* mushrooms

4 ounces *prosciutto*

4 ounces boiled ham

1 medium-sized red onion, peeled

6 tablespoons (3 ounces) sweet butter

1 pound fresh tomatoes or 1 pound canned imported Italian tomatoes, drained

Salt and freshly ground black pepper

½ cup heavy cream

FOR THE STUFFING

½ pound veal brains

Coarse-grained salt

4 tablespoons (2 ounces) sweet butter

5 sage leaves, fresh or preserved in salt (see Note on page 43)

Salt and freshly ground black pepper

4 ounces *prosciutto*

4 tablespoons freshly grated *Parmigiano*

1 extra large egg yolk

4 ounces ricotta, preferably whole milk ricotta

Pinch of freshly grated nutmeg

FOR THE PASTA

4 cups unbleached all-purpose flour

5 extra large eggs

Pinch of salt

TO COOK THE PASTA

4 quarts homemade chicken broth

Coarse-grained salt

PLUS

8 tablespoons freshly grated *Parmigiano*

Prepare the sauce: Soak the mushrooms in a bowl of lukewarm water for ½ hour. Drain them and be sure that no sand is still attached to the stems. Coarsely grind the mushrooms, *prosciutto,* and boiled ham together using a meat grinder.

Finely chop the onion on a board.

Melt the butter in a large heavy casserole over medium heat and, when the butter is completely melted, add the chopped onion and sauté for 2 minutes. Then add the ground ingredients and cook for 15 minutes longer.

Pass the tomatoes through a food mill, using the disc with the small holes, and add them to the casserole. Mix very well and taste for salt and pepper. Cover the casserole and cook for 20 minutes. When the sauce is ready, let it stand, covered, until the pasta is cooked before adding the heavy cream to it.

Prepare the stuffing: Blanch the brains in boiling water with coarse-grained salt for 2 minutes; then remove the large membranes under cold running water.

Melt the butter in a small saucepan and, when the butter is completely melted, add the brains and the sage. Taste for salt and pepper and sauté for 3 minutes. Remove the pan from the heat and let the brains cool for 15 minutes. Discard the sage leaves.

Use a meat grinder to coarsely grind the brains with their juice together with the *prosciutto* into a crockery or glass bowl. Add the *Parmigiano,* egg yolk, and ricotta to the bowl. Season with salt, pepper, and nutmeg and mix the ingredients together very well with a wooden spoon. Cover the bowl and set aside until the pasta is ready.

Prepare the pasta with the ingredients and quantities listed above, following the directions on pages 86–87.

Stretch the pasta to a thickness of less than 1/16 inch by hand, or with a pasta machine to the finest setting.

On a sheet of pasta about 5 inches wide, place dots of the filling (each 1 heaping teaspoon), starting an inch from the top and side edges, in two rows lengthwise. The dots of filling should be 2 inches apart. (For a narrower sheet of pasta, make only 1 row.) Lay a second sheet of pasta over the sheet with the dots of filling and press down the edges. Use a 1½-inch diameter cookie cutter, without a scalloped edge, to cut out the round *anolini.* Lift them out and seal the edges all around (see Note on page 96).

Bring the broth to a boil and taste for salt. Then add the *anolini.* Cook for 1 to 3 minutes, depending on the dryness of the pasta.

Meanwhile, heat the sauce and add the heavy cream. Mix very well to amalgamate all the ingredients. Taste for salt and pepper. Ladle half of the sauce onto a large warm serving platter; then, when the pasta is ready, transfer the *anolini* to the platter with a strainer-skimmer. Mix very well, pour the remaining sauce over the pasta, and sprinkle with *Parmigiano.* Serve immediately.

SERVES 8

*F*ish stuffing for pasta is not a recent invention of *nuova cucina*—witness these well-established, succulent triangular relatives of *tortelli* and *ravioli*. The fish for the stuffing is seasoned and baked first. An unusual feature is the marjoram sauce containing heavy cream.

Triangoli di pesce
PASTA TRIANGLES STUFFED WITH FISH

Prepare the stuffing: Clean the spinach very well, removing the large stems. Soak the spinach in a large bowl of cold water for ½ hour.

Bring a large pot of cold water to a boil and add coarse-grained salt to taste. Then add the spinach. Cook for 10 minutes. Drain the spinach and cool it under cold running water. Squeeze the spinach dry and chop it finely on a board.

Soak the fish in a bowl of cold water, with coarse-grained salt added, for ½ hour.

Preheat the oven to 375 degrees.

Finely chop the parsley and garlic together on a board.

Use the tablespoon of olive oil to oil the shiny side of a piece of aluminum foil. Put the fish on the oiled foil. Sprinkle the fish with the parsley and garlic and with salt and pepper. Wrap the fish completely in the foil and bake for 20 minutes. Remove from the oven and open the foil package on a plate.

Remove and discard the fish bones and skin. Mix together the meat of the fish and the cooking juices in a large bowl. Mix in the chopped spinach; then add salt and pepper to taste, the ricotta, egg, and egg yolk. Mix all the ingredients together very well. Cover the bowl and refrigerate until needed.

Prepare the pasta with the ingredients and quantities listed above, following the directions on pages 86–87.

Stretch the pasta to a thickness of less than ⅛ inch by hand, or with a pasta machine to the finest setting. Use a scalloped pastry cutter to cut the pasta into 2½-inch squares.

Put a heaping teaspoon of the stuffing in the middle of each square. Fold half of the pasta square over to form a triangle and seal them all around (see Note on page 96). Repeat until all the pasta squares are filled. Transfer the *triangoli* onto cotton dish towels and let them rest until needed.

Prepare the sauce: Finely chop the onion, garlic, and parsley together on a board.

Heat the oil and butter in a large heavy saucepan over medium heat and, when the butter is completely melted, add the chopped ingredients. Lower the heat and sauté for 20 minutes.

Meanwhile, bring a large pot of cold water to a boil; then add coarse-grained salt to taste. Add the *triangoli* and cook them for 1 to 2 minutes, depending on the dryness of the pasta.

Remove the *triangoli* from the boiling water with a strainer-skimmer and put them into the pan with the sauce. Add the cream, marjoram, and salt and pepper to taste. Mix gently and let the cream be absorbed by the pasta. Quickly transfer the pasta and sauce to a warm serving platter. Sprinkle with the basil leaves and serve immediately.

SERVES 8.

NOTE: *Cheese is optional with this dish. Most Italians prefer not to mix cheese with fish, but when an exception is made, it is because butter, cream, or milk is also prominent in the dish.*

FOR THE STUFFING

2 pounds spinach

Coarse-grained salt

1 slice nonoily fish, such as sea bass or striped bass, about 1 pound with bones

15 sprigs Italian parsley, leaves only

1 clove garlic, peeled

1 tablespoon olive oil

Salt and freshly ground black pepper

4 ounces whole milk ricotta

1 extra large egg

1 extra large egg yolk

FOR THE PASTA

4 cups unbleached all-purpose flour

5 extra large eggs

Pinch of salt

FOR THE SAUCE

1 small red onion, peeled

2 medium-sized cloves garlic, peeled

25 sprigs Italian parsley, leaves only

½ cup olive oil

4 tablespoons (2 ounces) sweet butter

½ cup heavy cream

1 scant tablespoon dried marjoram

Salt and freshly ground black pepper

TO COOK THE PASTA

Coarse-grained salt

TO SERVE

10 basil leaves, fresh or preserved in salt (see Note on page 43), torn into thirds

Opposite: The ingredients for Triangoli di pesce *(Pasta Triangles Stuffed with Fish).*

FOR THE PASTA

3½ cups unbleached all-purpose flour

2   extra large eggs

2   teaspoons olive oil or vegetable oil

1   heaping tablespoon boiled and finely chopped spinach (from ½ pound fresh spinach leaves, cooked after removing the stems)

   Pinch of salt

TO COOK THE PASTA

   Coarse-grained salt

2   tablespoons olive oil or vegetable oil

FOR THE TOMATO SAUCE

¼   cup olive oil

3   cloves garlic, peeled but left whole

2¾ pounds fresh tomatoes or 2¾ pounds canned imported Italian tomatoes, drained

   Salt and freshly ground black pepper

*L*ess well known than Naples' *Lasagne imbottite* (Stuffed Lasagne), which is often made with long, rather thick rectangles of dried pasta, this special lasagne—also from Naples—is a more refined version of the great Neapolitan dish. The squares of homemade fresh green pasta are thin and light, and the mozzarella is coarsely grated rather than sliced. There are no eggs or sausage in the stuffing, but rather the lightest of tomato sauces. As for any Neapolitan dish, the tomatoes, if canned, should be the imported San Marzano type, and if fresh, should be ripe and full flavored.

Lasagne verdi alla napoletana
GREEN LASAGNE NAPLES STYLE

Prepare the pasta with the ingredients and quantities listed above, following the directions on pages 86–87, placing the chopped spinach in the well in the flour together with all the other ingredients.

Stretch the pasta to the finest setting of the pasta machine. Use a scalloped pastry wheel to cut the sheets of pasta into squares of about 5 inches.

Precook the pasta squares in salted boiling water for 5 seconds after the water returns to a boil. Then transfer them to a large bowl of cold water to which the 2 tablespoons of olive oil have been added. When all the pasta squares have been boiled, lay them in a single layer on dampened cotton dish towels. Cover the pasta squares with additional dampened cotton dish towels.

Prepare the tomato sauce: Put the oil and garlic into a saucepan over medium heat. Sauté for 1 minute. When the garlic is very light golden brown, add the tomatoes. Lower the heat, cover the saucepan, and simmer for about 25 minutes. Taste for salt and pepper. Pass the contents of the pan through a food mill, using the disc with the small holes, and put the sauce back over medium heat. Cook, uncovered, to reduce for 15 minutes longer. Transfer the sauce to a crockery or glass bowl and let it cool completely (about 1 hour). The sauce may be prepared as much as a day in advance.

Prepare the cheese stuffings: Put the ricotta in a bowl. Add the *Parmigiano*, butter, and salt, pepper, and nutmeg to taste. Mix all the ingredients together with a wooden spoon.

Grate the mozzarella with a coarse grater and put it in a separate bowl. Season it with salt and pepper.

Preheat the oven to 375 degrees.

To assemble the dish, heavily oil a 13½- x 8¾-inch baking dish. Then fit in enough pasta squares to cover the bottom of the baking dish and to allow about 1 inch of the pasta to hang over all around the edges of the dish. Cover the pasta on the bottom of the dish with a quarter of the tomato sauce. Sprinkle a quarter of the basil leaves over the sauce (see Note). Add another layer of pasta to just cover the tomato sauce, but with no overhanging pasta. Cover this second layer of pasta with one third of the ricotta mixture. Then make another layer of pasta and top it with one third of the grated mozzarella. Keep making layers of pasta, alternating in between them the three different fillings in the same order. The last layer should be of mozzarella, covered with 3 pasta squares. Fold the ends of the pasta squares, which are hanging over the edges of the baking dish, in over the top of the last 3 pasta squares. Pour the remaining tomato sauce over the top of the pasta. Sprinkle the remaining basil leaves over the tomato sauce (see Note).

Place the dish in the oven and bake for 25 minutes. Remove the dish from the oven and let it sit for 15 minutes before serving.

SERVES 8 TO 10.

NOTE: *If fresh basil is not available and basil preserved in salt is substituted, add the basil leaves to the tomato sauce while it is cooking. Remove them before passing the sauce through the food mill.*

*T*he *timballo* of pasta is, perhaps, the most dignified of pasta dishes, appropriate for black-tie parties and formal dinners. The pastry drum is made differently according to what is to be presented in it. The flavorings in this pastry are nutmeg, a little sugar, and salt. The half-moon-shaped *tortelli* have a meat stuffing strongly flavored with cloves, which blends well with the nutmeg in the *timballo*. Even though the drum is for presentation rather than eating, the pasta baked in it absorbs some of the flavoring of the crust.

FOR THE RICOTTA STUFFING

15 ounces ricotta

4 tablespoons freshly grated *Parmigiano*

4 tablespoons (2 ounces) sweet butter at room temperature

Salt and freshly ground black pepper

Pinch of freshly grated nutmeg

FOR THE MOZZARELLA STUFFING

8 ounces whole milk mozzarella

Salt and freshly ground black pepper

PLUS

20 fresh basil leaves (see Note)

Timballo di mezzelune
TIMBALLO OF HALF-MOON PASTA

FOR THE PASTRY DRUM

12 tablespoons (6 ounces) sweet butter

5 cups unbleached all-purpose flour

2 extra large egg yolks

1 cup cold water

4 tablespoons olive oil

1 tablespoon granulated sugar

Pinch of salt

Pinch of freshly grated nutmeg

FOR THE GLAZE

1 extra large egg

FOR THE STUFFING

8 tablespoons (4 ounces) sweet butter

4 ounces boneless beef sirloin

2 cloves garlic, peeled but left whole

3 whole cloves

Salt and freshly ground black pepper

½ cup warm homemade beef broth

½ cup freshly grated *Parmigiano*

½ cup unseasoned bread crumbs

FOR THE SAUCE

4 ounces *prosciutto* in one piece

2 ounces *pancetta* in one slice

1 whole chicken breast, about 1 pound, skinned and boned

Make the pastry drum: Melt the butter in a small bowl, using a double boiler or *bagnomaria*. Let the butter cool for ½ hour.

Make a mound of the flour on a pasta board and make a well in the flour. Pour the melted butter into the well and then add the egg yolks, water, oil, sugar, salt, and nutmeg to the well. Use a fork to mix all the ingredients in the well together; then start incorporating the flour from the inside rim of the well until only 1 cup of the flour remains unincorporated. Use your hands to gather the dough together; then knead it for 2 minutes and form the dough into a ball. Put the ball of dough in a floured cotton dish towel and let it rest in a cool place for 2 hours.

Prepare the stuffing: Melt the butter in a small heavy saucepan over medium heat. Add the meat and sauté for 4 minutes. Then add the garlic, cloves, and salt and pepper to taste. Cover the pan and cook for 2 minutes. Add the broth, cover the pan again, and cook over low heat for 15 minutes longer. Discard the garlic and cloves. Grind the meat finely and return it to the pan with its juices. Mix very well. Put the pan over medium heat and mix again. Remove from the heat and transfer the contents of the pan to a crockery or glass bowl to cool completely (about 1 hour). Then add the *Parmigiano* and bread crumbs, taste for salt and pepper, and mix all the ingredients together very well. Cover the bowl and let it stand until needed.

Prepare the sauce: Coarsely grind the *prosciutto, pancetta,* chicken breast, and beef together with a meat grinder. Remove the skin from the sausage and put the sausage meat into a bowl. Add the ground meats to the same bowl and mix together with a wooden spoon.

Finely chop the carrot, onion, celery, garlic, and parsley on a board.

Heat the butter and oil in a casserole, preferably terra cotta, over medium heat. When the butter is completely melted, add the ground meats and sauté for 2 minutes; then add the chopped vegetables and sauté, stirring occasionally, until the onion is translucent (about 15 minutes). Add the wine and let it evaporate very slowly (about 15 minutes).

Dissolve the tomato paste in the hot broth and add it to the casserole. Taste for salt and pepper and simmer, covered, for 1½ hours, mixing occasionally. Let the sauce stand, covered, until needed.

Prepare the pasta with the ingredients and quantities listed above, following the directions on pages 86–87.

Stretch the pasta to a thickness of less than ¹⁄₁₆ inch or to the finest setting of the pasta machine.

To make the *tortelli,* make 2 rows of dots of filling 1 inch from each side, using 1 teaspoon of filling for each dot. Fold each side of the pasta over to cover the filling and press down around the dots of filling. Cut out half-moons or semicircles by placing only half of a round 2-inch jagged pastry cutter over each area of stuffing and seal them all around (see Note on page 96).

Preheat the oven to 375 degrees.

Finish the pastry drum: Unwrap the dough and knead it for 2 minutes

1	pound boneless beef sirloin in one piece	1	medium-sized red onion, peeled	
1	sweet Italian sausage, without fennel seeds, or 3 ounces finely ground pork	1	celery stalk	
1	large carrot, scraped	1	medium-sized clove garlic, peeled	

10 sprigs Italian parsley, leaves only

6 tablespoons (3 ounces) sweet butter

1 tablespoon olive oil

1 cup dry red wine

2 tablespoons tomato paste

2 cups hot homemade chicken broth

Salt and freshly ground black pepper

FOR THE PASTA

4 cups unbleached all-purpose flour

5 extra large eggs

Pinch of salt

TO COOK THE PASTA

Coarse-grained salt

PLUS

1 cup heavy cream

¼ cup freshly grated *Parmigiano*

4 tablespoons (2 ounces) sweet butter

on a pasta board. Sprinkle the board with the remaining flour; then cut the dough into 3 equal pieces. Using a rolling pin, roll out 1 piece to a thickness of a little less than ¼ inch. Make the "lid" of the *timballo* by placing the removable bottom of a 10-inch springform pan on the sheet of dough and cutting around it with a scalloped pastry wheel.

Butter a baking sheet and place the *timballo* lid on it. Use a fork to make punctures all over the lid so the dough does not rise while it is baking. Cut out a circle or square of dough of about 2 inches and place it in the center of the *timballo* lid to make a little handle.

Prepare the glaze: Beat the egg in a small bowl and use a pastry brush to spread it over the top of the lid.

Bake the lid for 35 minutes, or until the pastry is golden brown.

While the lid is baking, roll out a second piece of the dough to the same thickness as the first. Cut out a circular bottom for the *timballo* by placing the removable bottom of the springform pan on the pastry and cutting out a circle ½ inch larger than the bottom of the springform pan.

Put the springform pan together and butter it. Fit the bottom layer of the *timballo* into the springform; the ½-inch overlap of pastry should be curled up along the sides of the pan.

Take the third piece of dough and roll it out into a strip long enough to circle the inside of the springform pan. This strip will form the sides of the *timballo*. Use the rolling pin to stretch the strip of dough to a width of 3½ inches. Fit the strip of dough inside the springform, along the sides, fitting it inside the overlapping pastry from the *timballo* bottom.

Use the palm of your hand to press down the pastry hanging over the top edge of the pan. Then use a knife to cut around the top to remove the extra pastry.

Fit a piece of aluminum foil shiny side up loosely inside the *timballo*; then put in weights or dried beans to keep the pastry from rising as it bakes. Place the springform pan in the oven and bake for 1 hour.

By the time the pastry form is ready for the oven, the lid should have finished baking. Remove it from the oven and put it on a rack to cool.

When the pastry drum has almost finished baking, bring a large pot of cold water to a boil and add coarse-grained salt. Then add the pasta and cook it for 1 to 3 minutes, depending on the dryness of the pasta.

Remove the pastry drum from the oven and lift out the aluminum foil with the weights. Leave the pastry in the pan.

Use a strainer-skimmer to transfer the cooked pasta to the casserole with the sauce. Add the cream and *Parmigiano* and mix very well. Fill the *timballo* with the sauced pasta and distribute over it the 4 tablespoons of butter, which have been cut into pieces. Place the lid on the *timballo* and bake for 15 minutes.

Remove from the oven and allow to cool for 2 minutes. Then transfer the springform pan to a large platter and open and remove the form. Serve immediately, lifting the lid and spooning out individual servings.

SERVES 8.

Overleaf: Timballo di mezzelune *(Timballo of Half-Moon Pasta), with its homemade pastry shell complete with pastry lid and lid handle.*

The age-old method of preserving tomatoes in southern Italy, predating the age of canning and still practiced today, is to hang them in the open air to dry the skin very lightly and to then hang them indoors where they will last throughout the year. The skin gets very thin, an accentuation of the normal ripening process, and separates from the pulp. Although the skin softens slightly, the inside retains the quality and juiciness of a fresh tomato. (These are not the completely sun-dried tomatoes that can be purchased in jars.)

Cherry tomatoes are best preserved in this way, and, in fact, this type is not used fresh in Italy, but is reserved for the air-drying process. Cherry tomatoes are never used for salads or dips in Italy.

When making *Spaghetti alla Sangiovannino*, the preserved cherry tomatoes can be closely approximated by placing fresh ones on a baking sheet in a 375-degree oven for 5 minutes. The skin dries and separates from the pulp, and the result is very similar to the original. This dish is always made with dried rather than freshly made spaghetti.

Spaghetti alla Sangiovannino
SPAGHETTI WITH AIR-DRIED CHERRY TOMATOES

1 pound fresh ripe cherry tomatoes (as a substitute for air-dried cherry tomatoes)	1 teaspoon hot red pepper flakes
	Coarse-grained salt
3 cloves garlic, peeled	1 pound dried spaghetti, preferably imported Italian
½ cup olive oil	25 sprigs Italian parsley, leaves only
Salt and freshly ground black pepper	

Bring a large pot of cold water to a boil to cook the pasta.

Meanwhile, prepare the sauce: Preheat the oven to 375 degrees. Put the cherry tomatoes on a baking sheet and bake for 5 minutes.

Remove the tomatoes from the oven and let them cool for 10 minutes. Then cut the tomatoes in half, but retain the seeds and skin.

Coarsely chop the garlic on a board.

Heat the oil in a large casserole over medium heat. Add the garlic and sauté for 2 minutes; then raise the heat to very high and add the tomatoes. Sauté for 5 minutes longer. (Even over very high heat, the tomatoes will not dissolve completely.) Season with salt and pepper to taste and the hot red pepper flakes.

When the water for the pasta comes to a boil, add coarse-grained salt to taste. Then add the pasta, stir with a wooden spoon, and cover the pot to bring the water back to a boil as quickly as possible. Remove the lid and cook the pasta until it is *al dente* (9 to 12 minutes, depending on the brand).

Drain the pasta and transfer it to the casserole with the sauce. Sprinkle the parsley over all, mix very well, and serve immediately. No cheese should be used with this dish.

SERVES 4 TO 6.

The little ear-shaped pasta, *orecchiette*, is made by rolling the dough into a long cord, which is then cut into half-inch discs. Each disc is flattened with the thumb; then the thumb is turned clockwise to make the "little ear" shape.

Orecchiette con cavolfiore
ORECCHIETTE *WITH CAULIFLOWER*

1 pound dried *orecchiette*, preferably imported Italian, or fresh *orecchiette* made with the following ingredients:

FOR THE HOMEMADE PASTA

1 cup semolina flour

2 cups unbleached all-purpose flour

1 cup cold water

   Pinch of salt

FOR THE CAULIFLOWER

1 large cauliflower, about 2½ pounds, large leaves removed

   Coarse-grained salt

2 large cloves garlic, peeled but left whole

5 whole anchovies in salt, or 10 anchovy fillets in oil, drained

20 sprigs Italian parsley, leaves only

¾ cup olive oil

   Salt and freshly ground black pepper

OPTIONAL

½ teaspoon hot red pepper flakes

If using fresh *orecchiette*, prepare the pasta using the ingredients listed at left and following the directions given on pages 86–87 and above. (For further details, see *Giuliano Bugialli's Classic Techniques of Italian Cooking*, page 152.)

   Put the cauliflower in a large bowl of cold water and soak for ½ hour.

   Bring a large pot of cold water to a boil and add coarse-grained salt. Cut the cauliflower into flowerets, discarding the stems. Put the flowerets into the boiling water along with the garlic. Cook for 3 minutes; then drain, reserving the cooking water. Transfer the cauliflower to a bowl until needed. Discard the garlic.

   If using the anchovies in salt, clean them under cold running water, removing the bones and excess salt.

   Bring the cauliflower cooking water back to a boil.

   Meanwhile, finely chop the parsley on a board.

   Heat the oil in a large casserole over medium heat and, when the oil is warm, remove the casserole from the heat and add the anchovy fillets. Mash them with a fork.

   Add the pasta to the boiling water. If you are using dried pasta, cook it until it is *al dente* (9 to 12 minutes, depending on the brand). If the pasta is fresh, cook it for 5 to 10 minutes, depending on the dryness of the pasta.

   Drain the pasta and transfer it to the casserole with the anchovies. Put the casserole back over medium heat, stir very well, and add the cooked cauliflower. Taste for salt and pepper, mix all the ingredients together, and cook for 1 minute longer. If using the hot red pepper flakes, add them at this point. Sprinkle with the parsley and serve immediately.

SERVES 6.

Opposite: Orecchiette con cavolfiore *(Orecchiette with Cauliflower). Top: A street in Old Bari where a woman makes the local types of fresh pasta. Shoppers buy their daily supply as it is being made. Above: The* orecchiette *dry on a wire screen; at this point the pasta-maker checks them one by one to separate any that are stuck together. Underneath is a sheet of pasta made with parsley leaves.*

Fresh tuna and swordfish are readily available in the south of Italy and are prepared in a multitude of imaginative ways. They are eaten far more often than meat in this area. A favorite dish is dried tubular pasta combined with the fish and its marinade. A substantial tubular pasta, such as *rigatoni* or *penne rigate*, blends best with the chunky pieces of meaty fish. Both tuna and swordfish absorb well the piquant sauce of capers, olives, anchovies, and sweet peppers preserved in wine vinegar.

Pasta con tonno fresco
PASTA WITH MARINATED TUNA

1 slice fresh tuna or swordfish, about 2 pounds, with bone

Coarse-grained salt

2 bay leaves

5 whole black peppercorns

1 teaspoon red wine vineger

20 sprigs Italian parsley, leaves only

2 small cloves garlic, peeled

1 sweet red or yellow bell pepper in wine vinegar, drained

1 cup olive oil

½ teaspoon hot red pepper flakes

Juice of 1 lemon

Salt and freshly ground black pepper

1 pound dried short pasta, such as *rigatoni, penne rigate, fusilli, chicciole*, etc., preferably imported Italian

TO COOK THE PASTA

Coarse-grained salt

Wash the fresh tuna and put it in a bowl of cold water with some coarse-grained salt.

Put a casserole with 8 cups of cold water, 1 heaping teaspoon of coarse-grained salt, the bay leaves, peppercorns, and wine vinegar over medium heat. When the water comes to a boil, add the whole slice of fish and cook for 15 minutes.

Meanwhile, coarsely chop the parsley and finely chop the garlic and bell pepper together on a board. Put the chopped ingredients in a crockery or glass bowl and add the oil, hot red pepper flakes, lemon juice, and salt and pepper.

Use a strainer-skimmer to transfer the cooked fish from the poaching liquid to the bowl with the marinade. Let stand, covered, in the refrigerator for at least 2 hours.

Bring a large pot of cold water to a boil and add coarse-grained salt to taste. Add the pasta and stir with a wooden spoon to be sure the pasta does not stick together. Cover the pot to bring the water back to a boil as quickly as possible. When the water is boiling again, remove the lid and cook the pasta until it is *al dente* (9 to 12 minutes, depending on the brand).

Drain the pasta and transfer it to a large serving dish. Remove the bone from the fish and add the fish to the pasta; then add the marinade. The fish will break up when you toss it with the pasta. Serve immediately.
SEE PHOTO ON PAGES 38–39. SERVES 6.

*I*talian seaside resorts often subdivide the beaches into privately organized *bagni*, or clubs, which rent cabins, chairs, and umbrellas to their patrons, most of whom are regulars who return year after year. It is possible to rent boats from the *bagno* and to take swimming lessons from the *bagnino*, the supervising lifeguard. Some *bagni* have their own restaurant right on the beach, and, sometimes, these are the best restaurants in town—featuring fish and seafood, naturally.

Spaghetti della Pina is a specialty of Pina, the owner of Bagno Bruno in Forte dei Marmi.

Spaghetti della Pina
SPAGHETTI PINA STYLE

FOR THE SAUCE

1   pound mussels

1   pound clams

    Coarse-grained salt

1   lemon, cut in half

1   small piece lemon rind

15 sprigs Italian parsley,
    leaves only

2   medium-sized cloves garlic,
    peeled

½   cup olive oil

1   pound fresh tomatoes or 1
    pound canned imported Italian
    tomatoes, drained

4   basil leaves, fresh or preserved
    in salt (see Note on page 43),
    torn into thirds

    Salt and freshly ground black
    pepper

3   tablespoons red wine vinegar

1   pound dried spaghetti,
    preferably imported Italian

TO COOK THE PASTA

    Coarse-grained salt

TO SERVE

15 sprigs Italian parsley,
    leaves only

Carefully scrub the mussels and clams under cold running water; then put them together in a bowl of cold water with coarse-grained salt and the lemon halves.

Finely chop the lemon rind, parsley, and garlic together on a board.

Put a heavy casserole with ¼ cup of the oil over medium heat and, when the oil is warm, add the chopped ingredients. Sauté for 2 minutes. Drain the clams and mussels and add them to the casserole. Cover the casserole and cook for 10 minutes.

Meanwhile, cut the tomatoes into pieces and pass them through a food mill, using the disc with the small holes, into a small bowl.

Put a small saucepan with the remaining oil over medium heat and, when the oil is warm, add the strained tomatoes and then the basil leaves. Season with salt and pepper, cover the pan, and simmer for about 5 minutes.

Add the wine vineger to the casserole with the shellfish, taste for salt and pepper, and let the vinegar evaporate for 2 minutes.

Add the prepared tomato sauce to the casserole, mix very well, and cook for 2 minutes longer.

Bring a large pot of cold water to a boil and add coarse-grained salt to taste. Add the pasta to the boiling water, stir with a wooden spoon, and cover the pot to bring the water back to a boil as quickly as possible. Uncover the pot and cook the pasta until it is al dente (9 to 12 minutes, depending on the brand).

Drain the pasta and transfer it to a large warm serving platter. Pour the sauce with all the shellfish over the pasta and toss very well. Serve with the parsley leaves on top.

SERVES 4 TO 6.

Overleaf: Pesce alla griglia *(Whole Fish on the Grill) and* Spaghetti della Pina *(Spaghetti Pina Style) served with Tuscan white wine on the beach at Forte dei Marmi. Even in this informal setting, pasta would precede the fish and not be served with it. Both fresh and cooked rosemary adorn the fish.*

Lumachelle al tartufo (*Lumachelle Pasta with Black Truffle Sauce*). Both black and white truffles have become so popular in the last few years that now even canned ones, once relatively reasonable in price, are approaching luxury level prices outside Italy and France.

The sauce for the Umbrian dish *Lumachelle al tartufo*, Pasta with Black Truffle Sauce, is made with trout as well as with black truffles; the single trout that flavors the sauce is left whole and is removed after cooking. It would be sheer insanity, however, to throw away this delicately cooked fish, which is completely suffused with the nutty essence of the fresh black truffle. The trout can be eaten as an informal snack, but it should not be served at the same meal as the pasta.

As their name indicates, *lumachelle* are shaped like land snails. They resemble elbow macaroni a bit, but are slightly larger, with a curve on one end like the snails themselves.

Lumachelle al tartufo
LUMACHELLE PASTA WITH BLACK TRUFFLE SAUCE

1   medium-size red onion, peeled

2   cloves garlic, peeled but left whole

¼   cup olive oil

Cut the onion into eighths and put it with the garlic, oil, and butter in a heavy saucepan over medium heat. When the butter is completely melted, sauté for 5 minutes, or until the onion is translucent. With a slotted spoon, remove and discard the onion and garlic. Add the whole trout to the pan and sauté for 2 minutes on each side.

Pass the tomatoes through a food mill, using the disc with the small

116

holes, into a small bowl. Then add the tomatoes to the pan with the trout. Taste for salt and pepper and simmer for 15 minutes.

Meanwhile, bring a large pot of cold water to a boil and add coarse-grained salt to taste.

When the sauce is ready, remove the trout from the sauce, being careful not to leave in any pieces of the fish. Lower the heat to very low to keep the sauce warm.

Add the pasta to the boiling water, stir with a wooden spoon, and cover the pot to bring the water back to a boil as quickly as possible. Remove the lid and cook the pasta until it is *al dente* (9 to 12 minutes, depending on the brand).

Meanwhile, finely chop the truffle on a board and add it to the saucepan with the sauce. Mix very well, raise the heat, and cook the sauce for 4 minutes longer.

Drain the pasta and put it in the saucepan with the truffle sauce. Mix very well and cook for 20 seconds more. Then transfer the pasta and sauce to a warm serving platter and serve immediately.

SERVES 4 TO 6.

2	tablespoons (1 ounce) sweet butter
1	brook trout, cleaned, but left whole with head and tail on
1	pound canned imported Italian tomatoes, drained
	Salt and freshly ground black pepper
1	pound dried short pasta, preferably *lumachelle* (snails) or *conchiglie* (shells), and preferably imported Italian
	Coarse-grained salt
	About 1 ounce fresh or canned black truffle

Cooking *"al cartoccio"* is popular with fish, but the technique works beautifully with a special pasta dish as well. The under-cooked spaghetti is combined with a tomato sauce, "fillets" of fresh tomato, and black olives in individual parchment packages for each serving. The pasta absorbs the flavors and the sauce, while remaining moist though well baked.

Pasta al cartoccio (*Spaghetti Baked in Parchment Paper*).

117

Pasta al cartoccio
SPAGHETTI BAKED IN PARCHMENT PAPER

¼ cup plus 2 tablespoons olive oil

1 large clove garlic, peeled but left whole

2 cups canned imported Italian tomatoes, drained

Salt and freshly ground black pepper

½ teaspoon hot red pepper flakes

Coarse-grained salt

1 pound ripe fresh tomatoes

25 sprigs Italian parsley, leaves only

30 large black Greek olives, preserved in oil, pitted

1 pound dried spaghetti, preferably imported Italian

TO COOK THE PASTA

Coarse-grained salt

Heat the ¼ cup of oil in a heavy saucepan over medium heat. When the oil is warm, add the garlic and sauté for 2 minutes; then discard the garlic and add the canned tomatoes to the pan. Let simmer for 20 minutes, stirring occasionally with a wooden spoon. Season with salt and pepper and add the hot red pepper flakes.

Pass the contents of the pan through a food mill into a crockery or glass bowl, using the disc with the small holes. Return the sauce to the pan and reduce over medium heat for 10 minutes longer. Then remove from the heat and let stand until needed.

Meanwhile, bring a medium-sized casserole of cold water to a boil; then add coarse-grained salt to taste. Add the whole fresh tomatoes, lower the heat, and simmer for 3 minutes. Then use a slotted spoon to transfer the tomatoes to a bowl of cold water. Remove the tomatoes one by one and use a paring knife to peel them. Then cut the tomatoes into quarters, making the classical *filetti di pomodoro* (tomato fillets) and seed them. Put the tomatoes into a bowl and let stand until needed.

Coarsely chop 10 sprigs of the parsley and finely chop the remaining parsley, keeping the two types separated.

Bring a large pot of cold water to a boil and add coarse-grained salt to taste. Then add the pasta and cook a few minutes less than for *al dente* pasta (5 to 10 minutes, depending on the brand, instead of the usual 9 to 12 minutes).

Preheat the oven to 375 degrees. Prepare 4 to 6 pieces of parchment paper, depending on the number of individual servings you wish to make, and spread them out on a board.

When the pasta is ready, drain it and add it to the bowl with the tomato quarters. Add the remaining 2 tablespoons of oil, the olives, the prepared tomato sauce, and the finely chopped parsley. Taste for salt and pepper and mix all the ingredients together well.

Divide the contents of the bowl according to the number of servings you are making, placing the portions on the pieces of parchment paper. Close each paper tightly. Place the packages in a baking pan and bake for 15 minutes.

Remove the packages from the oven and place each on its own warm plate. Open each package with a pair of scissors and sprinkle some of the coarsely chopped parsley over each serving.

SERVES 4 TO 6.

C *respelle* (crêpes) are used all over Italy, from the *crespelle* of Abruzzi to the *cannelloni* of Florence, and the various kinds of *manicotti* of southern Italy. In Emilia Romagna, rolled stuffed pasta, such as the *Rotolo di pasta* and the *crespelle*-wrapped *cannelloni*, are sliced into pieces before they are put in the oven for the last phase of cooking. *Bocconcini di Parma* are also made in this way. The word *bocconcini*, meaning "little mouthfuls," is used to describe pasta and meat dishes that are divided into succulent morsels. Because of the small size of the pasta rolls, the stuffing tends to puff up in the oven, giving the dish a soufflé-like appearance.

Bocconcini di Parma
BOCCONCINI FROM PARMA

FOR THE *CRESPELLA* BATTER

1 tablespoon (½ ounce) sweet butter

1 cup unbleached all-purpose flour

2 extra large eggs

1 cup cold milk

Pinch of salt

Pinch of freshly grated nutmeg

Twist of freshly ground white pepper

FOR THE STUFFING

30 ounces ricotta, preferably whole milk ricotta

4 extra large egg yolks

1 extra large egg

¾ cup freshly grated *Parmigiano*

4 tablespoons (2 ounces) sweet butter at room temperature

Salt and freshly ground black pepper

Freshly grated nutmeg

PLUS

1 tablespoon (½ ounce) sweet butter to heavily butter the baking dish

Prepare the batter for the *crespelle*: Melt the butter in the top of a double boiler over hot water or in a *bagnomaria*. Then let the melted butter stand until it is cool.

Sift the flour into a crockery or glass bowl and make a well in the flour. Pour the cooled butter into the well. Stir carefully, absorbing some of the flour from the edge of the well. Add the eggs, stirring continuously with a wooden spoon and absorbing more flour. Start adding the milk a little at a time and keep stirring until all the flour is incorporated. Then add the salt, pepper, and nutmeg. Mix very well. Cover the bowl and put it in a cool place to rest for at least 1 hour to allow the gluten in the flour to expand.

Meanwhile, prepare the stuffing: Drain the ricotta and put it in a crockery or glass bowl. Add the egg yolks, whole egg, *Parmigiano*, and butter to the bowl; then add the salt, pepper, and nutmeg. Mix all the ingredients together with a wooden spoon. Cover the bowl and refrigerate until needed, but for at least ½ hour.

Using an 8-inch crêpe pan and ¼ cup of the batter for each one, prepare the *crespelle*, buttering the pan each time. Stack the prepared *crespelle* on top of each other, separated by wax paper.

To stuff the *crespelle*, place each one on a board and spread about 3 heaping tablespoons of the stuffing along one side. Then roll it up, starting with the end with the stuffing. Place the rolled up *crespella* seam side down on a baking sheet. Repeat until all the *crespelle* are rolled and on the sheet. Refrigerate for ½ hour.

Preheat the oven to 375 degrees. Use the tablespoon of butter to heavily butter a 13½- x 8¾-inch baking dish.

Use a very sharp knife to cut off the ends of each *crespella*; then cut each one into thirds (or into pieces about 2½ inches long). Arrange them standing up in the buttered baking dish, side by side. Bake for 20 minutes and serve hot.

SERVES 8.

Bocconcini di Parma *(Bocconcini from Parma)*.

RICE

Although rice has been eaten in India and China since the beginning of recorded time, it only reached Western Europe in the eighth century, when it was introduced into Spain by the Arabs. Rice was brought to Italy directly from the Orient by the Venetian ships during the Crusades. It did not, however, take firm root until the mid-sixteenth century.

The best types of rice for *risotto* are grown near Novara in Piedmont. (*Larousse Gastronomique* calls Italian rice Piedmont rice.) Rice is generally divided into three categories in Italy: *comune*, *semifino*, and *fino*. The *fino* type is best for *risotto* because it absorbs the liquid while retaining its shape. Among the subtypes of *fino* are *Vialone*, *Razza*, and *Arborio*. *Arborio* is the type most exported and, therefore, most available outside Italy.

Although Piedmont is the source of northern Italy's rice, it is the Lombard way of preparing *risotto* that has become the classic method. The Piedmont procedure varies from the norm in that the rice, once sautéed, is no longer stirred; the pot is covered, and the liquid is left to be absorbed. The result is something between *risotto* and rice pilaf. In the Lombard technique, the rice is never covered, and the stirring continues until all the liquid is absorbed.

Authentic *Risotto alla milanese* has as its principal ingredients, in addition to the rice and broth, saffron, veal or beef bone marrow, and abundant butter added at the end with *Parmigiano*.

Opposite and overleaf: The gardens of the legendary Villa d'Este, on the shore of Lake Como near Milan, is the setting for a meal that will feature Risotto alla milanese. The villa was built in the mid-sixteenth century for Cardinal Tolomeo Gallio In 1893, it became a luxury hotel and continues to attract famous guests from all over the world.

Risotto alla milanese
RISOTTO MILAN STYLE

Heat the broth in a large casserole and, when it comes to a boil, add the bones and simmer for 20 minutes. Take the casserole off the heat. Remove the bones and put them on a board. Using a long handled fork, carefully lift out the marrow from each bone and put it on a plate. Discard the bones.

Wet a piece of heavy cheesecloth or a cotton dish towel and chill it in the freezer for 5 minutes. Then stretch the cheesecloth over a colander and strain the broth through it to remove any impurities. You will have ample strained broth to prepare the *risotto*, as only about 4½ cups are needed.

Cut the marrow into small pieces. Finely chop the onion on a board.

Melt the butter in a heavy casserole over low heat and, when the butter is melted, add the marrow and then the chopped onion. Sauté until the onion is translucent (about 4 minutes); then add the rice and sauté for 4 minutes. Add the wine and let it evaporate (about 3 minutes).

Meanwhile, reheat the broth. Start adding it a little at a time, stirring gently each time. Do not add additional broth until the broth that has been previously added has been completely absorbed.

After the first cup of broth has been used, measure out 3½ cups of broth and add the saffron to it. The broth should continue to boil in order to dissolve the saffron threads.

Season the rice with salt and pepper. Keep adding broth until the rice is cooked but still *al dente* (about 18 minutes from the time the first broth was added).

Remove the casserole from the heat, add the butter and *Parmigiano*, and mix very well with a wooden spoon until the butter is completely melted and the cheese absorbed. Serve with additional *Parmigiano* if desired.

SERVES 6.

8	cups homemade beef broth
3½	pounds veal or beef bones from the upper leg, cut into pieces
1	medium-sized white onion, peeled
6	tablespoons (3 ounces) sweet butter
2	cups raw rice, preferably Italian Arborio
½	cup dry white wine
	About 30 saffron threads
	Salt and freshly ground black pepper

PLUS

2	tablespoons (1 ounce) sweet butter
½	cup freshly grated *Parmigiano*

OPTIONAL

6	tablespoons freshly grated *Parmigiano*

Opposite: A peaceful view of one of the side canals in Venice. Risi e bisi (Rice with Fresh Peas) will be accompanied by local wine, enjoyed in wine glasses made in Venice on the island of Murano.

R*isi e bisi,* one of Venice's signature dishes, was traditionally offered to the Doges on the nameday of St. Mark, the patron saint of the city. It is the northern counterpart of the Pugliese *Piselli e paternostri* (see page 57). In Venice, the fresh peas are prepared with *risotto* rather than with pasta, and the proportion of peas is smaller than in the southern dish. But there is a distinctive feature in common: The pea pods are cooked separately and that water is reserved for cooking the rest of the dish. In the south, the pasta is cooked in it; in Venice, it is added to the broth for making the *risotto.*

This dish was originally called *Minestra di risi e bisi* (Venetian dialect for rice and peas), a thick soup with the rice cooked in broth. But in recent centuries, possibly because of the influence of neighboring Lombardy, its method of preparation has become more like that for *risotto.*

Risotto is begun by making the *soffritto,* the sautéed chopped vegetables. For the Venetians, making the *desfrito,* as they call it in their musical dialect, is a particular and loving art, and, indeed, they are the masters of it.

Risi e bisi
RICE WITH FRESH PEAS

2	pounds fresh peas, unshelled
1	tablespoon unbleached all-purpose flour
	Coarse-grained salt
1	medium-sized celery stalk
10	sprigs Italian parsley, leaves only
4	tablespoons (2 ounces) sweet butter
2	tablespoons olive oil
4	ounces *pancetta* or unsmoked bacon, cut into small pieces
	Salt and freshly ground black pepper
½	cup dry white wine

FOR THE *RISOTTO*

3	cups homemade beef broth
2	cups raw rice, preferably Italian Arborio
	Salt and freshly ground black pepper

PLUS

3	tablespoons (1½ ounces) sweet butter
3	heaping tablespoons freshly grated *Parmigiano*

Shell the peas, reserving both the peas and the pea pods. Put the peas in a bowl of cold water with the flour. Stir the flour into the water and let the peas soak for ½ hour.

Wash the pea pods carefully. Put them in a pot with 4 cups of cold water and coarse-grained salt to taste. Put the pot over medium heat and simmer for 1 hour.

Drain the peas and rinse them under cold running water.

Finely chop the celery and parsley together on a board.

Heat the butter and oil in a saucepan and, when the butter is completely melted, add the *pancetta* and sauté for 5 minutes; then add the chopped vegetables and sauté for 5 minutes longer. Add the peas, mix very well, and cook for 5 minutes. Taste for salt and pepper and add the wine. Cover the pan and cook over low heat for 20 minutes. By that time the peas should be cooked but still firm. Remove from the heat and let the peas stand in the pan, covered, until needed.

Pour the cooking water from the pea pods into a pot and set it aside. Discard the pea pods.

Prepare the *risotto:* Pour the pan juices from the cooked peas into a large heavy casserole, which will be used to cook the rice. Transfer the peas, which will be used later, to a crockery or glass bowl and cover them with aluminum foil. Set them aside until needed.

Combine the beef broth with the cooking water from the pea pods and heat the mixture.

Bring the pan juices in the heavy casserole to a boil. Then add the rice and sauté for about 4 minutes. Start adding the broth mixture a little at a time, stirring gently each time, until the rice has absorbed all but ¼ cup of the liquid. Then add the peas and the remaining ¼ cup of the broth. Taste for salt and pepper when the broth is absorbed. Remove the casserole from the heat and add the butter and *Parmigiano.* Mix very well and serve immediately.

SERVES 6.

$\mathcal{V}$enice is above all the Grand Canal, with its famous bridges, the great palaces like Ca' d'Oro and Ca' Barbaro, and even Peggy Guggenheim's modern museum. (No Venetian can forget her pigeon-shaped, diamond-covered sunglasses.)

Next to the most famous bridge of all, the covered Rialto bridge, is Venice's central market, jammed with vendors of fish, produce, and the glass animals made as souvenirs on Murano island. Among the delicious fresh shellfish offered are the sweet and tender Adriatic lobsters and shrimp, prepared in one of Venice's most characteristic *risotti*. In this dish the lobster meat is removed from the shell and incorporated into the rice along with whole shrimp. The *risotto* is made with a delicate chicken broth.

Risotto con aragosta e gamberi
RISOTTO WITH LOBSTER AND SHRIMP

2	pounds medium-sized shrimp or prawns, unshelled	1	pound fresh tomatoes or 1 pound canned imported Italian tomatoes, drained
	Coarse-grained salt		Salt and freshly ground black pepper
2	tablespoons olive oil		
6	tablespoons (3 ounces) sweet butter	2	cups raw rice, preferably Italian Arborio
¼	pound boiled lobster meat	4	cups hot homemade chicken broth
½	cup dry white wine		

Put the shrimp in a bowl of cold water with coarse-grained salt and soak for ½ hour.

Bring a small saucepan of cold water to a boil and add coarse-grained salt. Then add the shrimp in the shell and simmer for 3 minutes. Drain the shrimp and shell and devein them.

Prepare two casseroles, each with 1 tablespoon of the oil and 3 tablespoons of the butter. Put one of the casseroles over medium heat and, when the butter is completely melted, add the lobster meat and the shrimp. Sauté for 2 minutes. Then add the wine and let it evaporate for 2 minutes longer.

Meanwhile, pass the tomatoes through a food mill, using the disc with the small holes, into a small saucepan. Taste for salt and pepper and simmer for 3 minutes.

Put the second casserole over medium heat and, when the butter is completely melted, add the rice and sauté for 4 minutes. Then start adding the hot broth a little at a time, stirring gently. Do not add more broth until the broth previously added has been completely absorbed. After the first cup of broth has been incorporated, add half of the tomato sauce; then continue adding broth to the rice until the rice is cooked but still *al dente* (about 18 minutes from the time the first broth was added). Taste for salt and pepper. Mix very well and transfer the *risotto* to a buttered ring mold. Let stand for 2 minutes.

Meanwhile, reheat the lobster and shrimp; then unmold the *risotto* onto a large warm serving platter. Pour the remaining tomato sauce over it and place all of the fish in the center of the ring. Serve immediately.

SERVES 6.

Zucchini blossoms are prepared in a variety of ways in Italy: whole, fried in batter, and stuffed and then fried. There are still other dishes in which the blossoms are just an ingredient, for example, *frittata* of zucchini blossoms and *risotto* made with them. The flavor of the blossoms is more prominent in these dishes than in those in which the blossoms are fried whole, where shape and texture are more important. *Risotto con fiori di zucca* is a true traditional dish, not a faddish one like those made with rose petals, violets, or exotic flowers.

Risotto con fiori di zucca
RISOTTO WITH ZUCCHINI BLOSSOMS

Right: A zucchini blossom, wide open in the early morning; the flower closes later in the day when the sun gets warm. Next to the flower is a round zucchino, *the preferred type for stuffing in Italy. Surprisingly, it is not cultivated abroad. Opposite: The finished dish,* Risotto con fiori di zucca *(Risotto with Zucchini Blossoms).*

20	zucchini blossoms
4	ounces *prosciutto,* in one piece
4	tablespoons (2 ounces) sweet butter
2	tablespoons olive oil
15	sprigs Italian parsley, leaves only
2	cups raw rice, preferably Italian Arborio
4	cup homemade chicken broth
	Salt and freshly ground black pepper

PLUS

2	tablespoons (1 ounce) sweet butter
⅓	cup freshly grated *Parmigiano*

Clean the zucchini blossoms, removing the stems and the pistils. Wash the blossoms in cold water and drain them on paper towels. Cut them into large pieces.

Cut the *prosciutto* into tiny pieces.

Put a heavy saucepan with the butter and oil over medium heat.

Meanwhile, finely chop the parsley on a board.

When the butter is completely melted, add the *prosciutto* and the parsley to the pan and sauté over low heat for 5 minutes. Add the rice, raise the heat to medium, and sauté the rice for 4 minutes.

Heat the broth until it comes to a boil. Then start adding the broth to the rice a little at a time, stirring gently without adding more broth until the broth which has previously been added has been completely absorbed.

After adding the second cup of broth, add the zucchini blossoms. Season the *risotto* with salt and pepper.

When all the broth has been added and the rice is cooked but still *al dente* (about 18 minutes), remove the casserole from the heat and add the butter and *Parmigiano.* Stir very well and transfer the *risotto* to a large warm serving platter and serve hot.

SERVES 6.

POLENTA

Maize, which is ground into cornmeal for *polenta*, like wheat, is grown in small quantities on farms all over the country. In the Friuli region, even more than the neighboring Veneto, *polenta* is central to the diet. It is so popular there that it is even eaten for breakfast, dipped in milk. (Coffee is rarely taken at breakfast in Friuli.) In both Friuli and Veneto, grilled or broiled slices of *polenta* accompany the main course in place of bread.

The meal is made from both white and yellow corn and may be ground coarse, medium, or fine. It may be cooked in water, milk, broth, or even in wine, depending on the dish. Its texture varies from loose to very thick, again depending on what it is to be used for.

Polenta dishes range from the many very rustic ones to such a refined dish as *Polenta con mascarpone e tartufi*. For each serving of this dish, a small mound of cold *mascarpone* cheese is completely covered with hot *polenta*, and shavings of white truffle are scattered on top. The dish is most beautiful when it is cut through to reveal the different colors of the white and yellow layers and the soft tan of the truffles. It may be eaten either as a first course or as a main course. If served as a first course, it may be difficult to follow it with a main dish of equal lusciousness.

Piping hot **polenta** *ladled over cold* **mascarpone,** *topped with shavings of white truffles.*

Polenta con mascarpone e tartufi
POLENTA WITH MASCARPONE AND FRESH WHITE TRUFFLES

If the truffle is fresh, clean it very carefully with a truffle brush to remove all the sand.

Heat the broth in a large pot over medium heat and, when the broth comes to a boil, add coarse-grained salt to taste. Then start pouring in the cornmeal in a very slow stream, stirring continuously with a flat wooden spoon. Be sure to pour the cornmeal slowly and to keep stirring, or the *polenta* will easily become very lumpy. Stir slowly, without stopping, for 45 to 50 minutes from the moment the last of the cornmeal was added to the pot. If some lumps form, push them against the side of the pot to crush them with the spoon.

Use the 2 tablespoons of butter to lightly butter 8 dinner plates. Put 1 heaping tablespoon of *mascarpone* in the center of each plate. Put the plates in the refrigerator until needed.

When the *polenta* is cooked, taste it for salt, and then remove the pot from the heat. Immediately ladle some of the *polenta* over the cheese on the prepared plates. The *polenta* should cover the cheese completely.

Use a truffle cutter to slice the truffle over the *polenta* on the plates. Serve immediately.

SERVES 8.

1   medium-sized fresh or canned white truffle

3   quarts homemade beef broth

    Coarse-grained salt

1   pound coarse or stone-ground Italian yellow cornmeal

2   tablespoons (1 ounce) sweet butter

8   heaping tablespoons *mascarpone*

Fish and Shellfish

OCTOPUS AND SQUID

Preceding overleaf: Fresh Mediterranean fish and a variety of herbs, ready for the grill, balance on a rocky harbor setting near Bari, across the bay from an old stone lighthouse.

The lore of the sea and its fishermen have been the subjects of poetry and legend since ancient times, and many old local traditions remain connected with the preparation of certain fish. One of these traditions is the method, actually the rite, of preparing octopus in Puglia.

It begins with the picturesque sight of a small boat and a single fisherman bringing in his early morning catch of octopus from close to the shore. To prepare the octopi for the market, the fisherman first violently throws each one against the stone pavement fifty or sixty times. Next he uses a wooden paddle to beat it. In the final phase, the octopi are placed in a wicker basket and vigorously shaken until they fall into place. (In Bari the octopus is thrown and beaten in order to have it fall into a flower shape.) At this point, the octopi are so tender that some vendors sell the small ones at special stands right in the market, where they are eaten raw.

Fresh sea urchins are also sold in the markets. When sprinkled with lemon juice and eaten raw, the flavor and texture of the roe is light and delicate.

One of my memorable experiences was diving for sea urchins in the clear water off the rocky far side of the island of Giglio (off the Tuscan coast), to search for those of grayish color, which are the edible ones. We ate the roe on the spot, sitting with our feet dangling in the clear pools formed in the depres-

A fisherman approaches the dock of the Bari fish market, where he will prepare the octopi and later sell them himself.

Preparing the octopus for sale. Clockwise from top left: The fisherman throws the octopus on the shore, beats it with a wooden paddle, then shakes the basket so the octopi fall into an appealing flower shape, and finally offers one to a customer.

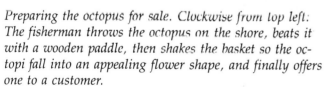

Small, inexpensive cuttlefish called "allievi."

sions in the rocks. In Bari people stand at long white marble tables in the market to enjoy the sea urchins just out of the water. It is amusing to see businessmen eating the roe with their hands—all the while being careful not to spot their ties.

The small cuttlefish that are so loved in the Bari region are called by the nickname *"allievi,"* meaning students, perhaps because of their diminutive size. The smallest ones are used whole in the mixed fish dish, *Fritto misto di mare.* The rounded shape of the stomach differentiates cuttlefish, or inksquid (*seppie*), from the long squid (*calamari*), which have cone-shaped stomachs.

Squid, cuttlefish, and octopus are combined in this flavorful main-course salad together with chick-peas and hard-boiled eggs. The chief herb is tiny whole mint leaves, the flavor of which pervades the fish. The dried chick-peas, soaked and boiled together with aromatic vegetables, combine marvelously with the various fish.

Insalata di calamari, seppie e polpi con ceci
SALAD OF SQUID, INKSQUID, AND OCTOPUS WITH CHICK-PEAS

TO COOK THE CHICK-PEAS

1½ cups dried chick-peas

2 tablespoons olive oil

1 medium-sized clove garlic, whole and unpeeled

1 medium-sized carrot, scraped

1 celery stalk, without leaves

1 medium-sized red onion, peeled

Coarse-grained salt

TO COOK THE FISH

1 pound cleaned squid

1 pound cleaned inksquid (cuttlefish)

1 pound octopus

Coarse-grained salt

3 quarts cold water

5 tablespoons red wine vinegar

Juice of 1 lemon

Soak the chick-peas in a bowl of cold water overnight. The next morning, rinse the peas and put them in a heavy casserole with the oil, garlic, carrot, celery, and onion. Add enough water to completely cover all the ingredients. Cover the casserole and put it over medium heat. Bring to a boil and add coarse-grained salt to taste. Cover again and simmer until the chick-peas are cooked but still firm (about 1 hour, depending on the dryness of the chick-peas).

Meanwhile, carefully rinse the squid, inksquid, and octopus to make sure that no sand remains attached to them. Put the fish in a bowl of cold water with a little coarse-grained salt and let them soak for ½ hour.

Pour the 3 quarts of cold water into a heavy casserole and bring it to a boil over medium heat.

Cut the squid and inksquid stomachs into rings about ½ inch thick. Cut the tentacles into 2 or 3 pieces. Cut the octopus into 1-inch pieces.

When the water comes to a boil, add coarse-grained salt to taste, the vinegar, and the lemon juice. Then add the octopus pieces, lower the heat, and simmer for ½ hour. Add the squid and the inksquid and simmer, covered, for ½ hour longer. Test for tenderness, because, even when cut into pieces, squid, and especially octopus, may require a longer cooking time if the original fish were large and, therefore, less tender.

Drain the fish, saving 4 tablespoons of the poaching broth, and transfer the fish to a crockery or glass bowl.

Prepare the sauce for the fish: Finely chop the parsley on a board and mix it with the fish pieces in the bowl. Add the olive oil, hot red pepper flakes, lemon juice, the 4 tablespoons of the poaching broth, and salt and pepper to taste. Mix very well, cover, and let stand until needed.

When the chick-peas are cooked, drain them, discarding all the aromatic herbs. Put the chick-peas in a second bowl and season them with the ¼ cup olive oil and salt and pepper to taste. Cover and let stand until cool.

Cut the hard-boiled eggs in half lengthwise. Prepare the serving platter by placing the fish with all the juices in the center of the platter. Then make a ring of the egg halves all around the fish. Then make an outer ring of the chick-peas. Sprinkle the mint and basil leaves over all and serve.

SERVES 8.

FOR THE SAUCE FOR THE FISH

15 springs Italian parsley, leaves only

¾ cup olive oil

½ teaspoon hot red pepper flakes

Juice of 1 lemon

4 tablespoons broth from poaching the fish

Salt and freshly ground black pepper

FOR THE SAUCE FOR THE CHICK-PEAS

¼ cup olive oil

Salt and freshly ground black pepper

PLUS

8 hard-boiled extra large eggs

10 whole fresh mint leaves

5 fresh basil leaves, torn into thirds

Insalata di calamari, seppie e polpi con ceci (*Salad of Squid, Inksquid, and Octopus with Chick-Peas*).

SCALLOPS

Preceding overleaf: The picnic lunch basket readied for a boat ride departing from Chioggia includes scallops served in their own shells and crusty rings of bread.

Above left: A regiment of fishmongers open scallop shells with a special knife designed only for that purpose. Above right: Nets are pulled taut by the abundant catch of sea scallops.

Opposite: Canestrelli di Chioggia (*Scallops Chioggia Style*).

In Italy, scallops are called by many different names: *canestrelli, ventagli, cape sante, pellegrini* (pilgrims). This last is probably a shortened form of still another name, *pellegrini di San Giacomo,* and therein lies a tale. This name, like the French *coquilles St. Jacques,* derives from the fact that pilgrims going to the holy sites, specifically to Santiago (or San Giacomo or Saint Jacques) di Compostella in northern Spain, carried the scallop shells as their drinking vessels.

One of the typical ways to prepare *canestrelli* is to sauté them *in bianco,* with wine, parsley, and garlic as well as the usual addition of a little brandy or *grappa.* (*Grappa* is the strong, very dry drink made from the seeds left over after the grapes have been crushed for the wine. *Grappa* is a favorite in the Veneto and in Friuli and is often drunk after dinner.) Although the cooking time varies according to the size of the scallops, they should be cooked only briefly or they will become tough. Sea scallops, rather than the small bay type, are closer to the variety found along the Adriatic coast around Venice and Bari. The finished dish is served in scallop shells, which can be kept and reused.

Canestrelli di Chioggia
SCALLOPS CHIOGGIA STYLE

18   sea scallops, about 1½ pounds

½   tablespoon coarse-grained salt

2   medium-sized cloves garlic, peeled

10   sprigs Italian parsley, leaves only

⅓   cup olive oil

Salt and freshly ground black pepper

¼   cup dry white wine

2   tablespoons brandy

Juice of 1 lemon

PLUS

15   sprigs Italian parsley, leaves only, finely chopped

1   lemon, cut into slices

Put the scallops into a bowl of cold water and add the coarse-grained salt. Let the scallops soak for ½ hour.

Finely chop the garlic and the 10 sprigs of parsley together on a board.

Drain the scallops and pat them dry with paper towels.

Heat the oil in a frying pan over medium heat. When the oil is warm, add the chopped ingredients and sauté for 2 minutes. Then add the scallops, lower the heat, cover the pan, and cook for 5 minutes. Season with salt and pepper. Add the wine and let it evaporate for 5 minutes; then add the brandy and cook for 5 minutes longer.

Heat the scallop shells in which you will be serving the dish in the oven for a few minutes.

When the brandy has evaporated, add the lemon juice and mix it in very well. Transfer the scallops to the heated scallop shells and serve immediately with the 15 sprigs of chopped parsley leaves and the lemon slices.

SERVES 6 AS AN APPETIZER, OR 3 AS A MAIN COURSE.

SHRIMP

Shrimp salads are popular in Italy, but rarely is *maionese* mixed through the salad, even when it is used to accompany it. Most often the shrimp are mixed with another ingredient, such as a vegetable, and are seasoned with oil and fresh herbs. Mediterranean shrimp have a strong, sweet flavor and need only a light dressing.

No matter how they are prepared, the shrimp are always cooked in the shell, and, except for salads, they are almost always served in their shells, even when part of a fish soup. The small shrimp may even be eaten without removing their tender shells when they are fried as part of *Fritto misto di mare*.

The first salad presented here combines fresh celery, cut into large pieces, with the shrimp marinated in tasty olive oil with fresh mint leaves and served cold.

The second salad, in which diced boiled carrots and potatoes accompany the poached shrimp, is dressed simply with a little oil and lemon juice to emphasize the main accompaniment of the dish, homemade *maionese*. Half of the shrimp are diced into the salad, and the remainder are used whole to top each serving.

The intensely greenish-yellow–colored homemade *maionese* is made with deep green virgin olive oil and yellow egg yolks and is flavored simply with lemon juice and salt. The texture of the *maionese* is stiffer and more solid than the mayonnaise of French cuisine. The rich taste of this dressing is enough to turn any poached fish into a noble dish.

Homemade maionese.

The *maionese* is presented in a sauceboat and is served on the side, not mixed in, to emphasize its important and independent position. When *maionese* or *salsa verde* accompanies a dish, a vegetable is never served at the same time.

Insalata di gamberi alla menta
SHRIMP SALAD WITH FRESH MINT LEAVES

2	pounds medium-sized shrimp or large prawns, unshelled	½	cup olive oil
	Coarse-grained salt		Salt and freshly ground black pepper
1	tablespoon red wine vinegar	15	sprigs Italian parsley, leaves only
1	bunch celery		
3	lemons	15	whole fresh mint leaves

Perfect

Wash the shrimp very well and put them in a bowl of cold water with coarse-grained salt and let them soak for ½ hour.

Bring a medium-sized casserole filled with cold water to a boil. Add coarse-grained salt to taste and the vinegar. After the water has boiled for 2 minutes, drain the shrimp and add them to the casserole. Cook for 3 minutes. Use a strainer-skimmer to transfer the shrimp to a bowl. When the shrimp are cool enough to handle, shell and devein them. Let the shrimp stand until needed.

Wash and clean the celery; you will be using only the inner white stalks of the bunch. Remove the leaves from the stalks and cut the stalks lengthwise into thirds. Then cut each piece into 1-inch pieces. Put the celery into a bowl of cold water with the juice of 1 lemon and let it soak for ½ hour.

Transfer the shrimp to a crockery or glass bowl and add the olive oil and salt and pepper. Drain the celery and add it to the bowl. Add the juice of the remaining 2 lemons and mix. Cover the bowl and refrigerate for ½ hour before serving.

Coarsely chop the parsley leaves on a board. Sprinkle the chopped parsley and the whole mint leaves over the salad, mix very well, and serve.

SEE PHOTO ON PAGE 39.   SERVES 6.

Gamberi, carote e patate con maione

SALAD OF SHRIMP, CARROTS, AND POTATOES WITH HOMEMADE MAYONNA

Gamberi, carote e patate con maionese (Salad of Shrimp, Carrots, and Potatoes with Homemade Mayonnaise) combines whole shrimp and pieces of shrimp in a lovely multicolored salad.

FOR THE SHRIMP

2	pounds medium-sized shrimp or large prawns, unshelled

Coarse-grained salt

8	cups cold water
½	cup dry white wine
5	whole black peppercorns
1	bay leaf

FOR THE CARROTS

1 pound carrots

Coarse-grained salt

FOR THE POTATOES

Coarse-grained salt

2 tablespoons red wine vinegar

1 pound boiling potatoes (not new potatoes)

PLUS

6 tablespoons olive oil

Juice of 2 lemons

Salt and freshly ground black pepper

FOR THE *MAIONESE*

3 extra large egg yolks

1 cup olive oil

Salt

½ tablespoon lemon juice

TO SERVE

Boston lettuce leaves and red *radicchio* leaves

Wash the shrimp very well and put them in a bowl of cold water with a little coarse-grained salt and let them soak for ½ hour.

Bring the 8 cups of cold water to a boil in a medium-sized casserole. Add coarse-grained salt to taste and the wine, peppercorns, and bay leaf. Add the shrimp and cook for 3 minutes. Drain the shrimp and, when they are cool enough to handle, shell and devein them. Place the cleaned shrimp on a plate. Cut half of them into 1-inch pieces and leave the rest whole. Let the shrimp stand until needed.

Meanwhile, soak the whole carrots in a bowl of cold water for ½ hour. Bring a small pot of cold water to a boil and add coarse-grained salt to taste. Then add the soaked carrots and boil them for about 15 minutes, or until they are cooked but still firm. Drain the carrots and cool and clean them by gently pushing off the outer skin under cold running water. Cut the cleaned carrots into 1-inch pieces and put them on a second plate. Let them stand until needed.

Bring a third small pot of cold water to a boil and add coarse-grained salt to taste and the wine vinegar. Peel the potatoes and cut them into 1-inch cubes. Cook them in the boiling water for about 6 minutes, or until cooked but still firm. Drain the potatoes and put them on a third plate. Let them stand until needed.

In a small bowl, mix the 6 tablespoons of olive oil with the lemon juice and salt and pepper to taste.

Use one third of the oil-lemon juice mixture to season the carrots, potatoes, and all the shrimp separately.

Mix the carrots, potatoes, and cut up shrimp together in a large bowl.

Line a large glass serving bowl with the Boston lettuce leaves and the *radicchio* leaves and put the carrot-potato-shrimp mixture in the middle. Arrange the whole shrimp around the rim of the bowl.

Prepare the *maionese:* Put the egg yolks into a crockery or glass bowl. Use a wooden spoon to mix them slowly, always in the same direction, in a smooth, rotating motion. When the yolks are well mixed, add the first drop of olive oil and stir slowly until it is absorbed. Continue adding oil a few drops at a time, always stirring slowly in the same direction, and only adding more oil when that already present has been well absorbed. As the emulsion begins to thicken, add the oil a few more drops at a time. Be careful not to add too much oil too soon. At this point, the emulsion should begin to resist as you stir it, and the mixture should be quite thick. When all the oil is added and the emulsion is perfect, stir the salt into the half tablespoon of lemon juice in a small bowl. Slowly add the salted lemon juice to the *maionese* while stirring thoroughly. Present the *maionese* in its own sauceboat or bowl.

SERVES 6.

145

FOR THE CRUST

8	ounces unbleached all-purpose flour
4	ounces sweet butter
	Pinch of salt
4	tablespoons cold milk

FOR THE STUFFING

½	pound sea bass fillets (the yield from a 1-pound fish)
½	pound small shrimp, unshelled
	Coarse-grained salt
1	tablespoon olive oil
	Salt and freshly ground black pepper
	Large pinch of hot red pepper flakes
1	tablespoon red wine vinegar
2	tablespoons (1 ounce) sweet butter
1½	cups homemade chicken broth
2	tablespoons unbleached all-purpose flour
1	large clove garlic, peeled
2	whole bay leaves
2	extra large egg yolks

*E*njoying a low-alcohol apéritif, such as Campari or Punt e Mes, before a meal is an almost universal custom in Italy, where cocktails are still looked on as an exotic though stylish importation. Salted or slightly spicy cold and hot dishes, such as the Fish and Shrimp Tart that follows, are often served with apéritifs.

Torta di pesce
FISH AND SHRIMP TART

Prepare the crust: Sift the flour onto a board and arrange it in a mound. Cut the butter into pieces and place them over the mound. Let stand for ½ hour, or until the butter softens. Start mixing the flour into the butter with your fingers; then finish incorporating it by rubbing it with the palms of your hands.

Make a well in the flour mixture and add the pinch of salt and the milk to the well. Mix with a fork and start adding the flour-butter mixture little by little, until all the ingredients are incorporated.

Form the dough into a ball with your hands and knead the dough gently for 1 minute. Slightly dampen a cotton dish towel and wrap the ball of dough in it. Let the dough rest in a cool place or on the bottom shelf of the refrigerator for 1 hour.

Meanwhile, prepare the stuffing: Preheat the oven to 375 degrees.

Soak the sea bass and the shrimp in 2 separate bowls with cold water and a little coarse-grained salt for 15 minutes.

Put a small saucepan with 5 cups of cold water over medium heat.

Drain the sea bass, pat it dry with paper towels, and put it on the shiny side of a piece of aluminum foil. Sprinkle the oil, salt and pepper to taste, and the hot red pepper flakes over the fish. Wrap the fish in the aluminum foil and bake for 30 minutes.

When the water in the saucepan comes to a boil, add coarse-grained salt to taste and the wine vinegar. When the water returns to a boil again, drain the shrimp and add them to the pan. Cook for 3 minutes. Remove the pan from the heat and let the shrimp stand in the poaching water for ½ hour.

Remove the bass from the oven and let it stand in the closed foil for ½ hour.

Shell and devein the shrimp; then cut them into 3 pieces each.

Transfer the contents of the aluminum foil to a small bowl and break up the fish, incorporating it with the juice. Add the shrimp pieces to the bowl and mix very well.

Melt the butter in a small saucepan over medium heat. When the butter is completely melted, add the fish and sauté for 2 minutes over low heat.

Meanwhile, heat the broth in a second saucepan. Finely chop the garlic on a board.

Add the flour to the fish, stir very well, and sauté for 1 minute. Add the hot broth all at once. Then add the garlic and bay leaves and stir very well. Simmer for 15 minutes over low heat. Transfer the contents of the saucepan to a crockery or glass bowl and let stand until cool (about 1 hour). Discard the bay leaves.

Butter a 9½-inch tart pan with a removable bottom.

Dust a board with a little flour. Unwrap the dough and knead it for 1 minute on the board. Then, using a rolling pin, roll out the dough into a circle about 16 inches in diameter. Roll up the dough circle onto the rolling pin and unroll it over the buttered pan. Fit the dough into the pan. Move the rolling pin over the pan to cut off any overhanging pastry. Use a fork to make punctures all over the pastry. Fit a sheet of aluminum foil shiny side down loosely over the pastry; then distribute dried beans or baking weights over the foil to keep the pastry shell from puffing up while it is baking. Refrigerate the pastry for ½ hour.

Preheat the oven to 375 degrees. Bake the pastry shell for 35 minutes.

Meanwhile, add the egg yolks to the cooled stuffing and taste for salt and pepper.

When the crust is ready, remove it from the oven and pour the stuffing into the shell. Return the pan to the oven and bake for 25 minutes. Remove the tart pan from the oven and let it stand for 2 minutes before removing the tart from the pan. Transfer the tart to a serving dish and serve, sliced like a pie.

SERVES 6 TO 8.

FISH

For baking, broiling, poaching, and even sautéing, Italians almost always use the whole fish and cook it with the head and tail on to retain maximum flavor. Slices of fish with bone are used when the fish is a very large one—for poached *palombo*, sautéed or grilled swordfish, or even preparations of fresh tuna. Smaller filleted fish are reserved for special dishes and for frying. However, even sole, if they are very small and young, are fried whole.

In addition to the simpler cooking methods, fish are also cooked in a variety of sauces, including a number of sweet-and-sour sauces called *in saor* or *in carpione*. The word *savori* was used in medieval times to mean sauces thickened with ground

Men fishing in the sweet, but slightly saline waters of the Ombrone River right at the point where it passes through the Maremma on its way to the sea.

nuts and a little bread, usually heavily spiced and often combining sweet flavors with salty, spicy, or sour ones.

In certain regional fish dishes in Italy, the word *savore* has hung on, referring to marinated fish. The most famous of these is the Venetian *Sardelle o sogliole in saor,* Marinated Fried Sardines or Sole (*saor* is the Venetian dialect word for *savore*). This is a sweet-and-sour dish that has almost converged with the *in carpione* treatment of fish in neighboring Lombardy, although the Venetian version is made with saltwater fish rather than with freshwater lake fish. The pink trout of Lake Garda, called *carpione,* are often cooked in Lombardy in a sweet-and-sour sauce. Other dishes using this sauce are called *in carpione.*

Sogliole in saor *(Marinated Fried Sole Venetian Style).*

150

Sogliole in saor
MARINATED FRIED SOLE VENETIAN STYLE

2	pounds small sole or flounder fillets	1	cup cold water
4	extra large eggs		Salt and freshly ground black pepper
	Pinch of salt	15	sprigs Italian parsley, leaves only
¼	cup cold milk		

FOR THE SAUCE

1	large white onion, peeled	2	medium-sized cloves garlic
½	cup olive oil	¼	cup raisins
4	tablespoons (2 ounces) sweet butter	2	tablespoons pignoli (pine nuts)

PLUS

10	whole black peppercorns
5	bay leaves
½	cup white wine vinegar

1	cup unseasoned bread crumbs, preferably homemade
1	quart vegetable oil
4	tablespoons (2 ounces) sweet butter

Cut the fillets into pieces not larger than 2 by 4 inches.

With a fork, lightly beat the eggs and the pinch of salt and the milk in a bowl. Add the fish pieces to the bowl, mix very well, and let the fish marinate for 1 hour, mixing occasionally.

Meanwhile, prepare the sauce: Cut the onion into very thin rings and put them in a bowl of cold water to soak for 5 minutes.

Heat the oil and the butter in a heavy saucepan over medium heat and, when the butter is completely melted, drain the onion rings and add them to the pan. Sauté over low heat for 5 minutes, or until the onion is translucent. Add the peppercorns, bay leaves, and wine vinegar to the pan. Cook slowly for 2 minutes. Then add the water and simmer for 30 minutes. Season with salt and pepper to taste. Keep the sauce warm while cooking the fish.

Finely chop the parsley and garlic together on a board. Soak the raisins in a bowl of lukewarm water for 15 minutes.

When the fish has marinated for an hour, heat the vegetable oil with the butter in a deep-fat fryer. Lay a sheet of aluminum foil on a board and spread the bread crumbs on the foil. Remove the fish pieces one at a time from the eggs, and bread them on both sides, pressing the fish pieces all over with the palm of your hand to make sure that both sides are coated uniformly.

When the butter is completely melted and the oil is hot (about 375 degrees), add the fish pieces and cook for 1 minute on each side. Transfer the cooked fish to a large serving platter (do not line the platter with paper towels). When all the fish pieces are cooked and on the platter, sprinkle them with the chopped ingredients.

Drain the raisins, pat them dry with paper towels, and spread them all over the fish along with the pine nuts. Pour the reduced hot sauce over everything. Cover the platter with aluminum foil and let stand for at least 1 hour before serving.

SERVES 6.

Above: A busy side canal in Chioggia. The open arches on the left lead to still more markets on the water. All the windows have the solid wooden shutters called scuri; in the Venice area they are usually painted green.
Opposite and right: Chioggia fishermen select and arrange the night's catch, dividing sardines from anchovies.

$\mathcal{W}$hile fish *in saor* subordinates the flavor of the fresh fish to the marinade and spices, many Italian fish preparations are dedicated to maintaining the fresh flavor and to that end use only those seasonings that will enhance the taste of the fish. Italians think of *in saor* as a city dish, made with fish that has traveled a little distance from where it was caught, and of the marinade as almost a preserving sauce. In contrast, two other preparations are considered seaside dishes—Fish Flamed with Fresh Herbs and Whole Fish on the Grill. Using fish that has just come out of the water, the cooking is meant to bring out the flavor of the sea itself.

In the first dish, the whole fish is baked with no flavorings except salt and pepper. Then it is flamed and smothered in an abundant variety of fresh herbs, which impart a subtle and completely sufficient richness to the dish.

In the second preparation on page 156, the whole fish—sea bass or red snapper—is simply grilled over a wood fire (or in a broiler) with sprigs of fresh rosemary stuck into the skin and a whole bay leaf in the cavity of the fish.

Flaming the grilled fish with fresh herbs for Pesce alle erbe.

Pesce alle erbe
FISH FLAMED WITH FRESH HERBS

1	sea bass or red snapper, about 2½ pounds, cleaned but left whole with head and tail on
	Coarse-grained salt
	Salt and freshly ground black pepper
15	sprigs Italian parsley
1	bunch fresh dill
10	fresh sage leaves
2	sprigs fresh rosemary, or 2 tablespoons fresh rosemary leaves
5	sprigs fresh mint
5	large bay leaves
5	large fresh basil leaves
½	cup light rum

Clean the fish well and soak it in a bowl of cold water with a little coarse-grained salt for ½ hour.

Preheat the oven to 375 degrees.

Drain the fish and pat it dry with paper towels. Put a large sheet of aluminum foil on a board shiny side up. Sprinkle the foil with a little salt and pepper and lay the fish on the foil. Wrap the fish completely in the foil and put it in a baking dish. Bake for 16 minutes; then turn the fish over and bake for 16 minutes longer.

Unwrap the fish and transfer it to a large serving platter, adding the juice from the foil. Place the herbs on the fish.

Warm the rum over low heat. Then pour the rum all over the fish and flame it. Serve immediately, including some of the flamed herbs with each portion of fish. (Loosen the fish flesh with a spatula; do not slice it with a knife.)

SERVES 4.

*A*lthough recipes for meat cooked together with vegetables are common to all regions of Italy and are especially popular in the South, fish baked with vegetables is a more unusual southern specialty. This dish may be made with various whole fish, including Mediterranean *dentice* or its Atlantic cousins bream or porgy. The fish is baked in the oven surrounded by fresh artichokes cut into pieces.

154

Pesce al forno con carciofi
BAKED FISH WITH ARTICHOKES

Put the artichokes in a bowl of cold water, with the juice of 2 of the lemons and the squeezed lemon halves. Let them soak for ½ hour.

Clean the artichokes, following the directions on page 51. Then cut them into small pieces and return them to the water with the lemon juice.

Bring a medium-sized pot of cold water to a boil; then add coarse-grained salt to taste and the remaining lemon, cut in half. Dissolve the flour in ½ cup of cold water in a small bowl and stir the mixture into the boiling water. Add the artichoke pieces and blanch them for 1 minute. Drain the artichoke pieces and transfer them to a bowl of cold water to stand until needed.

Meanwhile, wash the fish very well and put it in a bowl of cold water with a little coarse-grained salt. Let the fish soak for 15 minutes.

Finely chop the garlic on a board.

Remove the fish from the water and pat it dry with paper towels.

Preheat the oven to 375 degrees.

Put the fish in the middle of a poacher or baking dish, leaving room at the sides for the artichoke pieces. Season the cavity of the fish with salt, pepper, and half of the chopped garlic. Pour 4 tablespoons of the oil over the fish and season it with salt and pepper.

Drain the artichokes well, transfer them to a bowl, and pour the remaining 4 tablespoons of the oil over them. Season the artichokes with salt and pepper. Mix very well and arrange the artichoke pieces in the poacher around the fish. Sprinkle the parsley and the remaining chopped garlic over the fish and artichokes. Cover the pan and bake for 45 minutes, stirring the artichokes occasionally to be sure they cook evenly.

Remove the poacher from the oven and serve the fish and artichokes directly from the pan, adding a wedge of lemon to each serving.

SERVES 4.

4	large artichokes
3	lemons
	Coarse-grained salt
1	tablespoon unbleached all-purpose flour
1	2½ pound whole fish, such as porgy, sea bass, or red snapper, cleaned but left whole with head and tail on
2	cloves garlic, peeled
	Salt and freshly ground black pepper
8	tablespoons olive oil
15	sprigs Italian parsley, leaves only

TO SERVE

| 1 | lemon, cut into wedges |

Pesce al forno con carciofi *is prepared by baking the whole fish with artichokes.*

155

Pesce alla griglia
WHOLE FISH ON THE GRILL

Preheat the broiler to 400 degrees (see Note).

Wash the fish in cold salted water; then pat it dry with paper towels.

Cut each clove of garlic into 4 pieces. Make 2 slits on each side of the fish and insert some of the rosemary and 3 pieces of the garlic in each slit. Place the bay leaf in the cavity of the fish with the remaining garlic and rosemary. Sprinkle the cavity of the fish with salt and pepper. Then sprinkle the outside of the fish with salt and pepper.

Put the fish directly on the middle shelf of the oven, placing a jelly roll pan or baking tray under the shelf to catch the drippings. Grill for 18 minutes; then, using a long metal spatula, turn the fish over and cook for 18 minutes longer.

Remove the fish from the oven and transfer it to a large serving platter. Serve, sprinkling 1 tablespoon of oil on each serving and accompanying each serving with 1 or 2 lemon wedges.

SEE PHOTO ON PAGES 114–115.   SERVES 4.

NOTE: *If you cannot regulate your broiler or grill, place the fish on a rack in a pan 6 inches from the heat and broil for about 15 minutes on each side.*

1	sea bass or red snapper, about 2½ pounds, cleaned but left whole with head and tail on
	Coarse-grained salt
4	cloves garlic, peeled
4	sprigs fresh rosemary, or 2 tablespoons fresh rosemary leaves
1	bay leaf
	Salt and freshly ground black pepper
4	tablespoons olive oil
	Lemon wedges

*I*nvoltini, the stuffed rolls so often made with veal *scaloppine*, are equally popular in the South when they are made with fish. Swordfish is the most adaptable for this dish because its dense, solid flesh does not fall apart during the cooking. Indeed, it becomes stronger and more compact. Swordfish, along with fresh tuna and sardines, is the most common fish in southern Italy and Sicily.

The stuffing of bread crumbs flavored with fresh garlic and capers preserved in wine vinegar suffuses the fish, which is cooked on a skewer with slices of fresh tomato and lemon.

Although the fish *involtini* are usually cooked over a wood fire, the skewers of fish may be cooked in the oven with excellent results.

Involtini di pesce spada
ROLLED STUFFED SWORDFISH CUTLETS ON SKEWERS

3	pounds swordfish with bone, cut into 3 slices ½ inch thick
¼	cup olive oil
	Salt

FOR THE STUFFING

2	medium-sized cloves garlic, peeled
3	heaping tablespoons capers in wine vinegar, drained
½	cup unseasoned bread crumbs, preferably homemade
	Juice of ½ lemon
	Salt and freshly ground black pepper

Cut each slice of fish into 2 pieces, removing the bone in the center. Put the 6 pieces of fish in a bowl and add the olive oil. Sprinkle salt over the fish and let it stand for ½ hour, turning the pieces over two or three times.

Prepare the stuffing: Finely chop the garlic and coarsely chop the capers on a board. Put the chopped ingredients in a small bowl and add the bread crumbs, lemon juice, and salt and pepper to taste. Mix all the ingredients together with a wooden spoon.

Preheat the oven to 375 degrees.

Remove the fish slices from the bowl and lay them on a platter. Place one sixth of the stuffing in the center of each slice.

Cut the lemons and tomatoes into ½-inch-thick slices.

Thread a large skewer starting with a slice of tomato, then the lemon, and then a slice of the fish folded like a package. Repeat until all the ingredients are used. Brush everything threaded on the skewer with the oil left in the bowl and then sprinkle with salt and pepper.

Put the skewer on a jelly roll pan or baking tray and put it on the middle shelf of the oven. Bake for 20 minutes. Then raise the temperature to 500 degrees and cook for 3 minutes longer. Remove the skewer from the oven and transfer it to a serving platter. Serve with the lemon wedges and parsley leaves.

SERVES 6.

PLUS

2 lemons

3 large ripe but not overripe
tomatoes

Salt and freshly ground black
pepper

TO SERVE

Lemon wedges

18 sprigs Italian parsley, leaves
only

A colorful pattern is formed by the alternating slices of stuffed swordfish, bright yellow lemons, and juicy red tomatoes on a skewer.

Red mullet, *triglia* in Italian, *rouget* in French, is a delicate Mediterranean fish. When they are available, the tiny red mullets are one of the important components of *Fritto misto di mare;* and the larger ones are often wrapped in *pancetta* and baked in oiled parchment paper. *Triglie* are not available fresh away from the Mediterranean, but other half-pound fish may be substituted.

Triglie al cartoccio
RED MULLET COOKED IN PARCHMENT PAPER

2   fresh *triglie* (red mullets), about ½ pound each, or any small white-fleshed, nonoily sea fish, cleaned but left whole with head and tail on

Coarse-grained salt

3   tablespoons olive oil

2   slices *pancetta* or *prosciutto,* about 3 ounces each

2   pinches dried thyme

Salt and freshly ground black pepper

4   whole black peppercorns

2   large bay leaves

Triglie, *ready to be wrapped in parchment paper for* Triglie al cartoccio.

Wash and clean the fish very well and place them in a bowl of cold water with a little coarse-grained salt. Let the fish soak for ½ hour.

Preheat the oven to 375 degrees.

Drain the fish and pat them dry with paper towels.

Lay a large piece of parchment paper on a board. Brush the paper with 1 tablespoon of the oil. Place the *pancetta* slices on the paper. Then lay 1 fish on top of each slice of *pancetta*. Season the cavity of each fish with the thyme, salt and pepper, black peppercorns, and bay leaves. Wrap each fish with its *pancetta* slice and pour the remaining oil over them.

Make a package with the parchment paper, being sure to seal all the edges completely. Place the package in a baking dish and bake for 25 minutes. Serve immediately, opening the package at the table.

SERVES 2.

Baccalà (dried salt cod), once eaten in all parts of the world, has never lost its popularity in Italy. *Baccalà* perhaps originated as a practical way of preserving fish, but the aging process gives it such a unique flavor that even where fresh cod is available, *baccalà* does not yield to it.

Mantecare is a word used primarily to describe the churning motion with which butter and cheese are incorporated into *risotto* in its last stages. It may originally have meant the churning involved in butter-making. The churning of the flesh of the poached fish breaks it up and creates a texture resembling a dough, which is then arranged in a mound.

Baccalà mantecato ("Churned" Salt Cod) bordered with leaves of Italian parsley.

Baccalà mantecato
"CHURNED" SALT COD

Soak the dried salt cod in a bowl of cold water for at least 12 hours, changing the water four or five times.

Rinse the fish very well under cold running water; then put it in a large casserole filled with cold water, cover the casserole, and put it over medium heat. When the water comes to a boil, add a little coarse-grained salt and cook the cod, covered, for 5 minutes. Remove the casserole from the heat and let the fish stand in the poaching water, covered, for 1 hour.

Meanwhile, finely chop the parsley and garlic together on a board.

Drain the fish and place it on the board. Remove the skin and bones and put the flesh in a large bowl. Start mixing the fish with a wooden spoon in a rotating motion, adding the oil a little at a time. Keep stirring and adding the oil until the fish becomes almost like a coarse dough. Add the chopped ingredients and salt and pepper to taste and incorporate them thoroughly into the fish.

The fish may be transferred to a serving platter and served immediately. Serve accompanied by the parsley and lemon slices. If served later, keep the fish covered in the mixing bowl in the refrigerator. When ready to serve, mix it very well before transferring it to a serving platter.

SERVES 8 TO 12.

2 pounds dried salt cod

    Coarse-grained salt

20 sprigs Italian parsley, leaves only

2 large cloves garlic, peeled

1 to 1½ cups olive oil

    Salt and freshly ground black pepper

TO SERVE

15 sprigs Italian parsley, leaves only

1 lemon, cut into slices

159

Left: A swift trout is nearly cam-
ouflaged in a freshwater stream in
Umbria.

Above: Umbria is also black truffle
country, and two of the specialties of
this region are **Trote al tartufo**
(Trout with Black Truffles), left, and
Lumachelle al tartufo (Lumachelle
Pasta with Black Truffle Sauce),
right (see recipe on page 116).

*I*talians always speak of *acqua dolce*, "sweet water," when referring to fresh water as opposed to salt. The freshwater fish in the Italian rivers and lakes include tench, pike, carp, perch, trout, pink trout, eels, and even freshwater shrimp. Sturgeon and salmon are now rare, but they were once easy to find in large rivers like the Po.

One of the sights that constantly surprises visitors to Rome and Florence is the sight of Sunday fishermen, lined up along the streets above the riverbanks and even on the bridges in the heart of the city, casting their lines down into the river below. When occasionally a fish weighing three pounds or so is caught, the fisherman becomes a short-time celebrity, as his photograph with the fish usually ends up in the local paper.

Urban fishing scenes in Florence, with the shouts and calls of the fishermen and onlookers, were written down as early as the fourteenth century in little musical pieces that are still performed. These pieces have two voices in canon and a third one played by an instrument.

One of the most popular freshwater fish is trout; it is inexpensive but of high quality and available in many areas. A local dish in Umbria, Trout with Black Truffles, has achieved such a reputation with *buongustai* (gourmets) that visitors will make a detour just to stop in Scheggino to eat the dish.

Trote al tartufo
TROUT WITH BLACK TRUFFLES

3 brook trout, about ½ pound each, cleaned but left whole with head and tail on	crumbs, preferably homemade
1 tablespoon red wine vinegar	2 tablespoons olive oil
15 sprigs Italian parsley, leaves only	Salt and freshly ground black pepper
1 lemon	About 1 ounce fresh or canned black truffle
5 tablespoons unseasoned bread	PLUS Lemon wedges

Clean the trout carefully and put them in a bowl of cold water with the vinegar. Let soak for ½ hour.

Preheat the oven to 375 degrees.

Finely chop the parsley on a board and squeeze the lemon. Combine the chopped parsley, lemon juice, and bread crumbs in a small bowl. Add the oil and season with salt and pepper to taste. Mix all the ingredients together.

Drain the trout and pat them dry with paper towels. Stuff each trout with one third of the prepared stuffing.

Place the trout on the middle shelf of the oven and put an empty baking dish on the bottom shelf of the oven to catch the drippings. Bake for 15 minutes; then, using a metal spatula, turn the trout over and raise the oven temperature to 400 degrees. Cook the trout for about 5 minutes longer.

Meanwhile, finely chop the truffle on a board.

Remove the trout from the oven and transfer them to a warm serving platter. Place one third of the chopped truffle in the cavity of each fish on the other stuffing. Serve immediately with lemon wedges.

SERVES 3.

161

The city of Mantua, on the southern finger of the Po valley, is set among lakes. From the upper floors of the Castello San Giorgio, in the Piazza Sordello, you can see the entire city laid out beneath you, the subdued terra cotta roofs blending subtly into the misty northern landscape.

When the lakes are not stormy, the local pike is one of the best catches. The oldest and best-loved dish is poached pike with its unique Mantua green sauce, made of coarsely chopped vegetables and herbs. Actually, the sauce is not very green here; "green sauce" is simply another way of saying herb sauce, and in most other areas the sauce lives up to its name, as more of the greener herbs are included.

Luccio alla mantovana
POACHED PIKE WITH GREEN SAUCE MANTUA STYLE

FOR THE *SALSA VERDE ALLA MANTOVANA*

2 hard-boiled extra large eggs

2 medium-sized carrots

1 small celery stalk

2 whole anchovies in salt, or 4 anchovy fillets in oil, drained

2 tablespoons capers in wine vinegar, drained

1 tablespoon pignoli (pine nuts)

20 sprigs Italian parsley, leaves only

10 gherkins (*cetriolini* or cornichons) in wine vinegar, drained

1 sweet red bell pepper in wine vinegar, drained

1 medium-sized clove garlic, peeled

½ cup olive oil

Salt and freshly ground black pepper

FOR THE FISH

2 carrots, scraped

2 celery stalks

2 cloves garlic, peeled

10 sprigs Italian parsley

2 large bay leaves

1 teaspoon dried thyme

1 cup dry white wine

2 tablespoons coarse-grained salt

4 quarts cold water

2 pike, 2 pounds each, cleaned but left whole with head and tail on

Prepare the sauce: Shell the eggs and cut them into quarters. Put the eggs on a chopping board.

Scrape the carrots and the celery, removing the large threads from the celery, and put them in a bowl of cold water to soak for ½ hour.

If the anchovies are in salt, clean and fillet them under cold running water, removing the bones and excess salt. Put the anchovies on the board with the eggs.

Transfer the carrots and celery to the board, adding the capers, pine nuts, parsley, gherkins, and sweet red pepper. Coarsely chop everything except the eggs together. When all the vegetables and aromatic herbs are chopped, coarsely cut up the eggs and transfer everything to a crockery or glass bowl.

Finely chop the garlic and add it to the bowl along with the olive oil and salt and pepper to taste. Mix everything together with a wooden spoon. Cover the bowl with aluminum foil and refrigerate for at least ½ hour before serving.

Prepare the pike: Put all the ingredients except the fish in a fish poacher. Cover and place the pan over medium heat. Let the broth simmer for 30 minutes. Remove from the heat and use a slotted spoon to remove and discard the vegetables and herbs. Add the fish and return the poacher to the heat. After the water returns to a boil, cover the pan and simmer for 10 minutes. At that time the fish should be cooked but still firm. Transfer the fish to a board and remove the flesh in small pieces, discarding the skin and bones. Arrange the fish pieces in the center of a platter.

Just before serving, surround the fish with a ring of the prepared sauce. An outer ring of aspic may also be added. (See the following recipe for the aspic, which must be prepared in advance.)

SERVES 6 TO 8.

FOR THE ASPIC

Put the water, beef, calf's foot, carrot, onion, leeks, celery, parsley, cloves, and bay leaf in a large stockpot. Bring to a boil over medium heat. Add the salt and peppercorns and half-cover the pot with its lid. Simmer for about 4 hours. By that time the water should have reduced to less than half. Taste for salt. Remove the pot from the heat.	12 cups cold water
	2 pounds beef for boiling
Strain the broth through a cheesecloth placed in a large colander into a large bowl and let stand until cool (about 1 hour). Cover the bowl with aluminum foil and refrigerate until completely cold (at least 4 hours).	1 medium-sized calf's foot
	1 medium-sized carrot, scraped
Remove the bowl from the refrigerator and use a metal spatula to carefully remove the layer of fat from the top. Be sure that no fat remains in the broth.	1 small red onion, peeled
	2 medium-sized leeks, green parts removed, well washed
Using a wire whisk, beat the egg whites with about 3 tablespoons of the broth. Add the mixture to the bowl with the cold broth. Mix thoroughly; then transfer the contents of the bowl to a very heavy stockpot. Put the pot over very low heat and stir continuously with the whisk until the broth reaches a boil. Then half-cover the pot and lower the heat as low as it will go. Simmer for about 15 minutes.	1 celery stalk
	5 sprigs Italian parsley
	2 whole cloves
Wet a thick piece of cheesecloth with cold water and refrigerate it for about 15 minutes.	1 bay leaf
Pour the Marsala into the simmering broth and mix well.	2 teaspoons coarse-grained salt
Place the cold cheesecloth in a colander and rest the colander on a large bowl. Gently pour the broth into the cheesecloth-lined colander. The broth coming through into the bowl should be clear and transparent. Let the broth stand until it is cool (about 1 hour).	5 whole white peppercorns
	3 egg whites
Lightly oil a loaf pan and pour the cooled broth into the pan. Cover the pan and refrigerate until the aspic is firm (about 3 hours). Unmold onto a flat serving platter and cut the gelatin into 1-inch pieces. The gelatin can be refrigerated, covered, until needed.	2 tablespoons dry Marsala wine

Meat

CURED MEAT

Prosciutto is salted and air-dried fresh ham. This seasoning and aging process cures the ham completely so that cooking is unnecessary. Strictly speaking, it should be called *prosciutto crudo*, cured uncooked ham, as *prosciutto cotto*, boiled ham, is also available in Italy. But when we say simply *prosciutto*, we always refer to the uncooked ham—by far the most popular cured meat in Italy, and abroad, one of the symbols of Italian cooking.

Prosciutto curing does not include smoking, although there is a type of smoked *prosciutto* called *speck*, found in the extreme north of the country. In addition, a special *prosciutto* smoked with juniper berries is produced in parts of central Italy.

The hams for *prosciutto* come from the two hind quarters of the pig and contain the upper leg with the pig's foot removed. Shoulder hams from the front quarters (*prosciuttini de spalla*) are available, but they are neither as good nor as popular as the others.

The hams from one area of Italy differ in taste and texture from those of another as much as Chianti wine differs from Barolo. There are connoisseurs who enjoy *prosciutto* tasting, differentiating their hundreds of diverse flavors. The famous hams of the Parma area are a little bit sweet; those of the Chianti wine region are salty; the hams of San Daniele in Friuli have yet another flavor. There may be a notable difference even from one farm to the next, as with neighboring vineyards. The variations occur because of what the animals are fed, whether they are

Preceding overleaf: Rows of prosciutti di Parma *hung for aging in a cool room with a controlled flow of fresh air.*

Opposite: Unloading fresh hams.

Above: Rubbing salt into the fresh ham.

Left: Spreading sugna, *or pork fat, to seal the cut part of the ham.*

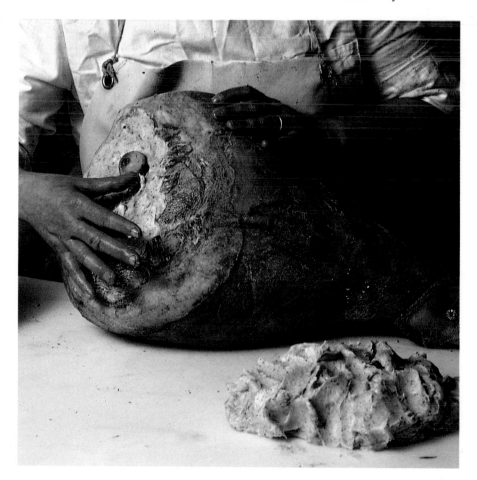

167

Top: A novice being introduced to the mysteries of prosciutto *making.
To make sure the hams are aging well without spoiling, testing is done
periodically. The instrument in my hand is a horse bone, which is
inserted into the ham and then checked for the proper smell. Above:*
Prosciutti *in three different stages; left, an unsalted fresh ham; center,
a salted* prosciutto, *aged six months, but not yet ready; and, right, a one-
year-old ham. Aging may last from ten months to two years.*

Right: At the factory of Citterio in Rho, a festival of salami, prosciutti,
and pancetta, *together with two air-dried beef* bresaole, *one round, the
other rectangular. The largest round sausage is the famous* mortadella *of
Bologna, the original bologna, stacked on a round, rolled* pancetta. *On
top, a pair of* prosciutti *and a similar* coppa, *made from the fore shank
of the pig.* Felino, *which is always cut diagonally, is the thin salami sitting on the board.*

kept indoors or outside, as well as the slight differences in the curing process itself. With the San Daniele type, the animals eat acorns and are kept outside; their meat is very lean. With the Parma type, the pigs eat the whey of the *Parmigiano* combined with some grain, and are kept indoors; their meat is sweeter and less lean. Interestingly, the pork dishes of the Parma area often contain cream and milk, undoubtedly because the combination of meat from milk-fed pigs with other dairy products is especially good. In this area, pigs are generally kept next to the *caseificio*, where the cheese is produced, and a pipe carries the whey directly from one building to the next.

The zone of production of various denominations of *prosciutto* is usually limited by law. The area of Parma ham is restricted to the land between the Taro and Baganza rivers, mostly coinciding with the *Parmigiano* cheese area. The air in this zone has unique properties for drying and curing, and the degree of humidity is so ideal that hams produced in neighboring zones are sent there to be air-dried and cured.

The various types of cured meat—produced from beef as well as pork—are used for different purposes in the *cucina*. *Bresaola* is popular not only in Lombardy, its place of origin, but has now become a favorite appetizer all over Italy. Salted, air-dried, and pressed, it may be made from a number of different cuts of beef. It may be served quite simply, sliced like *prosciutto* and dressed with a little lemon juice and oil. But a more intriguing presentation is "*cannelloni* style," in which the *bresaola* serves as the wrapping around a stuffing. In the following recipe, the filling uses the rich, soft *caprino* cheese of Lombardy, whipped with oil and pepper.

Preceding overleaf: The subtle and sweet prosciutto of Parma is perfectly paired with fresh figs. The fichi fiore, or flower figs, are the first early crop to blossom. The skin is thicker than in normal second-crop figs. The dish sits on a bed of fig leaves in a frescoed room of the castle of Torrechiara, on a hill next to the town of Langhirano, the capital of Parmesan ham production.

Opposite: Bresaola is served on the terrace of Villa d'Este, overlooking Lake Como. Writers from Vergil to Shelley have celebrated the lake's incomparable beauty.

Bresaola con caprino
BRESAOLA WITH CAPRINO CHEESE

18 thin slices *bresaola*

3   rolls *caprino* (7 to 8 ounces total weight)

10 tablespoons (½ cup plus 2 tablespoons) olive oil

    Salt and freshly ground black pepper

TO SERVE

6   Boston lettuce leaves

2   lemons

Lay all of the *bresaola* slices flat on a board.

On a plate, use a fork to mix together the *caprino* and to incorporate 4 tablespoons of the olive oil and salt and pepper to taste. Put the cheese mixture into a pastry bag with a ½-inch serrated tip.

Make a line of cheese along one narrow side of each rectangular *bresaola* slice and roll it up like *cannelloni*. Repeat the procedure with the remaining slices.

Place a lettuce leaf on each of 6 plates. Slice off both ends of each lemon. Cut the lemons in half vertically; then cut each half into 6 slices.

Arrange the *cannelloni* on each plate, alternating them with a lemon slice, until each serving consists of 4 lemon slices alternating with 3 *cannelloni*. Pour a little of the remaining oil over the *cannelloni* and serve immediately.

SERVES 6 AS AN APPETIZER.

BEEF

Chianina cattle, from the valley of the Chiana river in Tuscany, produce the meat of the true Florentine beefsteak, so admired all over Italy. Today, however, even in Florence itself one rarely finds this choice beef because of the great demand for it. *Chianina* beef used to be available for the filet section alone, but now it is too rare to be used for anything except the complete beefsteak *alla fiorentina,* which uses both the filet and the contrafilet. Even though the *Chianina* are more famous for beef than for veal, the lean tender meat is eaten quite young, and it is not hung long for aging. This breed, always white in color, has recently been interbred with Texas cattle in the United States, with great success.

A tender steak cut, not necessarily of *Chianina* meat, is also used in the marinated raw beef dish, *carpaccio. Carne al carpaccio,* a dish from Piedmont, probably means "beef in the style of the Carpathian Mountains," and whether such a Hungarian origin is real or exotically fanciful is not known. The name seems to have nothing to do with the Venetian Renaissance painter Carpaccio.

The marinade for *carpaccio* is always simply oil and lemon juice, and sometimes garlic. No other sauce should be added— not mustard sauce, *pesto,* or any of the others one sees too often abroad in inauthentic versions of the dish. The real *carpaccio* is always eaten with thin slices of *Parmigiano* and of raw mushrooms, preferably fresh *porcini* or *ovoli,* and if these are not available, domestic white champignons. In one particularly fine version of *carpaccio, Carne cruda all'astigiana,* the meat is ground and served with white truffles.

Right: The famous Chianina *cattle graze in the Val di Chiana. Always white, these cattle grow to great size and provide Italy with* bistecca alla fiorentina.

Below: The horned cattle of the Maremma range wild over central Italy and are a principal source of native beef there. Despite their impressive horns and great strength, the cattle are generally docile.

Carpaccio
CARPACCIO

Squeeze the lemons into a small bowl or cup.

Hold the garlic with a fork and rub it over the entire inside surface of a medium-sized crockery or glass bowl using a rotating motion. Then, with the other hand, slowly drip in all the olive oil, while continuing to rotate the fork with the garlic, using it to whip up the oil (about 3 minutes).

Add the lemon juice in the same way, using the rotating fork to mix it thoroughly with the oil (about 2 minutes longer). To this very light emulsion, add salt and pepper to taste. Let the sauce stand until needed.

Remove any soil clinging to the mushrooms with a damp paper towel; then thinly slice them and arrange them on the bottom of a crockery or china platter. Make an outer ring of the *Parmigiano* slices over the mushrooms; then lay the meat in the center, inside the ring of cheese. Pour the prepared sauce over all. Arrange the parsley on the platter and serve.

The dish may be prepared in advance and kept covered in the refrigerator, but the color of the meat and the mushrooms will darken.

SERVES 8.

Carpaccio *is served with thinly sliced mushrooms and* Parmigiano.

3   lemons

1   medium-sized clove garlic, peeled but left whole

½   cup olive oil

    Salt and freshly ground black pepper

1   pound champignon mushrooms

8   "scaglie" or thin slices *Parmigiano*, about 2 ounces each

8   very thin slices beef top round

8   sprigs Italian parsley, leaves only

*R*ump of beef is not only cooked longer than any other cut of beef, but it is usually also marinated for several hours before cooking, both to tenderize the meat and to infuse it with the fine flavors of wine and herbs. The same regional wine that is used in the marinade is always served with the meal in Italy. The versatile roast also adjusts well to each region's staple accompaniment—*polenta* in the North, beans in central Italy, and so on. In the South, the pasta first course may be dressed with the rich sauce from the roast, but pasta is never served as a side dish with the meat course.

Stufato al Barolo
RUMP OF BEEF BRAISED IN BAROLO WIN

3	pounds rump roast of beef or yearling
2	ounces *pancetta* or *prosciutto,* cut into strips
5	cups Barolo wine
2	carrots, scraped

1	large red onion, peeled
15	sprigs Italian parsley
1	sprig fresh rosemary, or 1 tablespoon rosemary leaves, preserved in salt or dried and blanched (see Note on page 43)

The uncooked rump of beef, darkened by the rich marinade of sage, fragrant vegetables, and a generous measure of fine Barolo wine.

6	large sage leaves, fresh or preserved in salt (see Note on page 43)	4	tablespoons (2 ounces) sweet butter	Salt and freshly ground black pepper

6   large sage leaves, fresh or preserved in salt (see Note on page 43)

3   bay leaves

2   large cloves garlic, peeled

2   medium-sized celery stalks

4   tablespoons (2 ounces) sweet butter

3   tablespoons olive oil

½   cup brandy

Salt and freshly ground black pepper

Freshly grated nutmeg

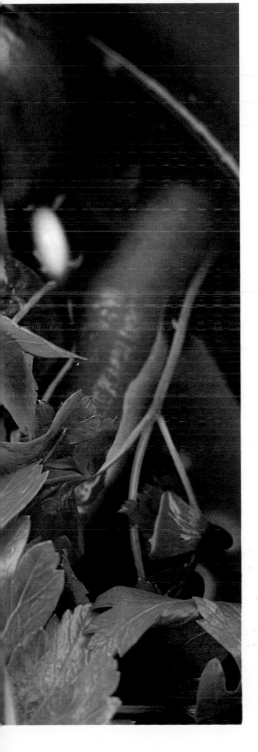

Using a larding needle, lard the meat with the strips of *pancetta;* then tie the meat like a salami (see Note).

Place the roast in a large terra cotta or crockery bowl and add the wine and all the vegetables and aromatic herbs. Cover the bowl with aluminum foil and refrigerate for at least 6 hours, turning the meat five or six times.

When the meat is ready, heat the butter and oil in a heavy casserole over medium heat. When the butter is completely melted, add the meat and sauté for 10 minutes, turning it until it is light golden brown on all sides. Add the brandy and let it evaporate for 5 minutes.

Remove and discard all the vegetables and aromatic herbs from the marinade, and start adding the marinade to the casserole 1 cup at a time, allowing about 35 minutes for each cup to evaporate. Cook, covered, until all the marinade is added and has evaporated and the meat is cooked and very juicy (about 3 hours). After the second cup of marinade has been added, season the meat with salt, pepper, and nutmeg.

Remove the meat from the casserole and discard the strings. If the sauce is very thin, reduce it.

To serve, cut the meat into slices 1 inch thick. Pour a little of the remaining sauce over each serving.

SERVES 6.

NOTE: *To tie like a salami, use a length of kitchen string about six times the length of the meat to be tied. Place one end of the string around the meat about 1½ inches from the end and knot it in the center of the meat. Bring the long end of the string down the meat another 1½ inches. Hold it in place, and pull the string under and around the meat again. Wrap the end of the string under, then over, the place where the string is held, without knotting it and pull the string tight. Stand the meat on end and pull the string under the bottom and over the top and fasten it again in the same way and place. Repeat the procedure every 1½ inches, and finally tie the two ends of the string together. The string can then be removed by cutting it only once.*

The filet cut of beefsteak is eaten in Italy as often as veal *scaloppine,* although abroad it is not usually associated with Italian cooking. The *filetti* are frequently cooked *alla griglia,* on the grill, and are sometimes served with a sauce, as in the following dish. They may also be sliced thin, lightly sautéed, and served with a sauce.

Steaks, whether *filetti* or *bistecca alla fiorentina,* are usually eaten quite rare, with the meat inside more red than pink. The filet is never used in the mixed grill, and when the whole *fiorentina* is used, its place in the ensemble takes precedence over the preference for rareness. But when cooked alone, even on a wood fire, special attention is paid not to overcook the meat. Since Italians prefer beef to be lean, they never wrap the filet in fat.

Filetti alla griglia (o alla brace) con salsa contadina
FILETS WITH VEGETABLE SAUCE

6 1½-inch-thick filets mignons

Salt

FOR THE *SALSA CONTADINA*

3 medium-sized celery stalks

3 medium-sized carrots, scraped

1 medium-sized red onion, peeled

1 clove garlic, peeled

15 sprigs Italian parsley, leaves only

4 basil leaves, fresh or preserved in salt (see Note on page 43)

1 bay leaf

1 whole clove

4 ounces boneless beef or veal in one piece

1 cup dry red wine

Salt and freshly ground black pepper

1 tablespoon sweet butter

3 tablespoons olive oil

Remove the meat from the refrigerator half an hour before cooking.

Prepare the sauce: Coarsely chop the celery, carrots, onion, garlic, parsley, and basil together on a board. Put all the chopped ingredients into a saucepan; then add the bay leaf and clove.

Put the meat on top of the vegetables and pour the wine over all. Cover the pan and cook over medium heat for ½ hour, without stirring. Season with salt and pepper, mix all the ingredients together, and cook, covered, for 15 minutes longer.

Remove the pan from the heat and discard the meat, bay leaf, and clove. Pass the contents of the pan through a food mill, using the disc with the medium-sized holes, into a small bowl.

Heat the butter and oil in a saucepan over medium heat and, when the butter is completely melted, add the passed vegetables. Taste for salt and pepper and simmer, uncovered, for 5 minutes, or until a smooth sauce has formed.

Preheat the broiler. Place the meat 2 inches from the heat and broil for 5 to 7 minutes on each side. (In Italy the meat is usually eaten medium-rare.)

Remove the meat from the broiler. If the filets are wrapped in fat, discard it. Place each filet on a bed of warm vegetable sauce on individual plates. Sprinkle a little salt on the meat before serving.

SERVES 6.

VEAL

Boneless veal *scaloppine*, which may be cut from any tender muscle meat, is, of course, eaten often in Italy; the boneless cuts adapt well to many different sauces and are fast and convenient to prepare. Many other cuts of veal, however, such as the shank and the breast, are equally appreciated.

Veal scallops sautéed with Belgian endive and served with fresh parsley is an unusual treatment. This type of endive, a close relative of *radicchio*, is covered during its growth to prevent it from developing color. Although this process was probably first applied to the vegetable in Belgium, Belgian endive is now grown all over Europe.

Opposite: The Filetti alla griglia con salsa contadina *(Filets with Vegetable Sauce) displayed on a centuries-old terra cotta bread oven.*

Left: Scaloppine di vitella con indivia *(Veal Scaloppine with Endives) in the* piazza *of the Cathedral of Spoleto, in the hills of Umbria. The thirteenth-century cathedral was built on the ruins of an earlier church, which was destroyed by Frederick Barbarossa, the Holy Roman Emperor, in the late twelfth century.*

Scaloppine di vitella con indivia
VEAL SCALOPPINE WITH ENDIVES

Opposite: A plate of Cotolette con funghi alla crema *(Veal Chops with Mushrooms in Cream Sauce) sits on the stone ledge of a terrace overlooking Parma's Piazza Garibaldi. In the foreground is* Bocconcini di Parma.

4   Belgian endives (about 1 pound total weight)

1   lemon

    Coarse-grained salt

1   cup unbleached all-purpose flour

10 sprigs Italian parsley, leaves only

8   veal *scaloppine* (about 1 pound total weight), pounded

2   tablespoons olive oil

4   tablespoons (2 ounces) sweet butter

    Salt and freshly ground black pepper

    Pinch of dried thyme

¾   cup Vinsanto wine or dry Marsala wine

TO SERVE

16 sprigs Italian parsley, leaves only

Clean the endives very well and cut them into 2-inch pieces. Put them in a bowl of cold water with the lemon, cut in half. Let stand until needed.

Bring a medium-sized pot of cold water to a boil and add coarse-grained salt. Dissolve 1 tablespoon of the flour in a small bowl with ½ cup of cold water. Add the dissolved flour to the boiling water and mix very well. Drain the endives and add them to the pot. Boil for 2 minutes. Then drain the endives and cool them under cold running water. Put the cooled endives on a platter and cover them with a dampened cotton dish towel. Let stand until needed.

Finely chop the 10 sprigs of parsley on a board. Lightly flour the *scaloppine.*

Heat the butter and oil in a large frying pan over medium heat. When the butter is completely melted, add the chopped parsley and then the *scaloppine.* Sauté for 1 minute on each side. Then taste for salt and pepper and season with thyme.

Add the wine to the pan, cover, and cook for 5 minutes longer. At that time the meat should be cooked and tender. Transfer the meat to a serving platter and cover it to keep it warm.

Add the endives to the sauce in the pan and sauté for 2 minutes. Taste for salt and pepper and then arrange the endives and the sauce over the meat. Serve immediately, with the 16 sprigs of parsley divided among the servings.

SERVES 4.

*T*his veal dish from Parma, *Cotolette con funghi alla crema,* for once does not include *Parmigiano*—because of the mushrooms. The flavor of the white cultivated champignon mushrooms is enhanced by cooking them in the soaking water of dried wild mushrooms as well as by adding a few of the wild mushrooms to the sauce.

The rib veal chop is cut in the Italian manner, that is, with the bone attached as in the classic *Cotoletta alla milanese.* However, the preparation differs in that the meat is not pounded thin and wide for the Parma dish.

Cotolette con funghi alla crema
VEAL CHOPS WITH MUSHROOMS IN CREAM SAUCE

1 ounce dried *porcini* mushrooms

10 sprigs Italian parsley, leaves only

1 small clove garlic, peeled

6 tablespoons (3 ounces) sweet butter

1 pound champignon mushrooms

Salt and freshly ground black pepper

3 tablespoons olive oil

6 loin veal chops

⅓ cup brandy

¾ cup heavy cream

Soak the dried mushrooms in a bowl with 4 cups of lukewarm water for ½ hour. Drain the mushrooms, saving the soaking water as well.

Clean the mushrooms very well, being careful that no sand remains attached to the stems. Pass the mushroom soaking water through several layers of paper toweling in order to thoroughly strain out all the sand.

Finely chop the parsley and garlic together on a board.

Melt 4 tablespoons of the butter in a casserole over medium heat. When the butter is completely melted, add the chopped ingredients and sauté for 5 minutes.

Meanwhile, clean the champignons with a damp paper towel; then cut them into slices about ¼ inch thick. Add them to the casserole and sauté for 5 minutes. Then add ¼ cup of the strained mushroom-soaking water and simmer for about 15 minutes, adding more mushroom water as needed. Taste for salt and pepper.

Heat the oil and the remaining butter in a frying pan over medium heat. When the butter is completely melted, add the chops and sauté them for 1 minute on each side. Season the chops with salt and pepper. Add the brandy to the pan and let it evaporate (about 2 minutes).

Transfer the chops to the casserole with the mushrooms and start adding the cream to the casserole, a little at a time, until all the cream is incorporated (about 10 minutes).

Transfer the meat and the sauce with the mushrooms to a warm platter and serve immediately.

SERVES 6.

*V*eal shank is rarely cooked whole in Italy, but rather is cut into slices, through the bone, so that each slice contains some bone and its marrow. These slices, called *ossibuchi*, are just as popular in Italy as are *scaloppine*, and may be prepared with as many different sauces. The best *ossibuchi* come from the shanks of the back legs, but the front shanks may also be used. The delicious cooked marrow within the bone is extracted with a special little fork, and, for real *ossobuco* fanciers, it is the greatest treat of all.

Ossobuco alle cipolle
OSSOBUCO WITH ONION SAUCE

6 large red onions, peeled

6 *ossibuchi* (veal shank cut into 1½-inch slices, with bone and marrow)

4 bay leaves

3 large cloves garlic, peeled but left whole

2 whole cloves

Cut the onions into slices less than ½ inch thick and put them in a bowl of cold water to soak for ½ hour.

Tie each *ossobuco* all around the side with string. Lay the bay leaves, garlic, and cloves on a small piece of cheesecloth and tie it into a bag.

Melt 4 tablespoons of the butter with the oil in a heavy casserole over medium heat. When the butter is completely melted, drain the onions and add them to the casserole. Cover and cook for 20 minutes, stirring occasionally. At that point the onions should be translucent.

Meanwhile, lightly flour the *ossibuchi* on both sides but not on the edges.

Ossobuco alle cipolle *(Ossobuco with Onion Sauce)*.

Use a slotted spoon to transfer the onions to a baking dish, leaving the cooking juices in the casserole. Add the remaining butter to the juices and, when it is completely melted, add the *ossibuchi*. Sauté until the meat is golden brown on both sides (about 3 minutes on each side). Add the wine and let it evaporate (about 2 minutes).

Preheat the oven to 400 degrees.

Transfer and arrange the meat in a single layer over the onions in the baking dish. Sprinkle the lemon rind over the meat; then pour in the warmed broth and the remaining sauce from the casserole. Season with salt, pepper, and nutmeg to taste. Put the bag of herbs into the baking dish. Cover the dish with aluminum foil and bake for 1½ to 2 hours. Shake the dish three or four times while baking without removing the foil to prevent the meat from sticking.

Finely chop the parsley, sage, and garlic together on a board and transfer the mixture to a small bowl. Add the grated lemon rind and mix all the ingredients together.

Transfer the cooked *ossibuchi* to a warm serving dish, remove the strings, and cover to keep the meat warm.

Discard the bag of herbs from the cooking juices and pass the onion and sauce from the baking dish through a food mill, using the disc with the medium-sized holes, into a saucepan. Put the saucepan over medium heat. Taste for salt and pepper and cook until the sauce is smooth and fairly thick (about 20 minutes).

While the sauce is cooking, prepare the rice if it is to accompany the dish: Bring a large stockpot with 10 cups of cold water to a boil. Then add coarse-grained salt to taste, the saffron, the peppercorns, and then the rice. Stir with a wooden spoon and let the rice cook until it is *al dente* (about 16 minutes).

Drain the rice. Pour the sauce into a large warm platter with sides and place the *ossibuchi* over it. Sprinkle the meat with the chopped ingredients and serve with or without the rice.

SERVES 6.

6	tablespoons (3 ounces) sweet butter
6	tablespoons olive oil
½	cup unbleached all-purpose flour
½	cup dry white wine
	Grated rind of 1 lemon
2	cups homemade chicken or beef broth, heated
	Salt and freshly ground black pepper
	Pinch of freshly grated nutmeg

TO SERVE

15	sprigs Italian parsley, leaves only
4	sage leaves, fresh or preserved in salt (see Note on page 43)
1	small clove garlic, peeled
	Grated rind of 1 lemon
	Coarse-grained salt
½	teaspoon ground saffron
15	whole black peppercorns
2	cups raw rice

Ossobuco alle verdure
OSSOBUCO IN A VEGETABLE SAUCE

2 medium-sized zucchini, ends trimmed

2 medium-sized carrots, scraped

1 medium-sized red onion, peeled

1 medium-sized celery stalk

20 sprigs Italian parsley, leaves only

6 *ossibuchi* (veal shank cut into 1½-inch slices, with bone and marrow)

½ cup unbleached all-purpose flour

6 tablespoons (3 ounces) sweet butter

2 tablespoons olive oil

2 tablespoons tomato paste

¼ cup lukewarm homemade chicken or beef broth

2 cups dry white wine

Salt and freshly ground black pepper

1 teaspoon dried thyme

FOR THE VEGETABLES

¾ pound fresh peas, shelled

¾ pound string beans

¾ pound carrots

¾ pound celery hearts

Coarse-grained salt

PLUS

6 tablespoons (3 ounces) sweet butter

2 tablespoons olive oil

Salt and freshly ground black pepper

Pinch of freshly grated nutmeg

Cut the zucchini, carrots, onion, and celery into small pieces and put them in a bowl of cold water along with the parsley. Let soak until needed.

Tie each *ossobuco* all around the side with string. Lightly flour the *ossibuchi* on both sides but not on the edges.

Heat the butter and the oil in a casserole over medium heat and, when the butter is completely melted, add the meat and sauté until it is golden brown on both sides (about 3 minutes on each side).

Meanwhile, dissolve the tomato paste in the broth; then add it to the casserole and cook for 2 minutes. Add ½ cup of the wine to the casserole and let it evaporate for 10 minutes.

Drain the vegetables and add them to the casserole. Cover and cook over medium heat for 20 minutes. Taste for salt and pepper. Turn the *ossibuchi* over and add the remaining wine and the thyme. Cover the casserole again and cook for at least 35 minutes longer.

Meanwhile, prepare the vegetables: Fill 4 bowls with cold water. Put the peas in one and let them soak for ½ hour. As each of the other vegetables is cleaned, put it in its bowl to soak for the same length of time.

Clean the string beans, removing the ends and the string.

Scrape the carrots and cut them into quarters lengthwise. Then cut each quarter into 2-inch pieces.

Remove the strings from the celery and cut each stalk into three long strips. Then cut each strip into 2-inch pieces.

Bring 4 small pots of cold water to a boil; then add coarse-grained salt. Place each vegetable in its own pot and boil them until each is cooked but still firm, about 15 minutes. Drain the vegetables and let them stand until needed.

When the meat is tender, taste for salt and pepper and transfer the meat to a serving platter. Cover the platter to keep the *ossibuchi* warm.

Pass the remaining contents of the casserole through a food mill, using the disc with the small holes, into a large bowl. Return the passed ingredients to the casserole and cook over medium heat for 15 minutes, or until a thick and smooth sauce is formed.

Meanwhile, heat the 6 tablespoons of butter and the oil in a saucepan. When the butter is completely melted, add the boiled vegetables and season them with salt, pepper, and nutmeg. Sauté gently for 5 minutes.

Return the meat to the casserole with the reduced sauce to reheat and to absorb some of the sauce.

Remove the strings from the *ossibuchi* and serve. Arrange each serving on a plate with an *ossobuco*, some of the sauce, and some of the sautéed vegetables.

SERVES 6.

*C*ima alla genovese, stuffed pressed veal breast, is a complex though not a technically difficult dish. Prepared in advance, it serves a large number of people and makes a *bella figura* (a fine impression) at a buffet. *Cima* is usually served cold, but in Genoa, where it is eaten often, the slices may be dipped in egg and deep fried for an occasional variation.

The stuffing in the following recipe emphasizes vegetables— peas, artichokes, and onions—and does not include *pancetta* or pistachio nuts as some others do. The hard-boiled egg in the center, which adds the attractive design in the slices, is a feature of all versions of the dish.

Ossobuco alle verdure *(Ossobuco in a Vegetable Sauce)*.

Petto di vitella ripieno
(Cima alla genovese con ripieno di verdure)
STUFFED PRESSED VEAL BREAST WITH VEGETABLE STUFFING

1 breast of veal, about 7 pounds with rib bones (about 4 pounds without bones)

FOR THE STUFFING

1 large artichoke

1 lemon

6 ounces sweetbreads or brains

Coarse-grained salt

8 ounces ground veal

8 ounces ground pork

½ cup freshly grated *Parmigiano*

1 tablespoon dried marjoram

6 slices white bread, crusts removed

1 cup cold milk

1 large red onion, peeled

½ cup olive oil

½ pound fresh peas, shelled

Salt and freshly ground black pepper

6 extra large eggs

Pinch of freshly grated nutmeg

2 hard-boiled extra large eggs

FOR THE COOKING BROTH

Coarse-grained salt

1 large red onion, peeled but left whole

1 medium-sized celery stalk

10 whole black peppercorns

2 whole cloves

2 bay leaves

1 small calf's foot

Bone the veal breast and prepare a pocket. (For detailed instructions on boning, see *Giuliano Bugialli's Classic Techniques of Italian Cooking*, page 250, or ask your butcher to prepare the breast for stuffing.)

Prepare the stuffing: Put the artichoke in a bowl of cold water with the juice of the lemon and the lemon halves. Let soak for ½ hour.

Blanch the sweetbreads in salted boiling water for 1 minute; then cool them under cold running water, removing the large membranes. Cut the blanched sweetbreads into small pieces on a board and put the pieces in a large bowl. Add the ground veal and ground pork to the bowl along with the *Parmigiano* and marjoram.

Soak the bread in the cold milk in a small bowl for 5 minutes. Then squeeze the milk out of the bread and add the bread to the bowl with the meat.

Slice the onion into thin rings.

Heat the oil in a small saucepan over medium heat. Add the onion and sauté for 5 minutes. Add the peas and cook for 10 minutes.

Clean the artichoke, removing the dark green outer leaves and the choke. Cut the artichoke into small pieces. (For complete instructions on cleaning artichokes, see page 51.) Add the artichoke pieces to the saucepan and cook for 5 minutes. Season with salt and pepper to taste.

Transfer the contents of the saucepan to a crockery or glass bowl and let cool completely (about 30 minutes).

When the vegetable mixture has cooled, transfer it to the large bowl with the other stuffing ingredients. Add the 6 eggs and season the stuffing with salt, pepper, and nutmeg. Mix all the ingredients together with a wooden spoon.

Place half of the stuffing in the veal pocket; then put the 2 hard-boiled eggs lengthwise in a row down the center of the stuffing. Spoon the remaining stuffing over the eggs and along the sides, being careful to keep the eggs in place. Sew up the pocket with a needle and thread. Use your hands to shape the flat stuffed pocket by rolling it until it looks like a loaf of bread. Wrap the stuffed breast in a piece of heavy cheesecloth or a cotton dish towel and tie it like a salami (see Note on page 177).

Prepare the broth: Bring a large pot or a large fish poacher with a large quantity of cold water to a boil; then add coarse-grained salt to taste. Put the onion, celery, peppercorns, cloves, bay leaves, and calf's foot into the boiling water. Simmer for 15 minutes; then turn off the heat and let the broth cool for 15 minutes.

Place the stuffed breast of veal in the broth and bring the poaching broth back to a boil. Simmer, covered, for 2½ hours. When cooked, remove the breast of veal and place it in a jelly roll pan or baking tray with a weight of at least 10 pounds on top. Let it cool for about 6 hours; then transfer it, still with the weight on it, to the refrigerator for at least 8 hours.

Unwrap the *cima* on a chopping board and slice it into slices of less than ½ inch thick, arranging them on a large serving platter. Serve it as is or with a cold parsley or basil green sauce. The *cima* may be accompanied by cubes of aspic, made from the clarified poaching broth (see page 163).

SERVES 18.

Considered by many people to be the humblest part of the veal, tripe is certainly one of the most delicious. Two types of tripe, from part of the veal stomach, are available in Italy. Both the lighter tripe and the darker type, called *lampredotto*, are sold in street stands for sandwiches or a snack. The tripe is kept warm in a broth and cut into pieces as needed.

The lighter, more common type is most often cut into strips and simmered in tomato sauce, sometimes together with cooked calves feet. It is also cut into strips and eaten cold with oil and lemon juice. In Naples it is eaten with lemon juice alone, with which it combines magnificently.

Lampredotto, which has its own traditional sauces, particularly one made with garlic and potatoes, is most appreciated in Florence. It is the Florentines who first gave *lampredotto* its name, which means a stomach in the shape of a lamprey eel. There are few things as comforting on a cold night as to find yourself in a simple Florentine trattoria presented with a steaming bowl of *lampredotto*—given to you without asking and gratis—accompanied by the pickled vegetables called *sottoacetti*.

Trippa con verdure
TRIPE COOKED WITH VEGETABLES

2	pounds fresh tripe, in one piece (see Note)			Salt and freshly ground black pepper
1	medium-sized red onion, peeled but left whole		½	teaspoon hot red pepper flakes
1	whole clove		2	bay leaves
	Coarse-grained salt			About 3 cups homemade chicken broth
3	medium-sized carrots, scraped		PLUS	
4	medium-sized celery stalks		12	medium-sized boiling potatoes (not new potatoes)
15	sprigs Italian parsley, leaves only			Coarse-grained salt
2	medium-sized cloves garlic, peeled		OPTIONAL	
¼	cup olive oil		6	tablespoons freshly grated *Parmigiano*

Tripe, cut into strips and simmered in broth with carrots, celery, and bay leaves, is accompanied by whole boiled potatoes. Tripe thoroughly absorbs the full flavor of a sauce and is characterized by a slightly chewy texture.

Rinse the tripe very well in cold water and put it in a pot of cold water with the onion and the clove. Put the pot over medium heat and, when the water comes to a boil, add coarse-grained salt to taste. Simmer, covered, for 2 to 3 hours, depending on how long the tripe had been precooked.

(The butcher will tell you how much additional cooking is required.) Transfer the tripe to a crockery or glass bowl and let it cool completely.

Meanwhile, cut the carrots and celery into quarters lengthwise; then cut each quarter into 1-inch pieces. Put the vegetable pieces in a bowl of cold water to soak for ½ hour.

Coarsely chop the parsley and finely chop the garlic on a board.

When the tripe has cooled, cut it into strips 3 inches long and ½ inch wide.

Heat the oil in a heavy casserole over medium heat. When the oil is warm, add the parsley and garlic and sauté for 4 minutes; then lay the tripe on top of the vegetables. Season it with salt, pepper, hot red pepper flakes, and the bay leaves. Add 1 cup of the broth and cook, covered, adding more broth as needed, until the tripe is tender (about 30 minutes).

Meanwhile, bring a pot of cold water to a boil and add coarse-grained salt to taste. Then add the whole potatoes and simmer for about 20 minutes, depending on the size of the potatoes, or until they are soft but still firm. Peel the potatoes. Serve the tripe in individual dishes, accompanying each serving with 2 potatoes. The cheese is optional.

SERVES 6.

NOTE: *All tripe is sold partially precooked.*

A specialty of Modena is boiled *polpettone*, a meat loaf of veal. In the following recipe, the *polpettone* is accompanied by a variety of boiled vegetables and topped with a special green sauce—one that is more typical in color, texture, and taste of northern Italy than of central Italy. This unusual meat loaf has heavy cream as one of its binding elements.

Boiled meat loaf of veal, polpettone, *is served with a piquant green sauce.*

Polpettone alla modenese
POACHED MEAT LOAF MODENA STYLE

Coarse-grained salt

1 pound celery hearts

1 pound carrots

1 pound string beans

1 pound boiling potatoes (not new potatoes)

6 small red onions

FOR THE MEAT LOAF

1½ pounds ground veal or beef

3 ounces ground fat from *prosciutto* or blanched salt pork

4 tablespoons (2 ounces) sweet butter at room temperature

5 tablespoons freshly grated *Parmigiano*

Juice of 1 lemon

⅓ cup heavy cream

3 tablespoons unseasoned bread crumbs, preferably homemade

3 extra large eggs

2 hard-boiled extra large eggs

Salt and freshly ground black pepper

Pinch of ground cinnamon

TO POACH THE MEAT LOAF

3 quarts homemade chicken or beef broth

Coarse-grained salt

FOR THE SAUCE

25 sprigs Italian parsley, leaves only

2 medium-sized cloves garlic, peeled

4 tablespoons capers in wine vinegar, drained

1 piece lemon peel (about 2 inches long)

4 hard-boiled extra large eggs

Salt and freshly ground black

pepper

Pinch of cayenne pepper

¾ cup olive oil

Bring 5 saucepans of cold water to a boil; then add coarse-grained salt to taste to each pan. As each vegetable is cleaned, put it in one of the pans of boiling water and boil until cooked but firm, about 15 minutes.

Scrape the large strings from the celery stalks and wash them. Cut the stalks lengthwise into three strips; then cut each strip into 2-inch pieces.

Wash the carrots but do not scrape them. Remove the skins under cold running water when the carrots are cooked.

Wash and remove the ends and strings from the string beans.

Peel the potatoes and onions, but leave them whole.

Drain the vegetables and let them cool completely, covered with a dampened cotton dish towel, until they are needed.

Prepare the meat loaf: Put the ground veal, *prosciutto*, fat, butter, *Parmigiano*, lemon juice, heavy cream, bread crumbs, the 3 eggs, and the 2 hard-boiled eggs, coarsely chopped, in a large crockery or glass bowl. Mix all the ingredients together with a wooden spoon. Add salt, pepper, and cinnamon and mix well again. Transfer the meat loaf mixture to a piece of heavy cheesecloth or a cotton dish towel. Shape the mixture like a loaf of bread. Wrap it twice with the cloth and tie the two ends with string. Refrigerate the prepared *polpettone* for ½ hour.

Bring the broth to a boil in a large pot and add coarse-grained salt to taste. Then put in the cold meat loaf and simmer, covered, for 35 minutes.

Let the *polpettone* stand in the poaching broth for another ½ hour. Then remove it from the broth and transfer it to a serving dish to cool for at least ½ hour longer.

Meanwhile, prepare the sauce: Finely chop the parsley, garlic, 2 tablespoons of the capers, and the lemon peel together on a board. Transfer the chopped ingredients to a bowl.

Coarsely chop the eggs and add them to the bowl along with the remaining capers. Season the mixture with salt, black pepper, and cayenne pepper. Add the oil and mix all the ingredients together with a wooden spoon. Cover the bowl and refrigerate until needed.

Unwrap the meat loaf and cut it into ¾-inch-thick slices. Arrange the boiled vegetables and the meat loaf slices in a large serving dish. Pour the sauce over all and serve.

SERVES 6.

PORK

The centerpiece at many grand celebrations in Italy has traditionally been a whole suckling pig, apple in mouth. The meat is so popular that it is still sold by the slice at country fairs and at street stands. In restaurants it is not unusual to find the whole roast pig occupying its own huge carving board.

For cooking, the meat is highly seasoned, inside and out, with great quantities of herbs, spices, and cured meats. The flavorings vary from region to region, but throughout the peninsula the piglet is cooked whole, either on the spit or in a very large oven.

Porchetta o maialino in porchetta
ROAST SUCKLING PIG

1   cup olive oil

2   pounds *pancetta* or *prosciutto*

6   pounds coarsely ground pork

About 60 fresh sage leaves

About 15 tablespoons fresh rosemary leaves

20   large cloves garlic, peeled

10   bay leaves

About 60 whole black peppercorns

Salt and freshly ground black pepper

1   suckling pig, about 60 pounds, cleaned but left whole with head and tail

About 2 cups homemade beef broth, heated

6   lemons

Preheat the oven to 375 degrees. Use ½ cup of the oil to oil a very large baking pan.

Coarsely grind the *pancetta* with a meat grinder. Put the ground *pancetta* in a very large bowl along with the ground pork, sage, rosemary, garlic, bay leaves, and peppercorns. Season with a large amount of salt and pepper. Use a wooden spoon to mix all of the ingredients together.

Stuff the pig with the contents of the bowl and transfer it to the prepared baking pan. Brush the pig with the remaining oil and sprinkle it with salt and pepper. Bake the pig for a minimum of 6 hours, brushing it with the warm broth as needed.

When the pig is cooked, squeeze the lemons and pour the juice over the pig. Raise the oven temperature to 450 degrees and roast the pig for 15 minutes longer.

Remove the pig from the oven and transfer it to a large serving platter or onto a board. Serve, slicing the meat from the meaty parts, such as the legs and the loin, and including some of the stuffing and the crisp, crackling skin with each portion.

SERVES A LARGE PARTY.

Porchetta (Roast Suckling Pig) served on a balcony at the Hotel Lungarno near the Ponte Vecchio in Florence.

LAMB

Lamb is the meat most often available in southern Italy, where meat in general is not eaten every day. The importance of lamb probably goes back to the time of the Greeks, whose culture left the strongest imprint on the area.

Lamb *spezzatino* with artichokes is an example of the meat-with-vegetables dish typical of the South. (*Spezzatino* refers to a dish made with cut up meat or fowl.) Vegetables form part of the dish itself, as they often do with pasta, for they are the mainstay of the southern diet. The quartered artichokes are sautéed briefly so that they keep their shape and add an attractive visual element to the dish.

Preceding overleaf: Sheep in a masseria *near Altamura in Puglia.*

Opposite: Quartered artichoke hearts and cubes of lamb produce an aesthetically appealing dish in Agnello con carciofi *(Lamb with Artichokes).*

Agnello con carciofi
LAMB WITH ARTICHOKES

6	medium-sized artichokes	20	sprigs Italian parsley, leaves only	3	pounds boneless lamb shoulder (from a 5-pound piece with bone in, trimmed), cut into 2-inch pieces
2	lemons	¾	cup olive oil		
2	medium-sized cloves garlic, peeled				Salt and freshly ground black pepper

2 cups dry white wine

PLUS

2 extra large egg yolks

1 tablespoon lemon juice

Soak the artichokes for ½ hour in a large bowl of cold water with the lemons, cut in half. Then clean the artichokes, removing the chokes and hair. Cut the artichokes into quarters and return them to the water with the lemons until needed. (For complete instructions on cleaning artichokes, see page 51.)

Finely chop the garlic and coarsely chop the parsley on a board.

Heat the oil in a large casserole, preferably of terra cotta or enamel so the artichokes do not turn dark, over medium heat. When the oil is warm, add the chopped ingredients and sauté lightly for 2 minutes. Add the lamb pieces, cover the casserole, and cook for 5 minutes. Stir the meat, cover the casserole again, and cook for 5 minutes longer. Taste for salt and pepper; then add ½ cup of the wine. Cover the casserole and cook for about 15 minutes longer, stirring occasionally and adding an additional ½ cup of the wine as needed. (When the meat is not baby lamb, even if it is called "spring" lamb, it may require a longer cooking time.)

When the meat is cooked, use a slotted spoon to transfer it to a bowl and cover to keep it warm.

Drain the artichokes and put them in the casserole with the leftover cooking juices from the meat. Sauté for 2 minutes; then taste for salt and pepper and add ½ cup of the remaining wine. Cover the casserole and cook over medium heat until the artichokes are cooked but still firm (about 25 minutes), adding the last ½ cup of wine as needed.

Use a fork to mix the egg yolks with the lemon juice in a small bowl.

With a slotted spoon, remove the artichoke pieces to a warm serving platter, arranging them in a ring on the outer rim of the platter.

Return the lamb to the casserole and reheat it in the sauce for 2 minutes. Then remove the casserole from the heat, pour the egg-lemon mixture over the meat, and mix well.

Arrange the meat with its sauce inside the ring of artichoke pieces and serve immediately.

SERVES 6.

Poultry and Game

The number and variety of Italian chicken dishes is probably greater than that for any other meat. Boiled and eaten with a variety of sauces; roasted on the spit, grill, or in the oven; cut into pieces with or without bone and sautéed; the whole bird boned and stuffed; the breast alone boned, rolled, and stuffed; the legs alone boned and stuffed; the livers, giblets, and other variety meats—all have their own repertory of dishes.

Turkey is also prepared in a number of ways, but because of the great differences in optimum cooking time between the breast and the dark meat, the two tend to be used separately in Italy. Duck lends itself best to roasting, stuffing, and also to boning whole for a variety of preparations. Wild ducks are most often roasted, while domesticated ducks get more complex treatment. Guinea hen, squab, and pheasant often appear in the mixed roasted course, and are also eaten separately in less elaborate meals. Capon is usually boiled, and Italians are particularly fond of its broth. Quail is plentiful and may even appear as part of such first courses as *risotto* and *polenta*. Rabbit is also popular: prepared whole, either boned or unboned, with many different stuffings; in pieces, usually with bone; and as the basis of sauces and pasta stuffings.

Preceding overleaf: A colorful piazza in little San Gusmè, one of the ancient hill towns facing Siena. The barbecue (alla griglia), grand finale of the hill towns' festivals, is a very old Italian method of cooking fowl and meat. Chicken, guinea hen, capon, lamb, beefsteak, and sausages are all cooked over a wood fire.

Opposite: A mugellese rooster. The great painter Giotto tended these chickens as a little boy, at his father's farm in the Mugello.

Below: Chickens and baby lamb spit-roasting in front of, rather than above, a wood fire. Allo spiedo (on the spit) is the second most popular roasting method in Italy. Neighborhoods have their own rosticcerie, where poultry and meat are quickly cooked in this manner for takeout.

CHICKEN

The small brown chickens of the Mugello, a mountainous area northeast of Florence, are used especially for hatching the eggs of other chickens and are rarely eaten. The tiny *mugellesi* hens have the unique ability to flatten themselves and spread out over a large area, covering more eggs at a time than the normal larger hens. When they spread out, their heads almost disappear into their bodies. They are regarded with affection all over central Italy for their plucky character, as they will fight off anyone who attempts to approach the eggs they are guarding.

It is the famous leghorn breed of chicken from Livorno in Tuscany, however, that is the main type for eating throughout Italy. This breed, mostly white in color with its characteristic yellow legs, has been exported and is now bred all over the world. It is regarded in Italy as the "classy" chicken, and the popular saying, "he (or she) has yellow legs," means the person is of high quality.

A mugellese *chicken on the alert, warning any would-be intruders to keep their distance. This small, feisty bird is a favorite among Florentines, who relish its ability to fend off larger opponents. The* mugellese's *own tiny brown eggs are prized, but it is difficult to pry them away from the hens.*

Unlike most dishes that have some lemon flavoring, this unusual chicken dish is based completely on lemon. The bird is marinated in the juice of four lemons without any oil. Seasoned only with salt, black and red pepper, and a little garlic, the roasted chicken absorbs the predominant lemon taste completely. Lemon halves are added during the roasting, both for their flavor and for the visual beauty they lend to the finished dish.

Pollo ai limoni *(Chicken Roasted with Lemon Halves).*

Pollo ai limoni

CHICKEN ROASTED WITH LEMON HALVES

Clean the chicken, removing the extra fat from the cavity. Open the chicken up by cutting it lengthwise through the breast bone, not down the back. Put the flattened bird in a large crockery or glass bowl. Squeeze the lemons and pour the juice over the chicken. Add the lemon halves to the bowl.

Finely chop the garlic and parsley together on a board and add them to the bowl with salt and pepper and the hot red pepper flakes. Let the chicken marinate for 1 hour in a cool place or on the bottom shelf of the refrigerator, turning it 4 times.

Preheat the oven to 400 degrees.

Transfer the chicken to a baking dish, preferably of terra cotta, and pour the marinade from the bowl over it. Arrange the lemon halves on the chicken and roast for 45 minutes.

Remove the chicken from the oven and serve immediately with a few sprigs of parsley.

SERVES 4.

1 chicken, about 3½ pounds

4 lemons

2 medium-sized cloves garlic, peeled

15 sprigs Italian parsley, leaves only

Salt and freshly ground black pepper

½ teaspoon hot red pepper flakes

TO SERVE

Sprigs of Italian parsley

Above: Chicken breast halves with spinach and balsamella *(béchamel) stuffing, before the top halves have been added. Right: The finished* Petti di pollo imbottiti con salsa al pepe verde *(Stuffed Chicken Breasts with Green Peppercorn Sauce).*

*I*n *Petti di pollo imbottiti,* a spinach and *balsamella* (béchamel) stuffing is sandwiched between chicken breast halves and the whole is then covered with bread crumbs and deep-fried in vegetable oil made from mixed seeds, especially those of the sunflower. (Peanut oil is rarely used in Italy.) The chicken breasts are first soaked in beaten egg, not only to make the crumbs adhere, but also to make the chicken especially tender. The bread crumbs should be unseasoned and toasted so they do not absorb the fat when the stuffed breasts are fried.

This dish can be served with lemon wedges only, but it is especially good with a spicy sauce, such as this one of green peppercorns, which blends well with the light flavor of the chicken and *balsamella.*

Petti di pollo imbottiti con salsa al pepe verde
STUFFED CHICKEN BREASTS WITH GREEN PEPPERCORN SAUCE

3	whole chicken breasts, skinned and boned	3	tablespoons unbleached all-purpose flour
3	extra large eggs	2	cups cold milk
	Pinch of salt	3	tablespoons freshly grated *Parmigiano*
FOR THE STUFFINGS			Salt and freshly ground black pepper
	The balsamella		
3	tablespoons (1½ ounces) sweet butter		Freshly grated nutmeg

Remove the fat from the chicken breasts and cut each into 2 halves.

Put the eggs in a crockery or glass bowl and add a pinch of salt. Beat the eggs lightly with a fork. Put the 6 chicken breast halves into the bowl and soak them for ½ hour.

Meanwhile, prepare the *balsamella*: Melt the butter in a heavy saucepan over low heat. When the butter froths, add the flour, mix well with a wooden spoon, and cook until the flour is light golden brown. Remove the pan from the heat and let stand while the milk is slowly heating just to a boil. Return the pan with the flour to the heat and add the hot milk all at once. Stir with a wooden spoon until the mixture boils. Cook for 12 to 14 minutes, adding the grated *Parmigiano*, and salt, pepper, and nutmeg to taste at the last moment, when the sauce is almost cooked. Let the sauce stand in a crockery or glass bowl, with a piece of buttered wax paper pressed down over the sauce, until needed.

Clean the spinach well, removing the large stems. Soak the cleaned spinach in a bowl of cold water for ½ hour. Then bring a large quantity of cold water to a boil; then add coarse-grained salt to taste. Add the drained spinach and cook for 10 minutes. Drain and cool the spinach under cold running water. Squeeze the spinach dry and chop it finely on a board.

Cut the garlic into small pieces. Heat the oil in a frying pan over medium heat and, when the oil is warm, add the garlic and sauté for 2 minutes. Then add the chopped spinach and season with salt, pepper, and nutmeg to taste. Sauté for 5 minutes. Transfer the spinach to a bowl and let it stand until cool (about ½ hour).

When the spinach is cool, add half of the prepared *balsamella* to it and mix very well with a wooden spoon. Taste for salt, pepper, and nutmeg.

Spread the bread crumbs on a sheet of aluminum foil; then take 3 of the chicken breast halves and press them down well on the bread crumbs. Be careful that the underside of each breast half is coated and that there are no crumbs on the uncoated side of the breast halves.

Place 1 tablespoon of the *balsamella* on each breast. Then put a heaping tablespoon of the spinach mixture over the *balsamella* and add another tablespoon of the *balsamella*.

Cover each breast with its other half and sprinkle bread crumbs evenly over the top. Be sure to press the edges of the 3 "sandwiches" together very well and make sure both sides are evenly coated with bread crumbs.

Prepare the sauce: Melt 4 tablespoons of the butter in a medium-sized heavy saucepan over low heat. When the butter is completely melted, add the peppercorns and sauté for 5 minutes.

Meanwhile, heat the broth.

Use a fork to incorporate the remaining butter into the flour on a plate and add the mixture to the peppercorns in the saucepan. Mix very well with a wooden spoon; then add 2 cups of the hot broth and mix thoroughly. Simmer for 10 minutes. Pass the contents of the pan through a food mill, using the disc with the medium-sized holes, into a bowl and then return it to the pan. Add the remaining broth and simmer for about 40 minutes, stirring occasionally with a wooden spoon. Taste for salt and pepper. At that point the sauce should be rather thick and smooth.

Transfer the sauce to a warmed sauceboat and serve immediately, sprinkling some of the chopped parsley on each serving.

Heat the oil in a deep-fat fryer and, when it is hot, gently place the stuffed breasts into the oil. Cook for about 2 minutes on each side.

Meanwhile, line a platter with paper towels. Transfer the cooked breasts to the prepared platter and, when all of them are cooked, remove the paper towels and serve the chicken immediately with lemon wedges or with Green Peppercorn Sauce.

SERVES 3.

The spinach

2   pounds spinach

    Coarse-grained salt

1   medium-sized clove garlic, peeled

4   tablespoons olive oil

    Salt and freshly ground black pepper

    Freshly grated nutmeg

PLUS

1   cup unseasoned bread crumbs, preferably homemade, toasted

1   quart vegetable oil

FOR THE *SALSA AL PEPE VERDE*

6   tablespoons (3 ounces) sweet butter

2   heaping tablespoons drained green peppercorns in brine

4   cups homemade beef broth

1   tablespoon unbleached all purpose flour

    Salt and freshly ground black pepper

TO SERVE

    Lemon wedges or *Salsa al pepe verde* (Green Peppercorn Sauce)

20 sprigs Italian parsley, leaves only, coarsely chopped

In a traditional chicken galantine, the chicken is boned and most of the meat is removed, leaving the whole chicken skin with just a little meat attached. In *Salsiccia di pollo tartufata*, however, the skin is removed in one piece from the unboned chicken and used as the casing for an elegant sausage. Only the breast meat is used in this dish; the rest of the naked bird must find its way into some more modest preparation.

The chicken breast, coarsely ground, is combined with pork, heavy cream, and above all, black truffles, in the stuffing, which is wrapped in a layer of *prosciutto* slices and inserted into the chicken skin. The only really appropriate sauce for this dish is the one made with black truffles given here. Otherwise, the dish should be served without a sauce.

Salsiccia di pollo tartufata *(Chicken Galantine-Sausage with Black Truffle Sauce) includes pieces of black truffle in the sausage as well as in the sauce.*

204

Salsiccia di pollo tartufata
CHICKEN GALANTINE-SAUSAGE WITH BLACK TRUFFLE SAUCE

Cut through the two tendons at the end of each of the two chicken legs. Cut the skin of the chicken lengthwise down the back and, using a paring knife, carefully remove the entire skin in one piece. Save the chicken for later use. Spread out the skin on a board with the inside of the skin facing up. Cover the skin completely with a layer of all the *prosciutto* slices.

Remove the skinned breast from the chicken and coarsely grind it in a meat grinder into a crockery or glass bowl. Add the ground pork and then the heavy cream. Season with salt and pepper to taste. Mix all the ingredients together very well with a wooden spoon.

Cut the truffle into tiny pieces and add them to the bowl. Mix again to incorporate the truffle with the other ingredients. Transfer the stuffing onto one end of the prepared chicken skin and roll it up like a salami.

Oil the shiny side of a large piece of aluminum foil and place the chicken galantine on the prepared aluminum foil. Wrap it completely like a package and refrigerate it for ½ hour.

Preheat the oven to 375 degrees. Bake the galantine-sausage in a baking dish for 1 hour, turning the package once. Remove from the oven and let rest, wrapped, for ½ hour.

Prepare the sauce: Finely chop the truffle on a board and transfer it to a small crockery or glass bowl. Add the oil and salt and pepper to taste. Mix all the ingredients well with a wooden spoon. Let stand until needed.

Finely chop the garlic and transfer it to a second crockery or glass bowl. Add the butter and the flour to the garlic and combine all the ingredients with a fork until a thick paste is formed. Then add the broth, lemon juice, and wine vinegar and mix again with a wooden spoon, adding a pinch of salt and pepper.

Transfer the contents of the first bowl to a small heavy saucepan and place it over low heat. Sauté gently for 5 minutes, stirring occasionally with a wooden spoon. Then add the contents of the second bowl and mix very well to be sure that no lumps have formed. Simmer for about 10 minutes. By that time a smooth sauce should have formed.

When the sauce is ready, unwrap the meat and cut it into 6 slices. For each serving, place 1 slice of the galantine-sausage on one side of a plate and spoon the sauce onto the other side of the plate, not over the meat. Serve immediately.

SERVES 6.

1	whole chicken, about 3½ pounds
¼	pound *prosciutto*, sliced very thin
¾	pound ground pork
1	cup heavy cream
	Salt and freshly ground black pepper
1	small fresh or canned black truffle (about 1 ounce)
1	teaspoon olive oil

FOR THE *SALSA AL TARTUFO*

1	fresh or canned black truffle (about 2 ounces)
4	tablespoons olive oil
	Salt and freshly ground black pepper
1	medium-sized clove garlic, peeled
2	tablespoons (1 ounce) sweet butter at room temperature
1	scant tablespoon unbleached all-purpose flour
¾	cup lukewarm homemade chicken broth
1	tablespoon freshly squeezed lemon juice
1	scant tablespoon red wine vinegar

CAPON

Capon has its own distinct flavor; it is not simply a chicken with high-quality meat. In Italy capon and chicken are not used interchangeably. Even capon broth has a special rich taste, and reducing chicken broth will not duplicate it.

The operation that produces a capon is well known and, for a brief period during my childhood when I thought I wanted to be a surgeon, the local farmers, at my father's instigation, taught me how to do this little chore with their excess young roosters. I'm not sure if this played a role in changing my career choices.

The capon salad in the following recipe is eaten cold as an appetizer or main course. It must be prepared at least a day in

advance so that it can marinate. The typically Renaissance sweet-sour flavor comes from combining raisins, nuts, and a touch of sugar with wine vinegar and olive oil.

The restaurant Il Cigno in Mantua keeps this dish on its menu, along with other old local and traditional ones.

Insalata di cappone
MARINATED CAPON BREAST

1	capon, about 4 pounds, yielding about 1½ pounds of breast meat		FOR THE MARINADE			Salt and freshly ground black pepper

1 capon, about 4 pounds, yielding about 1½ pounds of breast meat

TO BOIL THE CAPON

1 whole red onion, peeled

1 celery stalk

1 carrot, scraped

5 sprigs Italian parsley

Coarse-grained salt

FOR THE MARINADE

¾ cup olive oil

1 lemon

2 tablespoons red wine vinegar

3 whole cloves

2 whole bay leaves

3 tablespoons pignoli (pine nuts)

3 tablespoons raisins

Salt and freshly ground black pepper

1 tablespoon granulated sugar

A large pinch of hot red pepper flakes

PLUS

4 ripe but not overripe tomatoes

1 bunch chicory

OPTIONAL

A few red *radicchio* leaves to be mixed with the chicory

Clean and wash the capon very well, removing all the fat from the cavity.

Bring 6 quarts of cold water to a boil; then add the onion, celery, carrot, and parsley. When the water comes to a boil again, add coarse-grained salt to taste and then the capon. Cook for 2 hours, removing the foam that rises to the top.

Remove the capon and transfer it to a large platter. Let rest until completely cold.

Remove the capon breast in two halves. Cut the breast meat into thick strips and put them in a large crockery or glass bowl (see Note).

Pour the oil into a small crockery or glass bowl. Squeeze the lemon and add the juice to the oil. Then add the vinegar, cloves, bay leaves, pine nuts, and raisins and season with salt and pepper to taste. Mix all the ingredients together with a wooden spoon. Pour the sauce over the capon breast strips and sprinkle with the sugar and hot red pepper flakes. Mix very well so that all the capon strips are well coated with the sauce. Transfer the contents of the bowl to a glass jar. Cover and refrigerate for at least 12 hours before serving.

When needed, remove the jar with the capon from the refrigerator and let stand until it reaches room temperature. Discard the bay leaves.

Cut the tomatoes into quarters. Arrange the chicory and *radicchio* on a large platter, making a ring of tomatoes around the edge of the platter. Transfer the contents of the jar into the center of the platter and serve immediately.

SERVES 8 AS AN APPETIZER.

NOTE: *The rest of the capon meat may be sautéed in 2 tablespoons of olive oil with salt and pepper and served with the same sauce as that for* Melanzane carpionate *(see page 45). It should be served as an appetizer, but at a different meal than the one at which the eggplants are served or at which this dish is served.*

Opposite: Insalata di cappone *(Marinated Capon Breast), accompanied by a bowl of* Mostarda di Cremona, *the sweet and hot pickled fruit that is served with poached dishes.*

Overleaf: The kitchen of Il Cigno *(The Swan) restaurant in Mantua, with its old copper pots and molds that are still used in everyday cooking.*

Clarified capon broth is the basis for this simple, yet very classic, dish associated with the Grand Duke of Tuscany, Ferdinando I, and his villa La Ferdinanda at Artimino. The rich, clear broth is served with an egg floating in it, poached only by the heat of the boiling broth in the plate, whole fresh basil and parsley leaves, and bits of chopped capon breast. The whole ensemble gives an impression of lilies floating on a pond.

Zuppa ''La Ferdinanda''
GRAND DUKE FERDINAND'S SOUP

	Coarse-grained salt	1	pound boneless veal shoulder in one piece
1	medium-sized red onion, peeled	2	extra large egg whites
1	large carrot, scraped		PLUS
1	medium-sized celery stalk, without leaves	8	extra large eggs
15	sprigs Italian parsley	8	sprigs Italian parsley, leaves only
1	capon, about 4 pounds, cleaned	16	fresh basil leaves

Bring a large pot with 5 quarts of cold water to a boil and add coarse-grained salt. Then add the onion, carrot, celery, and parsley. When the water returns to a boil, add the whole capon and the veal. Cook, uncovered, over low heat for 2 hours, skimming off the foam that rises to the top of the broth every so often. Transfer the capon to a serving platter, cover with aluminum foil, and let rest until needed. Reserve the veal for another dish.

Discard the vegetables and aromatic herbs and reduce the broth for ½ hour longer. Then strain the broth into a large bowl and let it cool, uncovered, for 2 hours. Cover the bowl and chill in the refrigerator for 1 hour.

Clarify the broth: Remove the layer of fat from the top of the cold broth; then add the egg whites and, using a wire whisk, mix them with the cold broth.

Transfer the broth to a stockpot and place it at the edge of a burner. Bring the broth to a simmer and cook for 5 minutes.

Line a colander with a piece of heavy cheesecloth and fit it into a large bowl. Ladle the contents of the stockpot through the cloth. The broth passing through will be absolutely transparent and all the impurities will remain in the cloth. Return the broth to a clean stockpot and bring it back to a boil.

Meanwhile, remove the skin and bones from the cooled capon and finely chop the breast meat on a board (see Note on page 207).

Break the eggs into individual heated soup bowls and place some of the chopped breast meat next to each egg.

When the broth returns to a boil, taste for salt and pepper and add the parsley and basil leaves to the pot. Ladle the boiling broth over each egg, adding some parsley and 2 basil leaves to each bowl. Serve immediately.

SERVES 8.

Opposite: The villa La Ferdinanda at Artimino, which is shown behind the capon broth, was designed by the great Buontalenti in the late sixteenth century. The building is known as the ''villa with a hundred chimneys.'' Before the villa was built, the gardens and grounds of the estate were surrounded by a 32-mile wall erected by Cosimo I. In the first decade of the eighteenth century, Cosimo III defined the limits of the area used for the production of Carmignano wine, encompassing the hills from the wall up to the river Furba, thus establishing the first controlled denomination for wine in Europe.

GUINEA HEN

Guinea hens, called guinea fowl in Europe, were domesticated by the ancient Egyptians, and their Italian name, *faraona*, actually means "hen of the pharohs." Although now raised domestically, they still retain a somewhat gamy flavor. Like pheasants, they have wide breasts, so there is proportionally more white meat than on chickens. Available all year, guinea hens are popular in Italy, and most mixed roasts, cooked on the grill or spit, will include them as well as chickens. Like pheasant or other game, guinea hens must be cooked in ways that avoid dryness—in a sauce or wrapped in *prosciutto* or *pancetta*.

The special flavoring of this dish, *Faraona con polenta*, is an abundance of clove. The cooking procedure is curious in that the whole onion with the cloves is placed inside the bird. Sage is the chief herb used here and should be the only one included on the serving platter. Italian cooking does not usually garnish with an herb that is not used in cooking the dish.

The thick *polenta* served with the hens is prepared with broth rather than water—unusual for the far north of Italy. When *polenta* is to be cooled and then sliced and grilled—the usual way of eating it in this area—it is always prepared with water. *Polenta* cooked in broth is, however, common in other regions.

Stewed guinea hens on a bed of po-lenta are moistened with their own sauce and garnished with fresh sage and sausages.

Faraona con polenta
CLOVE-FLAVORED GUINEA HENS WITH POLENTA

2   small guinea hens, about 1¾ pounds each

4   medium-sized red onions, peeled

10 whole cloves

Salt and freshly ground black pepper

2   large celery stalks

¼   cup olive oil

4   tablespoons (2 ounces) sweet butter

2   sage leaves, fresh or preserved in salt (see Note on page 43)

1   cup dry white wine

1   pound fresh tomatoes or canned imported Italian tomatoes, drained

2   tablespoons tomato paste

FOR THE *POLENTA*

1½ quarts cold homemade chicken broth

½   pound coarse or stone-ground yellow cornmeal

TO SERVE

Several fresh sage sprigs

OPTIONAL

3   sweet Italian sausages, without fennel seeds, sautéed and cut in half

Clean and wash the hens very well. Then dry them with paper towels. Take 2 of the onions and push 5 of the cloves into each one. Place a clove-studded onion inside each hen, adding a little salt and pepper. Sew up the cavity of each bird with a needle and thread. Tie each hen with string so that the wings and legs are pressed to the body of the bird.

Finely chop the remaining 2 onions and the celery together on a board.

Put the oil, butter, and the chopped ingredients in a heavy casserole and place the hens on top of the vegetables. Cover the casserole and put it over medium heat. Cook for 15 minutes; then turn the hens over and stir the vegetables with a wooden spoon. Cover the casserole again and cook for 15 minutes longer. Add the sage leaves and the wine and let the wine evaporate in the uncovered casserole for 10 minutes.

Pass the tomatoes through a food mill, using the disc with the small holes, into a small bowl. Add the tomato paste to the casserole and stir very well. Then add the passed tomatoes. Season with salt and pepper to taste, cover the casserole, and cook for 15 minutes, stirring occasionally with a wooden spoon.

Meanwhile, bring the broth for the *polenta* to a boil. When the broth comes to a boil, start adding the cornmeal in a very slow, steady stream, simultaneously stirring with a long wooden spoon. Keep stirring without stopping for 55 minutes more.

When the hens have finished stewing, remove the casserole from the heat and let it stand until ready to bake the hens. Discard the sage leaves.

When the *polenta* is almost ready, preheat the oven to 400 degrees and transfer the hens to a baking dish. Bake for 15 minutes. Reheat the sauce in the casserole. Pour the *polenta* onto a warm platter; then place the hens on the *polenta* and pour the reheated sauce over everything. Place the sprigs of sage together in the middle of the platter and put the sausage halves, if used, on the *polenta*. Serve immediately.

SERVES 4.

SQUAB

Squab is not an unusual main dish in Italy, and its flavorful meat is also used for stuffing pasta and to flavor some sauces. In the following preparation, the concentrated, intense flavor of the dark-fleshed squab is brought out by cooking it in red wine with dried *porcini* mushrooms. This is one of the few dishes in which riced potatoes are treated like *polenta*, as a part of the dish to catch the rich sauce and stuffing.

Piccioni ripieni in umido
STUFFED SQUAB IN MUSHROOM SAUCE

Stuffed squab are served with riced potatoes and a sauce flavored with porcini *mushrooms.*

4   squabs

FOR THE STUFFING

2   sweet Italian sausages, without fennel seeds, or 6 ounces ground pork

2   slices white bread, crusts removed

4   ounces ground veal

    Salt and freshly ground black pepper

TO COOK THE SQUABS

1   small carrot, scraped

1 small celery stalk

1 medium-sized red onion, peeled

2 sage leaves, fresh or preserved in salt (see Note on page 43)

2 ounces dried *porcini* mushrooms

¼ cup olive oil

1 tablespoons sweet butter

½ cup dry red wine

1 cup canned imported Italian tomatoes, drained

2 tablespoons tomato paste

Salt and freshly ground black pepper

1 cup hot homemade chicken broth

TO SERVE

Coarse-grained salt

2 pounds boiling potatoes (not new potatoes)

A few sprigs of celery leaves

Clean and wash the squabs well. Then pat them dry with paper towels. Remove any extra fat from the cavities.

Prepare the stuffing: Remove the skin from the sausages and put the meat in a crockery or glass bowl.

Soak the bread in a bowl of cold water for 2 minutes; then squeeze the water out of the bread and add the bread to the bowl with the sausage meat. Add the veal and salt and pepper to the bowl and mix very well with a wooden spoon. Stuff the cavity of each squab with one quarter of the mixture. Use a needle and thread to sew up the cavity of each squab. Truss the birds by tying down the wings and legs with string.

Finely chop the carrot, celery, onion, and sage together on a board.

Soak the mushrooms in 2 cups of lukewarm water for ½ hour.

Heat the oil and butter in a casserole over medium heat and, when the butter is completely melted, add the chopped ingredients. Sauté for 5 minutes. Then add the squabs and sauté for 5 minutes, or until they are golden brown all over. Add the wine and let it evaporate over low heat (about 15 minutes).

Meanwhile, place a large pot with 10 cups of cold water over high heat.

Pass the tomatoes through a food mill, using the disc with the small holes, into a small bowl and combine the passed tomatoes with the tomato paste. Add this mixture to the casserole and cook for 5 minutes.

Drain the soaked mushrooms, saving the water for later use. Be sure no sand remains attached to the mushrooms; then add the mushrooms to the casserole. Taste for salt and pepper and cook, covered, until the squabs are tender (about 25 minutes), adding hot broth as needed.

As soon as the mushrooms are added to the casserole, pass the mushroom soaking water through a piece of heavy cheesecloth or several layers of paper toweling to strain out all the remaining sand.

When the pot of water reaches a boil, add the strained mushroom water and coarse-grained salt.

Peel the potatoes and put them into the boiling water. Boil until the potatoes are cooked, but still firm (20 to 30 minutes, depending on the size of the potatoes). The potatoes and the squabs should be cooked and ready at the same time.

Quickly pass the potatoes through a potato ricer onto a large warm serving platter and pour the sauce in which the squabs have cooked all over the layer of riced potatoes.

Untie the squabs and arrange them in the center of the platter over the potatoes. Arrange the sprigs of celery leaves in the middle and serve immediately.

SERVES 8.

TURKEY

Many old Italian turkey dishes are adaptations of dishes that had originally called for the meat of a peacock. Although peacocks still wander decoratively through the parks of noble villas and a few are kept by some modest farmers, they are not available for eating. Once, when I wanted to recreate a Renaissance recipe, I attempted to obtain a peacock for the dish. I couldn't find a farmer who was willing to sell me one until, after searching for some months, I finally met one whose heartlessness matched my own—and a peacock that had unfortunately lost nearly all his feathers met his fate as a *Pavone ripieno*. In the Renaissance the feathers were always put back on the cooked bird for presentation as a "live" peacock, and my poor featherless bird cut a very poor figure indeed. But when we ate it, I knew that George Eliot, who had described a peacock dish in her Florentine Renaissance novel *Romola* as tough and tasteless, had either not eaten one or had had a very poor cook. The noble bird was sweet and chewy, far from what I had expected. However, for aesthetic reasons, I don't intend to repeat the experience. I'll stay with turkey.

The turkey cutlet in the following *involtini* is wrapped around a sausage, tied, and sautéed. The cutlets are flavored like game, with sage and rosemary and a discreet amount of tomatoes. Covered with whole black olives, the dish has quite a complex flavor, much different from that of simple sliced turkey breast.

Opposite: Peacocks rarely appear in Italian dishes today, but they were popular during the Renaissance. (© Tom Stack/Tom Stack Associates)

Below: Turkey breast is often adapted to a variety of Italian dishes, including involtini *in which the cutlets are rolled and stuffed. Sausage helps keep the turkey moist.*

Involtini di tacchino
ROLLED STUFFED TURKEY CUTLETS

6 ½-inch-thick turkey cutlets, sliced from the breast

6 sweet Italian sausages, without fennel seeds, or 18 ounces ground pork

6 large sage leaves, fresh or preserved in salt (see Note on page 43)

1 medium-size clove garlic, peeled

2 tablespoons rosemary leaves, fresh or preserved in salt or dried and blanched (see note on page 43)

4 tablespoons olive oil

2 tablespoons (1 ounce) sweet butter

1 cup dry white wine

1 cup canned imported Italian tomatoes, drained

Salt and freshly ground black pepper

15 sprigs Italian parsley, leaves only

About 30 large black Greek olives in brine, drained

Pound the cutlets between two pieces of wax paper that have been dampened with cold water so the meat does not stick to the paper.

Lay out the pounded cutlets on a board and place a sausage on each one. Wrap the turkey cutlets around the sausages and tie these *involtini* like small salamis (see Note on page 177).

Finely chop the sage, garlic, and rosemary together on a board.

Heat the oil and butter in a casserole, preferably of terra cotta or enamel, over medium heat. When the butter is completely melted, add the chopped ingredients and sauté for 2 minutes. Put in the *involtini* and sauté for 5 minutes, turning them many times in order to cook them evenly, but keeping them very light in color.

Add the wine and let it evaporate for 15 minutes.

Pass the tomatoes through a food mill, using the disc with the small holes into the casserole. Season with salt and pepper and cook, covered, for 20 minutes longer.

Meanwhile, coarsely chop the parsley on a board.

Add the olives to the casserole and mix very well. Then add the parsley and cook for 10 minutes longer.

Remove the string from the *involtini* and transfer the contents of the casserole to a warm platter. Serve immediately.

SERVES 6.

DUCK

One year, when giving my fall cooking classes in Florence, I took the non-Italian students to a folk fair at Carmignano, where one of the games was to try to throw a ring around the neck of a gossipy, constantly moving live duck. We did not realize that the prize for making a ringer was the duck itself. Alas, we won a duck, which we had to lead on an improvised leash through the whole village back to the school, where it became our mascot. It was embarrassing to have guests drop in, because the duck would appear immediately and begin quacking. For those taking the course there was no question of my getting rid of the bird, which was even given a name, "Marietta," after one of the village women who had been especially vociferous during the contest at the fair. Finally, however, I was allowed to give Marietta to a friend with a country garden, where, for all I know, she may still be quacking away.

I would never have been allowed to use Marietta for a duck galantine; in fact, I did not dare do any duck dishes that year.

In this recipe for duck galantine, the duck is completely boned and opened down the back, but all the meat is left attached to the skin. Duck meat is more compact than that of chicken, so there is still room for the stuffing. The slices of *pancetta, prosciutto,* and chicken breast create an attractive pattern, especially when surrounded by cubes of aspic made from the duck poaching broth.

Galantina di anitra
DUCK GALANTINE

Wash and clean the duck, saving the liver for later use. Remove any extra fat from the cavity. Bone the duck, following the same technique for boning a chicken for galantine, but leaving all the meat attached to the skin. (For detailed instructions on boning, see *Giuliano Bugialli's Classic Techniques of Italian Cooking*, page 323). Save the bones of the duck.

Lay out the boned duck skin side down on a board.

Cut the *prosciutto, pancetta,* and chicken breast meat into ½-inch-wide strips. Finely chop the garlic and the reserved duck liver together on a board.

Arrange all the strips of the meats lengthwise on the duck; then sprinkle the chopped ingredients over them. Sprinkle with salt and pepper and Marsala. Fold the skin over on the two sides to overlap 1 inch. Roll up, starting from the hind end, being careful to keep all the stuffing inside. When completely rolled up, carefully lift onto a cotton dish towel and roll the towel around the *galantina* tightly. Tie the *galantina* with string like a salami (see Note on page 177).

Bring 6 quarts of cold water to a boil and add coarse-grained salt. Then add the peppercorns, bay leaves, vinegar, onion, cloves, celery, calf's foot, and the reserved bones of the duck. Boil for 15 minutes, then add the *galantina* and simmer covered for 2 hours.

Remove the pot from the heat and let the *galantina* rest in the broth for 3 hours. Then transfer the *galantina* to a flat serving dish, place weights (about 12 pounds) on top of it, and refrigerate for 24 hours.

Unwrap the *galantina* and slice it like a salami. The *galantina* may be served with aspic prepared with the reduced and clarified poaching broth (see page 163) or with a piquant sauce.

SERVES 8 TO 12.

1	domestic duck, about 5 pounds
½	pound *prosciutto* in one slice
½	pound *pancetta* or unsmoked ham, very lean if possible, in one slice
1	whole chicken breast (from a 3½-pound chicken), skinned and boned
3	medium-sized cloves garlic, peeled
	Salt and freshly ground black pepper
1	tablespoon dry Marsala wine

FOR COOKING THE *GALANTINA*

	Coarse-grained salt
10	whole black peppercorns
4	bay leaves
2	tablespoons red wine vinegar
1	medium-sized red onion, peeled
2	whole cloves
2	celery stalks
1	small calf's foot

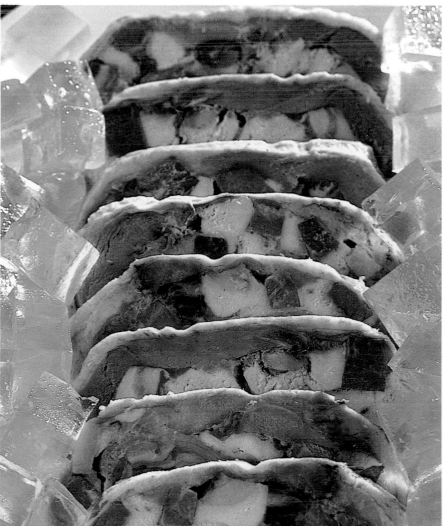

The Galantine of Duck is served with shimmering cubes of aspic.

219

GAME

Pheasants, both wild and domesticated, are available in Italy. In addition to the usual simple roasting, pheasants may be prepared in more complex dishes. In *Fagiano all'aretina*, the whole stuffed pheasants, when cooked, are opened and the stuffing and *prosciutto* slices are removed and returned to the casserole with the sauce. When the game birds are served, they are quartered and the thick sauce is arranged over them. It is unusual that in this very Tuscan dish from Arezzo, heavy cream is added to the sauce at the end.

Fagiano all'aretina
PHEASANT AREZZO STYLE

FOR THE STUFFING

4   ounces *prosciutto* or *pancetta* in one piece

4   ounces boneless lean pork in one piece

    Salt and freshly ground black pepper

TO COOK THE PHEASANT

1   pheasant, about 2 pounds, with its liver

3   slices *prosciutto* or *pancetta* (about 3 ounces total weight)

¼   cup olive oil

4   tablespoons (2 ounces) sweet butter

1   teaspoon rosemary leaves, fresh or preserved in salt (see Note on page 43)

5   sage leaves, fresh or preserved in salt (see Note on page 43)

3   medium-sized cloves garlic, peeled but left whole

½   cup dry Marsala wine

½   cup dry red wine

1½ cups homemade chicken broth

    Salt and freshly ground black pepper

1   cup heavy cream

Prepare the stuffing: Using a meat grinder, coarsely grind the *prosciutto* and pork together into a small bowl. Season with salt and pepper.

Wash the pheasant carefully and dry it with paper towels. Remove the liver and set it aside for later use. Stuff the pheasant with the prepared stuffing and sew up the cavity with a needle and thread. Place the *prosciutto* slices on the breast of the pheasant; then, using string, tie the legs and wings to the body of the bird, keeping the *prosciutto* slices in place.

Heat the oil and butter in a casserole over medium heat. When the butter is completely melted, add the rosemary, sage, and garlic. Sauté for 1 minute; then add the pheasant and sauté very slowly until it is golden brown (about 20 minutes). Add the Marsala and let it evaporate for 10 minutes.

Meanwhile, combine the red wine and the broth and heat the mixture in a small saucepan.

Start adding the wine-broth mixture to the casserole with the pheasant, a little at a time, until it has all evaporated (about 40 minutes). At that time the pheasant should be cooked and tender.

Transfer the bird to a plate, remove the string and the thread, and use poultry shears to cut the bird into quarters. Remove the stuffing and put it back into the casserole juices along with the cooked *prosciutto* slices from the breast of the bird.

Put the pheasant quarters on a warm serving platter and cover with aluminum foil to keep them warm.

Strain the contents of the casserole, pour the juices into a small sauce pan, and finely grind the stuffing and *prosciutto* along with the reserved liver. Warm the saucepan juices over medium heat; then add the ground ingredients. Taste for salt and pepper and add the heavy cream, stirring continuously with a wooden spoon. When the cream is completely amalgamated and the sauce is smooth and warm (do not let it reach a boil), unwrap the platter with the pheasant and pour the warm sauce over the pheasant quarters. Serve immediately.

SERVES 4.

*T*he combination of fruit and game is a classic one in Italy—the fruit-stuffed pheasant of Lombardy, game accompanied by baked apples in Mantua, and the coupling of quail with white grapes from the wine areas of central Italy. There, the wine grapes are used for the dish, but any white grapes with seeds may be used.

Quail arrive in temperate zones from the tropics in March and leave in October, preferring to fly low in open fields, hiding in the grain. Although they are among the most hunted of birds, they survive because they have one of the highest reproduction rates in nature. The quail has such a musical bird call that Beethoven included it in his Pastoral Symphony.

Quail are also raised commercially, and these birds are available most of the year. Despite the popularity of the birds, quail eggs, so fashionable elsewhere, are not used in Italian cooking.

Above: Fagiano all'aretina *(Pheasant Arezzo Style).*

Opposite: The decorative feathers of pheasants reflect the colors of the autumnal landscape during the hunting season. Like peacocks, the male pheasant has brighter plumage, but the meat of the female is choicer. The differing meats of the cock and hen have given rise to two entirely different groups of recipes.

221

In Tuscany, Quaglie con uva *(Quail with Grapes) is prepared with the local white wine grapes, such as the Trebbiano or Malvasia varieties.*

Quaglie con uva
QUAIL WITH GRAPES

2	ounces *pancetta* in one piece	½	teaspoon dried thyme
8	whole quail	1	cup dry white wine
	Salt and freshly ground black pepper	2	cups homemade chicken broth
¼	cup olive oil	2	tablespoons unbleached all-purpose flour
3	tablespoons (1½ ounces) sweet butter		Coarse-grained salt
2	tablespoons brandy	1	pound white grapes with stems (not seedless grapes)

Use a meat grinder to grind the *pancetta* coarsely.

Clean the quail very well and dry them with paper towels. Sprinkle a little salt and pepper inside each bird.

Heat the oil and 1 tablespoon of the butter in a casserole over medium heat and, when the butter is completely melted, add the *pancetta* and sauté for 1 minute. Then add the quail and sauté for 10 minutes, or until they are lightly golden brown all over. Add the brandy and season with salt, pepper, and the thyme. Let the brandy evaporate for 1 minute; then add the wine and simmer for 10 minutes, turning the quail occasionally with a wooden spoon. Add 1 cup of the broth, cover the casserole, and simmer until the quail are cooked (from 15 to 25 minutes, depending on the size of the birds and whether they are domestic or wild). Transfer the quail to a crockery or glass bowl, cover, and let rest until needed.

Meanwhile, reduce the leftover cooking liquid to 1 cup (about 15 minutes). Strain the reduced cooking liquid into a second casserole and place this second casserole over medium heat. When the liquid comes to a boil, add the remaining butter and, when the butter is completely melted, add the flour. Stir very well with a wooden spoon and cook for 2 minutes. Remove the casserole from the heat and let stand for 10 minutes.

Bring a small pot of cold water to a boil and add coarse-grained salt. Then add the grapes and simmer for 2 minutes. Cool the grapes under cold running water, remove their stems, and put the grapes in a small bowl.

Bring the remaining cup of broth to a boil. Put the casserole with the sauce back over medium heat and add the boiling broth. Stir very well and cook for about 5 minutes, or until a smooth and moderately thick sauce is formed. Taste for salt and pepper.

Transfer the quail to the casserole along with the grapes. Mix all the ingredients together gently and cook for 1 minute more. Transfer to a warm serving platter and serve hot.

SERVES 4.

*A*lthough many rabbit dishes are quite rustic, whole rabbit with a stuffing is an elegant treatment. The most complex and formal presentations involve boning the rabbit before stuffing and then rolling it. This elaborate rabbit dish, in which the meat is rolled and stuffed, would be appropriate for a formal Italian dinner.

Three stylish Tuscan game dishes in an elegant setting. On the plates is the elaborate and refined Coniglio ripieno con salsa di peperoni *(Boned Whole Rabbit, Rolled and Stuffed, with Sweet Pepper Sauce). On the credenza two other dishes are waiting,* Quaglie con uva *(Quail with Grapes) and* Fagiano all'aretina *(Pheasant Arezzo Style).*

Coniglio ripieno con salsa di pepero
BONED WHOLE RABBIT, ROLLED AND STUFFED, WITH SWEET PEPPER SAUCE

1   whole rabbit, about 3 pounds, skinned and cleaned

FOR THE *FRITTATA*

3   extra large eggs

     Salt

½   tablespoon olive oil

FOR THE STUFFING

1   large sweet red bell pepper

     Salt and freshly ground black pepper

20   sprigs Italian parsley, leaves only

1   medium-sized clove garlic, peeled

4   ounces *pancetta* or *prosciutto* in one piece

1   tablespoon olive oil

FOR THE *SALSA DI PEPERONI*

6   sweet yellow or red bell peppers

1   yellow or red pepper (use the same color as the fresh peppers), in wine vinegar, drained

2   tablespoons olive oil

2   medium-sized cloves garlic, peeled but left whole

1   cup homemade chicken broth

     Salt and freshly ground black pepper

Bone the rabbit. (For detailed instructions on boning, see *Giuliano Bugialli's Classic Techniques of Italian Cooking,* page 262.)

Prepare the *frittata:* Break the eggs into a small crockery or glass bowl, add salt, and beat them lightly without allowing air bubbles or foam to form.

Place a 10-inch omelet pan over medium heat. Add the oil to the pan and, when the oil is hot, add the beaten eggs. Keep making punctures in the bottom with a fork as the eggs set to allow the liquid on top to move through to the bottom. Cook for 1 minute; then, holding a plate firmly on top of the pan, reverse the pan and turn the *frittata* out onto the plate. Return the pan to the heat and carefully slide the *frittata* into the pan and cook the other side for 30 seconds. Then reverse the *frittata* out onto a round serving dish. Cut the *frittata* in half and let it cool until needed.

Roast and peel the red pepper, following the directions on page 26 *(Insalata di peperoni).* Remove the seeds completely with the stem. Finely chop the pepper on a board. Transfer it to a small bowl and add salt and pepper to taste. Mix very well with a wooden spoon.

Finely chop the parsley and garlic together on a board and cut the *pancetta* into small pieces.

Preheat the oven to 375 degrees.

Spread the boned rabbit open skin side down and sprinkle with the parsley and garlic. Arrange the *pancetta* all over; then place the 2 *frittata* halves on top. Sprinkle with salt and pepper. Make a line of the chopped pepper down the center of each *frittata* half, leaving an inch at the top and bottom. Roll up the rabbit and tie it like a salami (see Note on page 177).

Oil a large sheet of aluminum foil on the shiny side and sprinkle it with salt and pepper. Place the rolled up rabbit on the foil and roll up the foil around it, closing it tightly like a package. Place in a baking dish and bake for 1½ hours.

Meanwhile, prepare the sauce: Roast and peel the 6 peppers, following the directions on page 26. Remove the stems and seeds from both the roasted peppers and the pepper preserved in vinegar and coarsely chop all the peppers together.

Heat the oil in a small saucepan over medium heat and, when the oil is warm, add the garlic and sauté for 2 minutes; then add the chopped peppers and sauté over medium heat for 15 minutes longer. Pass the contents of the pan through a food mill, using the disc with the small holes. Return the peppers to the saucepan and add the broth. Taste for salt and pepper and reduce over medium heat for 15 minutes longer, stirring occasionally with a wooden spoon. Let the sauce stand until needed.

Remove the rabbit from the oven and allow it to cool for about 45 minutes; then refrigerate for at least 2 hours.

Remove the rabbit from the refrigerator, unwrap, and remove the string. Cut the boned stuffed rabbit into 1-inch-thick slices.

Reheat the sauce and prepare each serving with 1 slice of the rabbit and some of the sauce surrounding the slice.

SERVES 6 TO 8.

*M*aremma, with its great variety of meats, fowl, and game, has given birth to the very interesting *scottiglia,* a meat counterpart to mixed fish soups, such as *cacciucco* from Livorno or *bouillabaisse* from Marseilles. As many as fifteen different meats, cut into pieces, are stewed together in a spicy wine sauce that contains a little tomato. All the meats are cooked for the same length of time, so there are varying degrees of softness in the finished dish. Meats that might not blend well in twos or threes combine marvelously in this large ensemble. The stew is served over toasted country bread that has been rubbed with garlic. The name of the dish probably comes from the verb *scottare*, "to burn," referring most likely to the spiciness of the hot red peppers.

Scottiglia
SCOTTIGLIA

Cut the poultry into 8 pieces (leave the quail whole) and cut the meat into 2-inch cubes.

Coarsely chop the carrots, onions, parsley, celery, and garlic together on a board.

Heat the oil in a large casserole over medium heat and, when the oil is warm, add the chopped ingredients. Sauté for 5 minutes; then add the poultry and meat pieces and sauté for 10 minutes, stirring with a wooden spoon.

Squeeze the lemons and add the juice to the casserole. Raise the heat and cook for 2 minutes; then add the wine, lower the heat, and simmer for 10 minutes, stirring occasionally with a wooden spoon.

Pass the tomatoes through a food mill, using the disc with the small holes. Add the passed tomatoes to the casserole, cover, and cook for 35 minutes, stirring occasionally with a wooden spoon. Taste for salt and pepper and add the hot red pepper flakes. Cover again and cook for 15 minutes longer, adding some of the lukewarm broth if needed.

Meanwhile, preheat the oven to 400 degrees. Place the bread slices on a baking sheet and toast them for 10 minutes.

Finely chop the 20 sprigs of parsley on a board.

When the bread is toasted, rub each slice on both sides with the garlic and place the bread on a large platter.

Remove the casserole from the heat and let it stand for 2 minutes. Then pour the contents of the casserole over the toasted bread on the prepared platter. Sprinkle the parsley over all and serve immediately.

SERVES 8 TO 10.

Below: Scottiglia *combines a mélange of meats and poultry in a spicy stew.*

About 10 pounds of mixed fowl and meats, such as pheasant, quail, guinea hen, rabbit, hare, chicken, veal, pork loin, beef, lamb, etc.

2   large carrots, scraped

2   medium-sized red onions, peeled

25 sprigs Italian parsley, leaves only

3   large celery stalks

3   medium-sized cloves garlic, peeled

½   cup olive oil

3   lemons

1½ cups dry red wine

2   pounds fresh tomatoes or canned imported Italian tomatoes, drained

    Salt and freshly ground black pepper

½   teaspoon hot red pepper flakes

1   cup lukewarm homemade chicken or beef broth

PLUS

8   large slices crusty Italian bread (Tuscan type, see page 75), about 4 x 2 inches, 1 inch thick

20 sprigs Italian parsley, leaves only

2   cloves garlic, peeled but left whole

225

Wine

A DAY IN A CHIANTI VINEYARD

Driving from Florence to the vineyard we had decided to visit on a cool, crisp October morning, we passed orderly rows of grape vines, olive trees, and cypresses on the lovely hills of Chianti. We did not, however, pass a single person on our way to join the harvest, for everyone in Chianti was in the fields helping with the picking. When we arrived at the vineyard, we heard the sound of many voices, but nobody was visible among the tall, thick, yellowing vines.

Once we found the corridor between two rows of vines, people became visible—country folk, whose hands are so knowledgeable of the vines and so loving in their treatment of this source of their well-being. It was fascinating to watch the speed and yet the gentleness of their hands as they picked.

As we joined in the work, I noticed that even the pickers could not resist tasting some grapes from the luscious vines every so often. My companions were less blasé and started greedily tasting the grapes as soon as they arrived, trying to distinguish the flavors of the four or more different vines whose grapes are mixed to make the Chianti wine.

Those who have never worked in the grape harvest do not realize that the grapes are so rich and sugar-filled at the harvest stage that eating them in quantity, especially under the strong early morning sun, produces its own kind of drunkenness, or light-headedness, even though no alcoholic fermentation has taken place. My inexperienced friends were soon reeling around like so many Bacchuses—much to the amusement of the experienced harvesters—and they spent a good part of the morning resting in the shade of the mulberry trees.

As the grapes were collected, they were deposited in a basket and then brought to a large truck parked above the vines on the hill. The vines are planted so that the different types used in Chianti wine alternate in the correct percentages for making the wine. Thus, the pickers need not concern themselves with which type of grape they are picking; they simply pick the grapes as they find them and the mixture will be right.

By noon we were exhausted and starving. We noticed that the pickers had disappeared from the fields, only to reappear moments later with baskets containing a special harvest-time lunch. Since we were guests, our hosts set a stone table for us; the workers sat on the ground under the trees. We were further honored by being served a labeled bottle of some of the vineyard's finest old *riserva*. All the courses for the meal were placed

Preceding overleaf: This typical Tuscan landscape is a hillside of three shades of green—the verdant green of orderly rows of grape vines for wine; the deep, rich darkness of cypresses lining the crest of the hill; and, finally, the silvery green of olive trees, alternating on the hillside with the vines. This combination is unique to Tuscany, where vines and olive trees yield an equally fine result.

Opposite: A vineyard worker empties baskets of grapes into a harvest trough on a hilltop in Chianti. Traditionally, Chianti wine is a blend of Sangiovese, Canaiolo Nero, and Trebbiano Bianco and Malvasia Bianco grapes. In this vineyard, the vines are ingeniously planted so that the different grape varieties alternate in the correct percentages for making the wine.

229

Top: Harvesting grapes in Chianti. Above: Ripe grapes from a Chianti vineyard. Opposite: Schiacciata con uva (Schiacciata with Grapes).

together on the table. The grapes, served in bunches, had just been picked, and the flat bread called *schiacciata*, with abundant fresh grapes baked into it, was fresh from the oven.

Schiacciata con uva is a sign of the grape harvest in much of central Italy. It is eagerly eaten in the city as well as in the country during this brief period and may be found in the fanciest pastry shop or the simplest bakery. Even the most refined city people in Italy treasure their links with the rustic country traditions, and they are very happy to serve a dessert *schiacciata* or a fresh chestnut flour *castagnaccio*, which is also flat and pizza-like, after the most elegant dinner during the harvest season. They do not feel that a fine dessert must necessarily have cream, chocolate, puff pastry, or the texture of a soufflé.

Whether served as a dessert or as a snack, *schiacciata* should be made with wine grapes and a simple bread dough that will not detract from the grapes.

Schiacciata con uva
SCHIACCIATA WITH FRESH GRAPES

Prepare the sponge: Put the cup of flour in a bowl and make a well in it. Dissolve the yeast in the water and pour it into the well. Mix the dissolved yeast with a wooden spoon, incorporating the flour. Cover the bowl with a cotton dish towel and put it in a warm place away from drafts. Let stand until the sponge has doubled in size (about 1 hour).

Meanwhile, remove the stems from the grapes. Carefully wash the grapes in cold water. Then pat them dry with paper towels and put them in a large crockery or glass bowl. Add the sugar and fennel seeds. Mix well with a wooden spoon so that the grapes are well coated with the sugar. Let stand until needed.

Arrange the 2½ cups of flour in a mound on a pasta board; then make a well in the flour. Pour the sponge into the well along with the olive oil, salt, and water. Use a wooden spoon to mix together all the ingredients in the well. Then start mixing with your hands, absorbing the flour from the inside rim of the well little by little. Keep mixing until all but about 5 tablespoons of the flour is incorporated. Then knead the dough with the palm of your hand, incorporating the remaining flour in a folding motion, until the dough is homogeneous and smooth (about 2 minutes).

Oil a 14-inch pizza pan.

Divide the dough in half. With a rolling pin, roll out both pieces into round shapes, about 16 inches in diameter. Lay one piece on the bottom of the oiled pan, covering even the sides of the pan. Distribute half of the sugared grapes over the layer of dough, cover with the other layer of dough, and seal the two edges together all around by pressing them together.

Distribute the remaining grapes on top of the *schiacciata*, cover the pan with a cotton dish towel, and let rest until the *schiacciata* has risen to almost double in size (about 1 hour).

Preheat the oven to 375 degrees.

When the dough has doubled in size, remove the towel and bake the *schiacciata* for 1 hour. Remove from the oven and let cool completely (about 1 hour). Serve from the pan or on a board to preserve its rustic character, slicing it like a pizza.

SERVES 8 to 10.

FOR THE SPONGE

1   cup unbleached all purpose flour

1   ounce (2 cakes) fresh compressed yeast, or 2 packages (4 teaspoons) active dry yeast

¾   cup lukewarm or hot water, depending on the yeast

FOR THE DOUGH

2½ cups unbleached all-purpose flour

2   tablespoons olive oil

    Pinch of salt

    Scant ½ cup lukewarm water

PLUS

2½ pounds red wine grapes (not Concord) or 2½ pounds seedless ruby red grapes

1   cup granulated sugar

½   teaspoon fennel seeds

WINE MAKING

After the grapes are picked they must be crushed. Today this is done efficiently by machines, and some lament the passing of the legendary days when this work was done by very clean feet. Up until about fifty years ago, people really did crush the grapes by jumping on them, and their purple-stained feet had to be soaked in the fountain for hours in order to get them back to their normal color.

After the grapes are crushed, the juice *(il mosto)* and skins are placed in vats for the first short period of fermentation. Nowadays, the vats used for this first fermentation are constructed of stainless steel or cement on the outside and fiberglass inside. If there is a second fermentation, the *mosto* is transferred to wooden casks. The wine is stored in these large oak casks from six months to five years, according to the wine.

It is important that the wine be stored, before bottling, in a container of porous material, such as wood, which allows oxygen to enter and the alcohol to evaporate. The Italians generally prefer larger casks that allow for a slower maturation than the smaller ones favored by the French.

The wood for the casks is *rovere*, durmast, or leiblein oak, once plentiful in Italy but now obtained from Slavonia in north Yugoslavia. The wine takes on some of the flavor of the wooden cask. There is much controversy over the superiority of old versus new casks. Some vineyards change casks every ten years; others use centuries-old casks.

After the wine has been placed in the casks, many steps of vinification take place over a long period, varying according to the individual theory of the vineyard. To take one excellent vineyard as an example, at Signor Sergio Manetti's Monte Vertine, only the red Chianti grapes *sangiovese* and *canaiolo* are used, with the addition of a little *colorino*. (The white grapes *trebbiano* and *malvasia* are now utilized to make a Tuscan white, *Bianco di*

Preceding overleaf: Lunch in the vineyard includes Schiacciata, *on the right, and a bottle of Chianti riserva, which is aged a minimum of three years in a cask before bottling.*

Above: Grapes being crushed.

Below: An old oak cask. (© Ferri Cesare/Mac Film)

Opposite, top: The vinsanteria *of Castellare in Chianti.*

Opposite, bottom: Bunches of grapes drying for vin santo—*a dessert wine and an apéritif.*

Monte Vertine.) Signor Manetti is among those who believe that the older the vines, the better the wine. The only corrective added during the vinification is glycerin for stabilization. Monte Vertine takes a middle position on the age of barrels—neither are they changed every ten years, nor are they kept for a century. The normal vintages stay in the oak barrels for eighteen months, the *riservas* for twenty-four. Normal bottles are put on the market after three years, the *riservas* after four.

To be sure that oxygen does not enter through the opening in the top of the casks, they are traditionally "topped up" with the same wine to keep a constant level in the casks despite evaporation. A modern, and perhaps more efficient, alternative is topping up with inert carbon dioxide or nitrogen.

The time to bottle the wine is when the cask has not yet given it too "woody" a flavor and before too much oxygen has entered through the porous wood. The bottle allows less air to enter, and the slower aging strengthens the bouquet of the wine.

Red wines acquire their color from the skins that are left to ferment with the juice in the vats. After fermentation the skins are filtered out. The various shades of color are often described as ruby red, dark red, red with violet tints, brilliant red, garnet red, and light red; the different lusters are discussed as bright, sparkling, very clear and, undesirably, cloudy. Wine connoisseurs enjoy examining the color of a wine and evaluating the color in relation to the vintage.

When my father, who could tell by the aroma and look of a wine whether it came from the sunny or shady side of a hill, would open a bottle, his examination of its contents resembled a religious ceremony. He would start by sniffing the cork and measuring its size and porous quality. Then he would examine the same wine in different glasses to rule out the variations in the color of the glasses themselves. The family had to maintain total silence and reverence during this long service, all the while just hoping and waiting for a sip of wine.

Meanwhile, he would be making copious notes, which he kept on each bottle of wine. Finally, he would arrive at the stages of tasting, first with bread, then with bread and salt, and, finally, with bread and cheese. After fifteen or twenty minutes of examination, if he had decided the wine did not pass the test, he would refuse to allow us to have it and he would start all over again with another bottle. How relieved we were when a bottle had finally passed the test and we could fill our glasses.

The only time I ever saw my father cry was when, during the Second World War, a shell hit the wine cellars and all the barrels exploded. I remember the wine pouring out down the hill like an unruly river.

In those days, when wine was still "natural," the bottles of the same wine really could vary enormously. Quite a few did not survive the aging, but the best were more memorable than the more safely uniform wines of today.

LIQUEUR MAKING

While most wine is made in relatively large quantities in vineyards and wine cooperatives, liqueur making is still frequently a home activity. Grain alcohol, perfectly legal and accessible in Italy, is most often used as the basis.

Liquore al limone, Lemon Liqueur, is made with lemon peel generously soaked in alcohol. One of the simplest and most natural liqueurs, it used to be made by almost all families in southern Italy and was the drink offered to guests when they came to call.

Liquore al limone
LEMON LIQUEUR

4 lemons with thick skins	1 cup granulated sugar
3 cups pure grain alcohol or 3 cups unflavored vodka	

Put the lemons in a bowl of cold water and let them soak for ½ hour. Then remove them from the water and dry them with paper towels. Use a vegetable peeler to peel the lemons carefully, so that no white inner skin remains attached to the peel.

Put the lemon peels in a bottle with a large mouth or in a mason jar and pour 2 cups of the alcohol over them. Then cork the bottle and let it stand in a dark place for 72 hours.

Combine 2 cups of cold water with the sugar in a saucepan and put it over medium heat until it comes to a boil. Then remove the pan from the heat and let it cool completely (about 2 hours).

Add the water-sugar mixture to the jar with the lemon peels and mix well. Then, to remove impurities, filter the contents of the bottle through a coffee filter or through several layers of paper toweling into a bottle or jar. Put the lemon peels back into the liquid and add the remaining alcohol. Cork the bottle again and let it stand in a dark place for 36 hours.

Then filter the contents of the bottle again through a coffee filter or through several layers of paper toweling, returning only the liquid to a bottle. Let stand for 1 week before using.

MAKES ABOUT 5 CUPS.

Above: Liquore al limone (*Lemon Liqueur*).

Left: Lemon trees abound in southern Italy, and the fruit is a favorite cooking ingredient there.

Overleaf: Liquore al mandarino (*Orange Liqueur) in front of one of the world's greatest frescoes, painted by Mantegna between 1465 and 1474 and found in the Room of the Newlyweds, in Mantua's Castello San Giorgio.*

$\mathcal{M}$andarin oranges, hung in cheesecloth over—but not touching—the alcohol, impart a rich color and flavor to *Liquore al mandarino*.

Liquore al mandarino
ORANGE LIQUEUR

Below: Homemade Orange Liqueur. The cheesecloth suspends the oranges just above the alcohol.

Wrap the oranges in a piece of cheesecloth and tie the package together with string, leaving about 5 inches at each end of the string.

Pour the alcohol into a mason jar. Holding the cheesecloth by the two ends of the string, hang it in the jar, dangling over, but not touching, the alcohol. Wrap the string around the mouth of the jar and tie it tightly in

order to keep the cheesecloth sling in place. Close the jar tightly and put the jar in a dark place for 1 month.

After a month, it is time to add the sugar syrup. Put 3 cups of water into a small saucepan and heat it over medium heat until it comes to a boil. Then add the sugar and simmer for about 5 minutes. Remove the pan from the heat and let the syrup cool completely (about 2 hours).

Remove the oranges from the jar and pour the liqueur into a bottle. Add the cooled syrup to the bottle and let stand for 3 hours. Use a coffee filter to filter the liqueur into another bottle. Cork the bottle and let the liqueur stand for 3 days before using it.

To prepare punch, place about ¼ cup of the liqueur in a cup and heat it with the steam of an espresso coffee machine, using the spout that produces the foam for *cappuccino*. Serve immediately with a piece of orange peel.

MAKES ABOUT 8 CUPS.

3   mandarin oranges or tangerines

1   quart pure grain alcohol or unflavored vodka

3   cups granulated sugar

Cheese

I n the days before de Gaulle, when French governments were falling one after the other, Winston Churchill was fond of blaming the chaotic political situation on French cheeses, asking how a country with 500 different cheeses could get together on anything. What are we then to say of Italy, which has even more varieties of cheese than France does? In any event, falling governments are a small price to pay for the variety, richness, and excellence of Italian cheeses.

The Etruscans were probably the first to develop a cheese that could travel, for it was they who developed the hard-rind, long-aged cheeses that we now call the *grana* type, which include *Parmigiano-Reggiano* and *Piacentino* (also called *Grana Padano*), both of which are probably made much as they were by the Etruscans 2,500 years ago.

Perhaps the milk originally used for cheese was that of sheep, because it coagulates most easily. Quite likely the first rennet was taken from vegetables, such as wild artichokes, rather than from the gland of the suckling calf, as is now common. (Wild artichoke rennet is still used in some parts of Italy.)

Where there is artisan production of cheese, the product of each locality reflects its specific soil, air, and water, just as wine does. Thus it is not uncommon for the *Pecorino* of one farm to differ from that of a neighboring one only a few miles away. Even *Parmigiano*, with its highly controlled methods of production, changes a little in taste from one producer to another. Further variety is added by using not only the milk of cows, but also that of sheep and goats and by combining two or all of these types.

PARMIGIANO MAKING

Arriving early in the morning to watch a day of *Parmigiano* making, we were greeted by the traditionally distrustful watchdog, who growled on the arrival of these outsiders and who never ceased to regard us with suspicion the entire morning. He was doing his job well, for the small *Parmigiano* farms have a product regarded as well worth stealing. It is true that in times of inflation, people of the Parma-Reggio area store wheels of *Parmigiano* in bank vaults, because its value never diminishes and it has a financial market like gold, Old Master paintings, or antique furniture in times of cheap money.

It takes about 600 quarts of the milk of specially pampered

Preceding overleaf: Wheels of aging Parmigiano-Reggiano, *with the name incised into the crust, proudly proclaim its exclusiveness. This cheese may be produced only within the restricted area around Parma, Reggio Emilia, and Modena.*

Opposite: Aged 75-pound Parmigiano *wheels, cut open, stacked, and ready for sale.* Parmigiano *is popular throughout Italy, even in areas that have their own grating cheeses, such as* Pecorino.

cows to produce one 75-pound wheel of *Parmigiano*, which must then be aged from two to three years before being marketed. Each small, family-sized farm produces only four to twelve cheeses a day.

In order to earn a living following these traditional artisan methods, our hosts, the Martini family, must work every day of the year, and the entire family is involved in the cheese making.

When we arrived at 7 A.M., the Martinis were beginning the morning's work. But the first step had actually begun the night before when the milk had arrived from the evening milking. The rich cow's milk had been placed in huge, shiny, immaculate trays and left at room temperature overnight to allow the cream to rise to the top. In the early morning, before we arrived, the cream had been removed and the skimmed milk was ready as the first ingredient of the cheese.

We were lucky enough to arrive just as the product of the morning's milking was arriving. This whole milk is combined with the skimmed milk of the night before in copper kettles. The "starter," some whey from the preceding batch that had been left to begin fermentation, is now added, so that the coagulation of the new milk will begin more easily when the rennet is added later. The two milks are heated together to the first temperature of 33 degrees C (about 91 degrees F). The milk must be constantly stirred while it is being heated (this is now done electrically), and one family member must constantly watch the temperature.

The flat Parma landscape is very green for most of the year and provides perfect grazing for the cows whose milk is used for the Maggengo *type of* Parmigiano. *The name* Maggengo *was originally given to the cheese by the Etruscans, who produced it only in the month of May.*

Left: Skimmed milk from last night's milking and whole milk from this morning's are combined in huge copper kettles.

Below: The milky-white curds are broken up with a spino, *or ball-shaped whisk.*

All through this process, there was a continual background of activity—family members washing and scrubbing the building and all the containers, for everything must be kept immaculately clean.

Once the milk reaches 33 degrees C., the heat is shut off and the rennet is added. The coagulation begins and takes place completely in about 15 minutes.

A large, ball-shaped whisk, called a *spino,* is then used to break up the *cagliate,* or curds, into tiny uniform pieces so they will be better integrated when they are heated again. If the curds are not uniform, the body of the aging cheese will not be uniform and cracks could develop inside, which would affect not only the texture of the cheese but its taste as well.

The *casaro,* or cheesemaker—on this farm, signor Martini himself—must be a skilled artisan who can determine from the size and grain of the broken up curds how the cheese will eventually turn out. This art is still passed from father to son, and it takes years to develop the skill to recognize all the signs of possible problems.

The heat is turned on again, this time to bring the curd slowly to 45 degrees C (113 degrees F) and then very quickly over higher heat to 55 degrees C (131 degrees F). The pieces of curd have by now all settled on the bottom of the kettles. With the aid of two sticks, one member of the family skillfully maneu-

249

The moist curd is lifted above the kettle in cheesecloth and allowed to drain for about thirty minutes.

vers a strong cheesecloth under the curd.

After sitting in the cheesecloth at the bottom of the kettle until it is cool, the curd is then lifted by two people to the top of the kettle. The whole mass of curd is enclosed in the cheesecloth to make a compact bulk. The thin liquid whey remains below in the kettle.

I tasted the curd at this point, and it did not give even a hint of what would later be *Parmigiano.* It was rubbery in texture and very mild. In earlier centuries, the fresh cheese at this stage was used for cooking, often combined with the aged cheese, sliced or grated, as in the once famous *Torta alla parmigiana.* I persuaded the family to let me have enough of the fresh cheese to try this Medieval recipe in its original form. The dish was delicious and would be well worth reviving if we could easily obtain the fresh *Parmigiano.*

Each mass of curd is divided in half at this point, as each kettle yields enough to make two wheels of cheese. Each half of the cheese is then placed in its own individual cheesecloth. The two cheesecloths, each with enough curd to make a wheel of cheese, is hung above the kettle to drain.

At this point, the whey is pumped out, and most of it goes directly to the nearby barn where the pigs are kept. Although this particular whey is not used to make Ricotta, it is usual with most artisan-produced cheeses to move the whey to another container and to add more rennet to make the Ricotta, which is the second curd. Ricotta is then marketed fresh, not aged like a cheese, in its own little baskets. In its attractive, tightly packed form, it is dry and unsalted, but nevertheless has a distinctive sweet, rich flavor. Fresh Ricotta is not eaten alone, but rather appears as a component of a dish or mixed with something else.

While the cheese was draining, the family had a period of relaxation, and a second breakfast was served. It was only about 10:30 A.M., so I was surprised to see the wine arriving, together with generous slices of—what else—*Parmigiano.* The cheese was three years old, golden, and still moist, with a pineapple flavor that is rarely tasted away from the farms themselves. The wine was, of course, their own, not bottled. Despite the uniqueness of the milk of this area, we all looked with pity on one of my companions who chose to drink a glass of it instead of the wine. Not even the Martini family, Parmenese to the core, and certainly aware of the quality of their milk, could understand this!

Left: Still in its damp cheesecloth, the cheese is lowered into a wooden form, or a fascera, *where it is covered and pressed into shape for several hours.*

Below: After a short aging, the wheels of the Parmigiano-Reggiano *are soaked in brine.*

After draining for about thirty minutes, each individual cheese, still in its cheesecloth, is lowered into a wooden form called a *fascera* and is covered and then pressed into shape for several hours.

After this period, the cloth is removed and a special matrix with teeth is inserted between the cheese and the walls of the mold, where it will remain for several days. These teeth are arranged so that they impress the words *Parmigiano-Reggiano* all over the sides of the cheese.

The wheels of cheese, when set firmly enough to have the wooden form and matrix removed, are then put into a heavily salted brine. They remain there for twenty-five days; then the aging period begins. After a short exposure to the sun, they are placed on shelves of a cool *cascina* and turned often. After one season (the cheese-making season is November 15 to April 15), they are moved to adjoining storerooms for the slow maturation period lasting two to three years.

Our *Parmigiano*-making day was over at noon. The family left us to clean up, have lunch, and rest, as their next day would begin again with the evening milking.

SOUTHERN ITALY'S LAYERED CHEESES

True Mozzarella is made from the milk of the water buffalo, a type of wild ox that was domesticated in Asia over the course of several millennia. When the water buffalo was brought from India to Italy, some say by the Greeks, others say in the early Christian era, no one could have foreseen that the draft animal would become indirectly responsible for the toppings of count- less pizzas all over the world! But the buffalo, a cousin of the American bison, adapted well to the climate of southern Italy, and cheesemakers developed the unique Mozzarella cheese from its milk. Today, much of what is called Mozzarella is a cow's milk adaptation of the original process and is called *Fior di latte*. Today, even in Italy, the distinction between the true Moz- zarella and that made from cow's milk is rapidly fading, and Mozzarella now often refers to both types of cheese.

Mozzarella di bufala is porcelain white in color, soft but slightly firm outside, and moist inside. Not only is it whiter and creamier than *Fior di latte*, but it tastes completely different as well. Both mild and very flavorful, true Mozzarella has the slightest hint of both sweetness and sourness and though creamy, has a chewy texture.

Real Mozzarella has become too rare to be used in cooking. It is either reserved for dessert or cut into cubes for a delicious salad of cheese, fresh tomatoes, olive oil, and basil. For pasta, pizza, and other cooked dishes, Italian cooks now use *Fior di latte*.

Mozzarella, when cut open, resembles a thick strip wrapped into a ball. Italians refer to this type of curd as *pasta filata*, or "layered." In Mozzarella production, the curds that are formed after the milk has been cooked with rennet are crumbled and

placed on a slanted table to allow the whey to run off. The crumbled curds begin to dry and ferment naturally. But after about three hours, the solidified curd is cut into long strips, returned to the kettle, and covered with boiling water. As the strips float to the top of the kettle, bunches of them are seized, quickly torn to pieces, and formed into balls of one-half pound to one pound in weight. (Smaller balls of about one-quarter pound are called *bocconcini* or "little mouthfuls.") It is the tearing action, *mozzare* in Italian, that gives the cheese its name. The balls of torn curd are placed in cold water for several minutes and then transferred to a light brine for ten to twelve hours. Once removed, they are kept in their own whey and may be eaten immediately or up to two weeks later.

Other cheeses of southern Italy share the fascinating technique of layering, in which the curd is cut into strips before being pressed together. This group of cheeses includes *Treccia, Scamorze, Caciocavallo, Provola,* and *Provolone* among others.

Variations in the same basic technique distinguish *Provolone* and mozzarella. After the milk has been cooked for *Provolone*, the curds are not crumbled, but rather placed directly on a slanted table to drain. They are left to dry and ferment for a longer period than the Mozzarella curds—one to three days, depending on the weather. (The *casaro*, or cheesemaker, knows by touch when the curd is ready.) As with Mozzarella, the *Provolone* curd is cut into long strips, placed in a kettle and covered with boiling water. But the bunches of strips, once seized from the water, are cut with a knife, rather than torn. Then they are formed into a huge sausage shape that is quickly bathed in cold water. They are immediately placed in a strong brine for six to twelve hours, depending on the local custom. At this point, the *Provolone* is either smoked or tied up like a sausage and left to age.

Provolone dolce, the sweeter-tasting cheese, is aged for two to

Water buffalo are the source of the milk for true Mozzarella. The whey that is left after producing this cheese is much sought after to make a rare and truly remarkable type of Ricotta. (© Ferri Cesare/Mac Film)

three months; the sharper version, *Provolone piccante*, is aged for some months longer, according to the degree of sharpness desired. A third variety, *Provolone affumicato*, is smoked for a week and then aged for about two months.

Eaten with bread and sometimes with *prosciutto* or *mortadella* sausage, *Provolone* is a favorite snack in southern Italy. It is also used in cooking, as in the Sicilian dish *Focaccia ripiena*, a pizza stuffed with cheese and meat.

Caciocavallo is produced more widely than *Provolone* and in much the same way. *Caciocavallo*, however, is formed into 5-pound pear shapes that are tied together in pairs and slung over a piece of wood, *a cavallo*, "on horseback." Because of the word "horse" in its name, many say that *Caciocavallo* was originally made from mare's milk, but this is not true.

Scamorze are smaller than *Provolone*, but made in a similar way. They are usually eaten fresh, but are also sometimes smoked.

Spending a Saturday morning together with a family of cheesemakers near Bari, I watched them making *Scamorze*, using the process employed for all the layered cheeses. They make the cheese in the back of a tiny shop, in the middle of the small village of Putignano, where the family has followed this occupation since 1805. On Saturday morning, people from the surrounding area flock to this shop, which is furnished with only a large marble counter and a single chair. The shop sells only their own production of freshly made cheeses—*Scamorza, Burrata, Fior di*

The cooked curd for Scamorze *is chopped into strips with the* mezza-luna *chopper.*

254

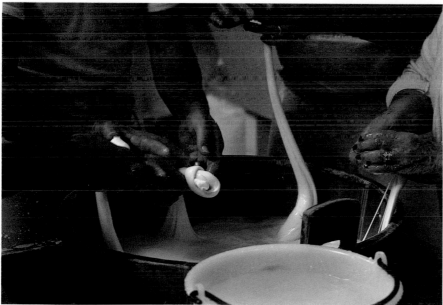

latte, Treccia. Since there is no display, the customers must know what to request, and when they do, the freshly made cheese is produced from the back of the shop. The cash register is tended by the grandmother.

The layered cheeses of this area are made from cow's milk. First the rough-textured *cagliata,* or curd, is cooked and cooled. Then it is chopped into strips rather than broken up, always with quick motions of the *mezzaluna* chopper. Only enough curd

Top: Stretching the curd on a stick. Above left: Forming the curd into a rope. Above right: Shaping the rope into a round bocconcino *and into a braided* treccia.

255

Right: Newly made pairs of Scamorze are strung over the arm of the cheesemaker.

Below right: Scamorze of differing ages—from a day old to a year old.

is chopped at one time for a single person to be able to work it.

The chopped *cagliata* is placed in boiling water, where it melts but still sticks together. Using a stick, the cheesemaker rotates the curd in and out of the water until it stretches into a long, smooth textured strip. Skillfully using the stick with a special technique, the cheesemaker creates a long, narrow sheet that eventually resembles a thick rope. The movements of the body, the arms, and the stick are coordinated in a beautiful choreography, and it is an aesthetic experience to watch it.

Once the rope is formed, other workers join in to shape the curd. The shaping is done while the piece of curd is still attached to the rope, and once shaped, it is literally torn off. A round *Bocconcino* may be formed, resembling a small balloon, or a braided *Treccia* may be shaped. For the *Treccia*, the rope is separated into two strands which are then braided together, while still forming a part of the long rope, and then torn off.

Once torn off, the shaped pieces are placed in brine for periods varying from a few minutes to two hours, depending on which cheese is being made. The *Scamorze* are then placed in nets and lifted out of the brine. The nets are attached in pairs and hung over a central stick.

The many varieties of layered cheeses are popular all over Italy. The well-aged ones also travel well and are shipped to many countries.

One of the most popular dishes using a layered cheese is *Spiedini alla romana*, a Roman dish in which the alternating slices of Mozzarella and bread are placed on skewers and cooked either on a wood fire, in the oven, or sautéed in a frying pan. Removed from the skewer, the overlapping layers of bread and cheese are arranged standing up on the plates. When they are ready, a delicious butter-anchovy sauce is poured over them. It is not a sandwich and should be eaten with knife and fork as an appetizer or as a light main course. The bread should be made of light rather than dark flour, and it should not be too crusty.

My friend Nika Hazelton, international food authority and a born Roman, showed me a Roman's way of making it in her recipe.

Spiedini alla romana
MOZZARELLA GRILLED ON SKEWERS ROMAN STYLE

1	thin loaf Italian bread		Salt and freshly ground black pepper		8	tablespoons (1 stick) sweet butter
3	medium-sized Mozzarelle (about 1½ pounds total weight)	8	whole anchovies in salt, or 16 anchovy fillets in oil, drained			TO SERVE
3	tablespoons olive oil				4	sprigs Italian parsley

Cut the bread and the Mozzarelle into ½-inch-thick slices. You will need 16 slices of Mozzarella and 20 slices of bread.

Preheat the broiler to 375 degrees.

Thread 4 skewers, starting with the bread and alternating 5 slices of bread with 4 slices of cheese. Press the end slices toward the center so that everything is closely packed together. Place the skewers on an oiled baking sheet. Brush the slices of bread and cheese with 2 tablespoons of the oil and season them with salt and pepper. Put the baking sheet on the middle shelf of the preheated broiler, or 5 to 6 inches from the flame if you cannot regulate your broiler. Broil for about 15 minutes, checking the *spiedini* occasionally to make sure the bread does not burn.

Meanwhile, if the anchovies are preserved in salt, clean them under cool running water, removing the bones.

Heat the butter and the remaining tablespoon of oil in a heavy saucepan, and, when the butter is completely melted, remove the pan from the heat. Add the anchovies and mash them with a fork until they are completely dissolved. Taste for salt and pepper.

Remove the skewers from the broiler, place each on an individual plate, and pour some of the sauce over each serving. Accompany with a sprig of parsley.

SERVES 4.

PECORINO

Tuscan *Pecorino* is still made with artisan methods on small farms, often Chianti vineyards. Each Tuscan shepherd has only fifteen to twenty sheep, lovingly cared for and moved from valley to mountain, from vineyard to the coastal Maremma. It is said, in Italy, that there are as many different sheep's milk cheeses as there are shepherds. Only a few of these cheeses are produced commercially or exported, but they are so special and so characteristically Italian that you must taste them when you travel to Italy.

The sheep's milk cheeses are classified as uncooked or semi-cooked, meaning cooked at a low temperature. Both types are often called *caciotta*, but this is an imprecise generic name, probably derived from the old Italian word for cheese, *cacio*. Technically, nowadays, *caciotta* refers to specific dimensions of either sheep's or cow's milk cheese: no more than 2 pounds in weight and round, oval, cylindrical, or fist-shaped. Originally all Italian sheep's milk cheeses were of the *caciotta* size and shapes; today such cheeses should be called *caciotte pecorine, pecora,* of course, being the Italian word for sheep. Whether the sheep's milk cheese is truly a *caciotta* or larger, like the *Pecorino Romano* used for grating, it may be called simply *Pecorino*.

These cheeses, when made in Livorno, Lucca, Pisa, and Pistoia, as well as some of those from Florence, are all called

Opposite: Spiedini alla romana (Mozzarella Grilled on Skewers Roman Style).

Pecorino, Pecorino Toscano, or *Caciotta.* Those from Carrara and Massa are labeled *Pecorino Massese,* after the Massese breed of sheep; this cheese is particularly delicate, rare, and much prized.

Marzolino, a white *Pecorino* cheese produced in the vineyards of Chianti Classico, was created by the Etruscans and probably has been produced in this area in the same way ever since. It is fist-shaped, weighs about 1¾ pounds, and is still made of pure sheep's milk. As it ages, the crust is kept oiled with pure olive oil, the other incomparable product of these same vineyards. The cheese attains its best flavor at four to eight months. When made with animal rennet, *Marzolino* remains rather mild, but when prepared with a vegetable rennet, it is sharp, even when fresh. A snack of cubes of *Marzolino* dressed with olive oil and black pepper, as in the recipe below, and accompanied by the marvelous local wine and crusty bread is unforgettable.

The many Tuscan *caciotte pecorine* comprise only one category of Italian sheep's milk cheeses. The other main type is *Pecorino Romano,* which is made in wheels of 16 to 40 pounds; it is salted and generally sharper than the Tuscan *Pecorino,* because of the particular herbs the sheep graze on around Rome, in Lazio. Ranging in color from white to light yellow, *Pecorino Romano* may be eaten as a dessert cheese at about four months of age, but is used more widely for grating after about eight months. When made in Sardinia, the same kind of cheese is called *Pecorino Romano Sardo,* usually shortened to *Sardo;* in Sicily it is spiced with whole peppercorns and called *Pecorino pepato.*

Pecorino marinato
MARINATED PECORINO

1 pound *Pecorino Toscano* (Tuscan *Pecorino*), crust removed	Abundant freshly ground black pepper
½ cup olive oil	

Cut the cheese into 1-inch cubes. Put the cheese on a serving plate and pour the oil and grind the pepper over it. Wrap the dish with aluminum foil and marinate for at least 1 hour before serving (see Note).

Unwrap the dish, mix the cheese gently but very well and serve 3 or 4 cubes of cheese on each plate.

SERVES 8 AS AN APPETIZER.

NOTE: *You can marinate the cheese in a cool place or on the bottom shelf of the refrigerator. If the cheese is refrigerated while it marinates, it must be brought back to room temperature before it is served.*

CHEESES OF LOMBARDY

Lombardy, with its ancient capital Milan, beautiful Lake Como, and the picturesque old towns of Bergamo, Cremona, Mantua, and Pavia, produces rich, buttery cow's milk cheeses with high fat content. These range in flavor from the mild, subtle, and soft *Stracchino* to the sharp, yet still creamy, *Gorgonzola.*

The name *Stracchino,* in its most restricted sense, denotes a young, buttery cheese aged from twenty to sixty days. Cooked but a short time, at a low temperature, *Stracchino* is classified with the fresh cheeses. It is made in the provinces of Brescia and Milano; most prized is that from Fonteno and the valley of the Tartano. A favorite dessert cheese throughout Italy, *Stracchino* is featured in Lombardy as a special course at Christmas Eve dinner, served with the fruit relish *Mostarda di Cremona*.

Derived from the Lombard dialect word *stracco*, meaning "tired," the term *Stracchino* has also long been used to describe a number of other cheeses made from the milk of cows that have just completed the long annual trip from the mountainside to winter quarters in the valley. It is part of Lombard folklore that this "tired" milk produces the finest results in many kinds of cheese-making.

The cows' important journey takes place in September and October, and the best cheeses are made during this period, although increased demand has resulted in year-round production. All *Stracchino* types are made from two separate milkings, and all have about a 50 percent fat content.

Stracchino Gorgonzola, most often known simply as *Gorgonzola*, after the town of its origin, is now produced in almost all parts of Lombardy. But the most celebrated examples still come from around the namesake town near Milan, where the earliest historical reference to the cheese is dated 879. The very best *Gorgonzola* is aged in the grottos or caves of the Valsassina. The cheese has internal flecks of mold, more green than blue, but it is creamier and milder than most of the blue-veined cheeses made in other parts of Europe.

Gorgonzola is prepared in layers. As each layer of curd cools, a new hot layer is placed over it. The adjacent layers must be at different temperatures during preparation to permit the layers to separate, allowing air to enter and to encourage the growth of mold. This mold is referred to as *erborinn*, the local dialect word for "parsley," which it is thought to resemble.

Much has been made of the distinction between *dolce* (sweet) and *piccante* (sharp) *Gorgonzola*, but the categories are not well defined. If, during preparation, the layers of curd are added slowly, the cheese will be milder. Flavor is also less sharp when the cheese is young, as the aging time may vary from 90 to 150 days. But since the younger cheeses are rarely exported, it is unlikely to find the real *dolce Gorgonzola* outside of Italy. An especially young cheese, allowed to age only 60 days, and not having a chance to form mold, is called White *Gorgonzola* or *Pannarone*; it is lighter and sweeter than the more aged cheeses.

Usually served as a dessert cheese, *Gorgonzola* is also used in cooking, as in a stuffing for *tortelli* or for *crespelle* (crêpes). It is also a component of the "four cheeses" sauce used with pasta and risotto. Recipes for the *crespelle* and risotto follow. It is not authentically Italian to mix *Gorgonzola* or any other cheese into salads or salad dressings.

Less sharp than most *Gorgonzola*, and without mold, *Taleggio* or *Stracchino Taleggio* is another celebrated dessert cheese. Its full flavor results from one of two processes: either the cooked curd is soaked in brine for about fourteen hours or else salt is rubbed into it. It is the salt that causes *Taleggio* to form a crust. The curd is cooked at 32 degrees C (89 degrees F).

Overleaf: A parade of Italian cheeses. Left, on the green plate, buffalo milk Ricotta, a compact form shaped by the basket in which it is kept. On the straw above it, a young white Tuscan Pecorino with a wedge cut out and Fontina Val d'Aosta. On the green glass with spoon, the creamy Mascarpone. In the basket, top, two pear-shaped young Scamorze. Then counterclockwise: A large wedge of the most refined Sweet Gorgonzola; brownish-smoked Scamorza, one of the many types of tomine from the pre-Alps, this one of goat cheese; the log-shaped Caprini, once made with the milk of capra (goat), but now more often with cow's milk; and a square-shaped, rich Robiola. Right of the basket, from front: the fist-shaped Tuscan sheep's milk Marzolino and the rich, soft Lombard Stracchino on the plate. The two behind are the yellowish Asiago, leading cheese of the Veneto, and a large toma from Piedmont. Behind them are two large, pear-shaped Provole, one yellowish, the darker one smoked. In the bowl are seven buffalo milk Mozzarelle sitting in some of their own whey; and in front to the right, a whole disc of aged small Sardinian Pecorino Caciotta and a wedge of Sicilian Pecorino pepato, with its dots of whole black peppercorns.

On the tray, upper right, a large wedge of three-year-old Parmigiano-Reggiano, with its own typical knife. Then a large disc of Provolone; a wedge of a young, large Pecorino Romano Sardo; and finally one of the best factory-made cheeses, Bel Paese.

261

In the old days, it was cooled in icy caves, but today it is refrigerated. The cheese should be aged two months and no longer. The choicest *Taleggio* comes from Abbiategrasso and the valley of the Erna.

 Mascarpone, the very rich, triple cream, fresh cheese, is produced in twenty-four hours. Mild in taste, it is slightly more yellow in color than cream, but its texture resembles that of solidified heavy whipped cream. *Mascarpone* is very widely used in Italian cooking, most often mixed with liqueur for pastries and desserts, but also as a richer substitute for whipped cream. One of the non-sweet dishes in which it is used is *Polenta con mascarpone e tartufi* (see page 131).

Crespelle al gorgonzola
CRÊPES WITH GORGONZOLA STUFFING

FOR THE CRESPELLE

2	tablespoons (1 ounce) sweet butter
2	cups unbleached all-purpose flour
4	extra large eggs
2	cups cold milk
	Pinch of salt
1	teaspoon granulated sugar

FOR THE STUFFING

4	tablespoons (2 ounces) sweet butter
2	tablespoons unbleached all-purpose flour
2	cups cold milk
2	cups heavy cream
4	ounces Gorgonzola
	Salt and freshly ground black pepper
	Freshly grated nutmeg
¾	cup freshly grated Parmigiano

FOR THE TOPPING

8	tablespoons (1 stick) sweet butter
½	cup unbleached all-purpose flour
3	cups cold milk
1	cup heavy cream
	Salt and freshly ground black pepper
	Freshly grated nutmeg

TO COOK THE CRESPELLE

About 4 tablespoons (2 ounces) sweet butter

TO ASSEMBLE THE DISH

1   tablespoon sweet butter

TO SERVE

½   cup freshly grated Parmigiano

Prepare the crespelle: Melt the butter in the top of a double boiler or in a bagnomaria over hot water and let stand until cool.

Sift the flour into a crockery or glass bowl and make a well in the flour. Place the cooled butter in the well. Stir very carefully with a wooden spoon, incorporating some flour from the edges of the well. Add the eggs, always stirring with a wooden spoon and incorporating more flour. Start adding the milk little by little and keep stirring until all the flour is incorporated. Then add the salt and sugar. Mix very well. Cover the bowl and put it in a cool place to rest for at least 1 hour to allow the gluten to expand.

Prepare the stuffing: Melt the butter in a heavy saucepan, preferably of copper or enamel, over low heat. When the butter reaches the frothing point, add the flour all at once. Mix very well with a wooden spoon. Then cook until the flour is completely incorporated (about 2 minutes). Remove the pan from the heat and let stand for 10 to 15 minutes.

While the butter-flour mixture is standing, combine the milk and the heavy cream in another pan and heat it until it is very close to a boil. Cut the Gorgonzola into small pieces.

Put the saucepan with the butter-flour mixture over low heat and add all of the hot milk-cream mixture at once. Stir and then add the Gorgonzola. Keep stirring until the cheese is completely melted and the stuffing is smooth (about 10 minutes). Add salt, pepper, and nutmeg to taste. Remove the pan from the heat, add the Parmigiano, and mix very well. Transfer the stuffing to a crockery or glass bowl, pressing a piece of buttered wax paper down over the stuffing to prevent a skin from forming. Let the stuffing cool completely.

Prepare the sauce for the topping, following the same procedure as that for the stuffing, but using the ingredients listed under topping.

Using an 8-inch crêpe pan and ¼ cup of the batter for each crespella, prepare them, buttering the pan each time. Stack the prepared crespelle one on top of the other, separated by wax paper.

When all the crespelle are ready, use the tablespoon of butter to heavily butter two 13½- x 8¾-inch baking dishes.

Preheat the oven to 375 degrees.

Use a spatula to spread 2 tablespoons of the stuffing over the entire surface of each crespella. Roll them up and arrange them in the baking dishes, one next to the other, with the seam on top. Gently pour the topping over them. Bake for about 25 minutes. Remove from the oven and serve immediately, sprinkling 1 tablespoon of Parmigiano over each serving.

MAKES ABOUT 24 CRÊPES; SERVES 8.

CHEESES OF NORTHERN ITALY

In the Alpine and pre-Alpine regions of northern Italy, cheeses have been produced since prehistoric times. Piedmont and Val d'Aosta, in the northwestern corner of the country, are particularly rich in venerable cheeses; the northeast areas of Veneto and Udine also have unique products.

Asiago, a commune at the foot of the Dolomites in Vicenza province, gives its name to the most famous cheese of the Veneto. Because aged *Asiago* is sometimes called *Pecorino,* one wonders whether the cheese's early history included some sheep's milk. All available documentation, however, refers only to cow's milk, taken either from two milkings, one skim, the other whole, or from one milking, partially skim. The forms are large, about 20 to 30 pounds, cylindrical and low. Cooked at low temperatures, the cheeses are placed in brine or dry salt before aging. The texture of the cheese is compact and dotted throughout with very small holes. Its color is the light yellow of straw.

When matured for six months, the cheese is called *Mezzanello* or *Asiago da taglio* and is served as a light piquant dessert cheese. When it becomes *vecchio* (old), twelve months, or *stravecchio* (very old) at eighteen months, it is more aromatic and may be used for grating.

Piedmont and Val d'Aosta produce several hundred varieties of cheese. The generic terms *toma, tometta,* and *tomino* encompass a breathtaking array of skim, part-skim, whole milk, and cream cheeses; fresh and aged; of cow's, goat's, and sheep's milk and as mixtures of two or three of these; large and small; firm and soft. Each mountain and valley produces a different variation, from the Camembert-Brie soft types, aged about forty-five days, to mild white cylinders, to large, firm, aged yellow cheeses. Unfortunately only a few of these varieties are known outside their localities and even fewer are exported.

The *tome* of the high mountains, produced between July and September, are the most celebrated. Experience has proven that they are good when they come from places above 6,500 feet. Among the most revered are the very sweet *Reblosson della Val di Susa,* which retains the herb and flower aromas of that especially fragrant cow-grazing area; the skim-milk *Toma del Maccagno,* aged for four months under a layer of mountain herbs but also good fresh; the sheep's milk *Toma di pecora della Val Stura;* and *Toma di Val Gressoney.*

A particular feature of the smaller *tomini* is that they are often cut into cubes and preserved in either oil and pepper or green sauce. The related cheese *Robiola* is especially excellent in the area of Roccaverano, where it is aged for a long time and preserved in basil, rosemary, thyme, flowering juniper, and fennel. Candele produces an excellent goat's milk *tomino* preserved with pepper. But it is possible to touch on only a few of the interesting *tome, tomine,* and *tomette.*

True *Fontina* is made only in the Val d'Aosta, although the cheese is widely imitated throughout Italy and in other countries. An ancient cheese, mentioned in *La Summa Lacticiniorum* (1477), it took its name either from the Alpine peak Fontin in the area of Quart, or from the village of Fontinaz. The whole milk used in this rich cheese must come from pure-bred Valdostana cows. The summer *Fontina*, made when the cows are able to graze at 10,000 feet on fresh grass and perfumed herbs, is best.

Although most *Fontina* is made in large cooperatives controlled by the local producers' consortium, the milk used must satisfy the same standards as those of the small farmers. A special feature of the cheese-making process is the slow salting of the outside of the 20- to 25-pound forms to produce the very mild flavor desired. The crust that slowly develops is of a unique brownish-orange color. The cheese itself is a straw color, yellower than *Asiago*; the texture is somewhat soft and elastic.

Fontina is often used after its minimum aging of four months, when it is mild though flavorful; but it may be aged as long as two or three years, and will become increasingly piquant. In recent times, the cheese has grown in favor as a dessert, but its classic use is in cooking. Above all, it is the basis for the classic *fonduta*, a whipped blend of melted cheese, butter, egg yolk, and milk that is eaten with small cubes of bread. *Fontina* is perhaps the dominating cheese in the *Risotto ai quattro formaggi*, Risotto with Four Cheeses, that follows. The four cheeses used in the *risotto* are *Fontina*, *Gorgonzola*, Mozzarella, and *Parmigiano*. Butter is also included, as it is in *Pasta ai quattro formaggi*, but in that recipe the butter has to be an honorary fourth cheese, as only three real cheeses are used.

Strangely, in the combination of seemingly mild *Fontina* with the assertive *Gorgonzola*, the *Fontina* dominates because, in cooking, the flavor of *Fontina* becomes stronger, while that of *Gorgonzola* diminishes.

The glass contains bocconcini, *small almost bite-size* Mozzarelle di bufala. *When cut through, one sees the layering and its moist interior, not a solid ball. It is a fresh cheese that should be eaten within a few days; in the meantime, it should be stored in its own whey. Other cheeses shown include, clockwise, the log shaped* Caprino, *Sweet* Gorgonzola, *and* Taleggio. (© *Franco Pasti*)

Risotto ai quattro formaggi
RISOTTO WITH FOUR CHEESES

4	ounces *Gorgonzola,* crust removed
4	ounces Mozzarella
4	ounces Italian *Fontina,* crust removed
1	cup lukewarm milk
30	unsalted shelled fresh pistachio nuts for cooking
	Coarse-grained salt
4	ounces (1 stick) sweet butter
1	tablespoon olive oil
2	cups raw rice, preferably Italian Arborio
3½	cups homemade chicken broth
	Salt and freshly ground black pepper
6	tablespoons freshly grated *Parmigiano*

Cut the three cheeses into cubes of less than ½ inch. Put the cubes in a small crockery or glass bowl with the milk and let stand until needed.

Blanch the pistachio nuts for 2 to 3 minutes in boiling salted water; then drain and skin them.

Heat the butter and oil in a flameproof casserole over medium heat. When the butter is completely melted, add the rice and sauté for 4 minutes.

Meanwhile, heat the broth to a boil in a separate saucepan. Start adding the broth to the rice, a small quantity at a time, stirring continuously and gently, until the rice has absorbed all the broth (about 12 minutes). Add the milk with all the cheeses to the pan and keep stirring until the milk and cheeses are well amalgamated with the rice (about 6 minutes). Taste for salt and pepper and add the pistachio nuts and the *Parmigiano*. Mix very well and transfer the risotto to a serving dish. Serve immediately.

SERVES 6.

*G*roviera, the cheese produced across the border from the Gruyère area, is fundamentally the same cheese as its Swiss and French counterparts. It melts very well and is good either cubed or grated for cooking. *Sformato di Groviera*, a mousse-textured cheese dish accompanied by a full-bodied meat sauce containing cubes of veal, may be a first or second course or even, in small portions, an appetizer.

Sformato di Groviera
SFORMATO OF GROVIERA

Prepare the *sformato*: Cut the *prosciutto* into cubes of less than ½ inch. Soak the *Groviera* in 1 cup of the milk for ½ hour.

Melt the butter in a heavy saucepan, preferably of copper or enamel, over low heat. When the butter reaches the frothing point, add the flour all

Right: Risotto ai quattro formaggi *includes* Gorgonzola, *Mozzarella,* Fontina, *and* Parmigiano.

Opposite: The Sformato di Groviera *is surrounded by a meat sauce.*

at once. Mix very well with a wooden spoon; then cook until the flour is completely incorporated (about 2 minutes). Remove the pan from the heat and let stand for 10 to 15 minutes.

While the butter-flour mixture is standing, heat the remaining 2 cups of milk in another pan until it is very close to a boil.

Put the first saucepan back over the heat and add all of the hot milk at once. Then add the soaked *Groviera* with its milk and stir very well until the cheese is completely melted and the sauce is smooth (about 10 minutes). Taste for salt, pepper, and nutmeg. Remove from the heat and transfer the sauce to a crockery or glass bowl, pressing a piece of buttered wax paper down over the sauce to prevent a skin from forming. Let the sauce cool completely.

Meanwhile, prepare the sauce: Heat the butter and olive oil in a flame-proof casserole over medium heat.

Cut the *prosciutto* slice into ½-inch cubes. Add the *prosciutto*, onion, and garlic to the pan and sauté for 15 minutes. Add the veal and sauté for 5 minutes longer. Discard the onion and garlic. Add the tomatoes and season with salt and pepper. Cover the pan and cook for about 15 minutes. Start adding the broth a little at a time and cook until the meat is tender (about 35 minutes). When ready, let the sauce stand, covered, until needed.

Blanche the pistachio nuts for 2 to 3 minutes in boiling salted water; then drain and skin them.

When the cheese sauce is cool, add the eggs, egg yolk, *Parmigiano*, *prosciutto*, and the pistachio nuts. Mix very well with a wooden spoon and taste for salt and pepper.

Butter and sprinkle a 2-quart tin-lined copper Turk's head mold with bread crumbs. Preheat the oven to 375 degrees and prepare a large oven-proof casserole with lukewarm water to make a *bagnomaria* for the mold.

Using an unlined copper bowl and a wire whisk, beat the egg white until stiff. Fold it into the cheese mixture, mixing very gently in a rotating motion until it is completely incorporated. Pour the contents of the bowl into the mold and place the mold in the *bagnomaria*. Bake for about 45 minutes.

Remove from the oven and let cool for a few minutes before unmolding onto a large serving dish. Reheat the sauce and arrange it on the plate around the *sformato*.

To serve, slice the *sformato* like a cake and spoon some sauce with meat alongside each serving.

SERVES 8.

FOR THE *SFORMATO*

2   ounces *prosciutto* in one slice

6   ounces *Groviera*, cut into ½-inch cubes

3   cups cold milk

6   tablespoons (3 ounces) sweet butter

1   cup unbleached all-purpose flour

     Salt and freshly ground black pepper

     Freshly grated nutmeg

     About 15 unsalted shelled fresh pistachio nuts for cooking

3   extra large eggs, whole

1   extra large egg, separated

½   cup freshly grated *Parmigiano*

     About ½ cup unseasoned bread crumbs, preferably homemade

FOR THE SAUCE

4   tablespoons (2 ounces) sweet butter

2   tablespoons olive oil

4   ounces *prosciutto* in one slice

½   medium-sized red onion, peeled, but left whole

1   medium-sized clove garlic, peeled but left whole

1   pound boneless veal (from the leg), cut into 1-inch cubes

5   fresh tomatoes, skin and seeds removed, or 5 drained canned imported Italian tomatoes, seeds removed

     Salt and freshly ground black pepper

     About 2 cups hot homemade beef broth

Desserts

Italy's landscape yields a rich cornucopia of fruits, from the orchards of fruit trees up and down the peninsula to the wild berries from the woods and the tropical fruits of the South. And it is fruit that is most often served for dessert at home, eaten informally at street stands, and offered a bit dressed up in elegant *ristoranti*. In summer and fall, fruit finds its way into pastries and *gelati*, where the fresh fruit flavor completely dominates its setting. It is no accident that so many of the decorative motifs in Italian frescoes and relief sculpture are fruit.

The wide array of prepared desserts includes creams, ice creams, custards, and, above all, an enormous variety of pastries. But these *dolci*, or sweets, are more often found in the cafés and pastry shops than at home, for they are eaten not after a meal, but at the traditional 11 A.M. and late-afternoon refreshment hours. In addition to the classic *alta cucina* (haute cuisine) pastries developed centuries ago, principally by Florentine and Lombard pastry chefs, there are hundreds of regional specialties, both rustic and fancy, which may be found just in one small area. The quest for these little-known pastries is particularly enjoyable if one leaves time to investigate the special architecture of the town, take in its often unique landscape, and savor the delicious specialties which may be unknown outside of that locality.

FRUITS

The great German poet Goethe expressed the northerner's longing for the Italian sun in a song sung by one of his characters, "Do you know the land where the lemon trees bloom?" Goethe may have seen the groves of lemon trees in Syracuse, forming a wave of pale yellow covering the hillside from the ancient Greek theater on the summit down to the vividly blue sea. Or he may have seen the neatly pruned lemon trees in rows of terra cotta pots in Tuscan gardens, pots that were brought inside in the winter to special buildings called *limonaie*, built just for that purpose.

The modern visitor to Sicily and southern Italy in February and March may also experience the snowy whiteness of the almond trees in bloom or eat the uniquely flavored Sicilian blood-red oranges called *tarocchi*. But the full outpouring of the Italian spring is heralded by the arrival of the first cherries. They are available from local orchards in much of the peninsula. The bitter cherries *amarene* and *visciole* come later, as do the speckled Queen Anne cherries. *Amarene* are used in the famous syrup containing whole cherries as well as in pastries. A Renaissance cherry soup was also made with this type.

Preceding overleaf: "The Hall of the Seasons" in the Ducal Palace in Mantua has trompe l'oeil marble, stuccoes, and niches containing ancient Roman statuary. The three types of cake are, from top to bottom: Sbriciolona, a crumbly almond pastry; Torta di amaretti e mele, a torte with bitter almond cookies and apples; and a sweet torte of pasta.

Opposite, clockwise from top left: Prickly pears from southern Italy; young lemons; a low relief stone carving depicting a fruit harvest in Lecce; cold watermelon; fichi e noci (dried figs and walnuts); and wild berries from the woods.

Above: Piazza San Marco as seen from Caffè Florian in Venice. Ice cream and ices have been favorites at cafés in Italy almost from the time cafés were first established in the seventeenth century.

Top: The combination of fruits served in southern Italy is especially fascinating, where the custom of including raw fennel, celery, and several other vegetables as part of the fruit course is still practiced. Above: The same sweet, pure water that nourishes the fruits and vegetables in Puglia is also available for drinking from communal fountains.

Opposite: Marinated pomegranates rest on a stone well in front of the side arcade of the Church of San Nicola in Bari.

A bit later in the spring, the first bounty of the woods—wild strawberries—appear in large numbers in the markets. By July there is the explosion of raspberries, currants, peaches, apricots, many kinds of plums, melons, the first eating grapes from the South, blueberries, and cultivated strawberries. In August the hot weather brings *Claudie*, sweet greenish-yellow plums, and blackberries. In the fall the mandarin orange comes, just in time for Christmas.

Pomegranates were eaten in biblical times, and their many fruit-covered seeds were long a symbol of fecundity. The juice extracted from the fruit was once extremely popular for cooking, especially in the Middle Ages. A type of dwarf pomegranate tree, whose fruit is not eaten, is among the most common backgrounds in Renaissance painting, often seen through the windows in subjects such as Last Suppers.

In Puglia the smooth, sensual pomegranate fruit are called *sete* (silk). The fruit-covered seeds, when marinated in lemon juice and liqueur, make a beautiful and very popular dessert.

"Sete" al liquore
MARINATED POMEGRANATES

3	medium-sized pomegranates	6	tablespoons granulated sugar
1	lemon	6	tablespoons lemon or orange liqueur or brandy

Remove the skin from the pomegranates and free the seeds. Put the seeds in a glass or crockery bowl. Squeeze the lemon and add the lemon juice, sugar, and liqueur to the bowl with the pomegranate seeds. Mix gently but thoroughly, cover the bowl, and refrigerate for at least 1 hour before serving.

The marinated pomegranate seeds may be served as is or on top of whipped cream or vanilla ice cream.

SERVES 6 TO 8.

The most versatile fruit for cooked desserts is pears. There are many different kinds and one type or another is available for almost the entire year. Earliest are the small green June pears, now quite rare, and these are the ones traditionally paired with cheese. From June until November different types appear, the final October-November ones lasting through the winter.

Cooked pears combine well with a variety of flavors, such as wine syrups, vanilla, chocolate, and caramelized sugar. In the first dish, the cored pears are poached, then stuffed with a chocolate cream, and finally glazed with their own reduced syrup and served with a chocolate sauce. This treatment is a good example of an Italian dessert that combines an unusual combination of tastes, which become well integrated in the finished dish.

In the second preparation, poached pears are stuffed with *mascarpone*, creating what must surely be the apotheosis of the classic pear-with-cheese dessert.

Pere ripiene al cioccolato
PEARS STUFFED WITH CREAM AND CHOCOLATE

6 large Bosc pears, ripe but not overripe

   Juice of 1 lemon

3 cups dry white wine

1 piece lemon peel (about 2 inches long)

   Juice of 3 oranges

2 whole cloves

1 cup granulated sugar

Peel the pears, leaving the stems on. Slice off the bottom of each pear so they can stand on the flat end. With a paring knife, cut all around the core and seeds from the bottom end of each pear. Be careful not to disturb the top with the stem, and leave the pears whole.

Fill the cavity of each pear with aluminum foil. Stand the pears in a small saucepan and pour in the lemon juice, white wine, and enough water to cover the fruit up to the stems. Add the lemon peel, orange juice, cloves, and sugar to the pan. Put the pan over medium heat and bring it to a simmer. Then lower the heat and simmer, covered, until the pears are cooked but still retain their shape (about 20 minutes, depending on the ripeness of the pears).

Individual servings of Pere ripiene al cioccolato *(Pears Stuffed with Cream and Chocolate).*

The syrup is poured over the poached pears just before they are surrounded with chocolate sauce.

Transfer the pears to a serving dish so that they are standing up. Cover the dish with aluminum foil and let stand until the pears are cool.

Remove the lemon peel and cloves from the poaching liquid and reduce it over low heat until a very thick syrup is formed (about 1½ hours). Then transfer the syrup to a crockery or glass bowl to cool completely.

Prepare the stuffing for the pears: Blanch the pistachio nuts in salted boiling water. Then drain the nuts and coarsely chop them.

Put the butter, cocoa powder, granulated sugar, and water in a small saucepan. Holding the pan at the edge of the burner, stir with a wooden spoon until all the ingredients are amalgamated. Simmer for about 10 minutes, by which time a cocoa syrup will have formed. Remove from the heat and let stand until cool.

Prepare the sauce: Melt the chocolate with the sugar and water in a small saucepan over low heat. Stir very well until the chocolate is completely melted and the sugar is dissolved (5 or 6 minutes). Then add the brandy and heavy cream and stir very well with a wooden spoon. Transfer the chocolate sauce to a wine bottle and refrigerate for about 1 hour.

Whip the heavy cream with the confectioners' sugar using a chilled metal bowl and a wire whisk until stiff. Refrigerate the whipped cream until needed.

When the pears and syrups are cool, remove the whipped cream from the refrigerator and add the cooled cocoa syrup and chopped pistachio nuts to it mixing very well.

Carefully remove the aluminum foil from the cavity of each pear and fill each cavity with the whipped cream mixture. Stand the pears on a serving platter lined with a piece of wax paper and refrigerate for at least ½ hour.

When the pears are ready, use a spatula to transfer them to individual plates. Brush them with the cooled wine syrup, pour the chocolate sauce around the pears, and serve.

SERVES 6.

FOR THE STUFFING

4 or 5 unsalted shelled fresh pistachio nuts for cooking

Coarse-grained salt

4 tablespoons (2 ounces) sweet butter

1 heaping tablespoon unsweetened cocoa powder

4 tablespoons granulated sugar

3 tablespoons cold water

½ cup heavy cream

1 tablespoon confectioners' sugar

FOR THE *SALSA AL CIOCCOLATO*

2 ounces baker's chocolate, cut into small pieces

4 tablespoons cold water

½ cup granulated sugar

4 tablespoons brandy

½ cup heavy cream

Pere al mascarpone
POACHED PEARS STUFFED WITH MASCARPONE

8 large pears, preferably Comice, ripe but not overripe

4 cups dry white wine

4 tablespoons granulated sugar

1 whole clove

FOR THE STUFFING

8 heaping tablespoons *mascarpone*

4 tablespoons granulated sugar

2 tablespoons confectioners' sugar

2 tablespoons brandy

2 amaretti cookies, coarsely crumbled

FOR THE SAUCE

8 extra large egg yolks

4 tablespoons granulated sugar

Wash the pears carefully and pat them dry with paper towels. Put the pears in a casserole and add the wine, sugar, and clove. Add enough cold water to completely cover the fruit. Cover the casserole, put it over medium heat, and simmer until the pears are cooked but still firm (about 20 minutes, depending on the ripeness of the pears). Transfer the pears to a platter and let them cool completely (about 1 hour).

Meanwhile, reduce the wine mixture to 2 cups over medium heat.

Prepare the stuffing: Put the *mascarpone* in a small bowl and mix in the granulated sugar, confectioners' sugar, and brandy. Refrigerate the bowl until needed.

When the wine mixture is reduced, remove the pan from the heat and pass the mixture through a piece of heavy cheesecloth into a crockery or glass bowl.

Prepare the sauce: Bring some water to a boil in the bottom of a double boiler. Put the egg yolks into a crockery or glass bowl and add the sugar. Stir with a wooden spoon, always in the same direction, until the sugar is completely incorporated and the egg yolks turn a lighter color. Then add the still-warm poaching wine from the pears and mix very well. Immediately transfer the contents of the bowl to the top part of the double boiler and insert it over the boiling water. Stir constantly with a wooden spoon, always in the same direction. Just before it boils, the sauce should be thick enough to coat the wooden spoon. Absolutely do not allow the sauce to boil.

Remove the top part of the double boiler from the heat and stir the contents for 1 minute longer; then transfer the sauce to a crockery or glass bowl and let it cool for 15 minutes. Pour the sauce into an empty wine bottle, cork it, and refrigerate the sauce for at least 1 hour.

Remove the cores of the pears from the bottom, using a paring knife and a small spoon. Fill a pastry bag with the prepared *mascarpone* filling and stuff the cavities of the pears with the filling. Put the stuffed pears on a large serving dish if they are to be served without sauce or whipped cream.

If the pears are to be served with the sauce, prepare individual servings by first distributing some of the sauce on individual plates and then placing a pear, cut into halves vertically, over it. Sprinkle the amaretti crumbs over the stuffing inside the pears.

If the pears are to be served with whipped cream, beat 2 cups of heavy cream until stiff in a chilled metal bowl with a wire whisk, adding in 4 tablespoons of granulated sugar and 2 tablespoons of confectioners' sugar. Arrange the whipped cream around the pears and sprinkle them with some coarsely crumbled amaretti cookie crumbs.

SERVES 8.

*D*uring the peach season, typical pastry displays in gourmet shops such as Il Salumaio in Milan feature the uncooked peach in all its freshness filled with a rich chocolate cream. Both chocolate and cream are often used to enhance the flavor of fresh fruits, but the unique feature of this dish is that the peach is uncooked.

Opposite and below: Poached Pears Stuffed with Mascarpone appear in the Teatro Farnese (1619) of the Palazzo della Pilotta, the royal palace in Parma. Famous for its remarkable movable stage made entirely of wood, the Teatro Farnese was designed by Giovanni Battista Aleotti, who based his plans on Palladio's Olympic Theatre in Vicenza.

Pesche ripiene
STUFFED FRESH PEACHES

8   large freestone peaches, ripe but not overripe

1   cup dry white wine

2   tablespoons brandy

FOR THE STUFFING

4   ounces bittersweet chocolate

2   tablespoons (1 ounce) sweet butter at room temperature

2   extra large egg yolks

1   tablespoon brandy

½   teaspoon peach extract

1   cup heavy cream

1   tablespoon confectioners' sugar

2   heaping tablespoons granulated sugar

PLUS

8   large amaretti cookies

Wash the peaches carefully and, leaving them whole, put them into a crockery or glass bowl with the wine, brandy, and enough cold water to cover them completely. Marinate for 1 hour.

Prepare the stuffing: Put the bottom part of a double boiler filled with some water over medium heat until the water reaches a boil.

Meanwhile, cut the chocolate into small pieces and put them in a metal bowl. When the water in the double boiler reaches a boil, lower the heat to very low and set the metal bowl over the pan to melt the chocolate. Mix with a wooden spoon and, when the chocolate is completely melted, add the butter and stir very well until all the butter is amalgamated with the chocolate. Remove the bowl from the heat and keep stirring while the chocolate cools for about 2 minutes. Add the egg yolks, stirring with a wooden spoon, always in the same direction, until the yolks are incorporated and the chocolate is smooth and almost whipped. Add the brandy and peach extract and stir well again.

Whip the cream with the confectioners' sugar and granulated sugar, using a chilled metal bowl and wire whisk. Then gently fold the whipped cream into the chocolate. Put the bowl in the refrigerator until needed.

Pesche ripiene (*Stuffed Fresh Peaches*), *topped with amaretti cookies.*

Remove the peaches from the marinade and pat them dry with paper towels. Cut off the top ½ inch of each peach and make the bottom level so that they will stand up.

Insert a long, thin knife through the center of the fruit, but only as far down as the bottom of the pit. Cut in a circular motion around the pit, loosening the pit itself and removing it with the bit of flesh attached above it, thereby making a cavity for the stuffing.

The peaches may be stuffed up to 2 hours before they are served. Use a pastry bag with a plain round tip to fill the cavities of the peaches with the prepared stuffing. Let the cream rise a little way above the top of the peach. Place an amaretto cookie on top of the stuffing in each peach. Arrange the peaches on a serving dish and refrigerate until needed.

SERVES 8.

MOLDED DESSERTS

Italians like the aesthetic shapes of molded desserts, even serving their soufflés out of the mold, neatly sliced. Molded custard and cream desserts are popular in restaurants as well as at home.

The molded cream dessert *Panna cotta* is a favorite in the Piedmont area. Half of the heavy cream is heated with the gelatin and, when cool, the other half in the form of whipped cream is folded in. In Italy, whipped cream is always sweetened with both granulated and confectioners' sugar, providing a more interesting taste.

Luscious Panna cotta *is richer than custard and elegantly creamy.*

Panna cotta
"COOKED CREAM" MOLDS

Heat 2 cups of the heavy cream with the 4 ounces of confectioners' sugar, the vanilla bean, and the lemon peel in a heavy casserole over medium heat.

Meanwhile, put the gelatin in a small bowl and pour the cold milk over it to soften the gelatin.

When the cream reaches a boil, remove the casserole from the heat and discard the vanilla bean and lemon peel. Add the rum and the softened gelatin. Mix very well with a wooden spoon to be sure that the gelatin is completely dissolved and no grains remain. Transfer the contents of the casserole to a large bowl to cool completely (1 hour).

Lightly butter twelve ½-cup *baba* molds.

In a small saucepan, preferably of unlined copper or enamel, heat 1 cup of the granulated sugar and the water over medium heat. Keep mixing with a wooden spoon until the sugar is completely dissolved. When the mixture starts to bubble, add the lemon juice and lower the heat, allowing the thick syrup to melt into a thinner one. When the syrup turns a light brown color, remove the pan from the heat and immediately distribute the caramelized sugar among the *baba* molds. Let the sugar in the molds cool.

Using a chilled metal bowl and a wire whisk, whip the remaining heavy cream with the remaining teaspoon of confectioners' sugar and the remaining tablespoon of granulated sugar, until stiff. Fold it gently into the cooled cooked cream. Ladle the mixture into the prepared molds, tap them on the counter to even them out, and refrigerate for at least 2 hours

Remove the molds from the refrigerator and unmold onto individual dishes. Serve immediately.

SERVES 12.

1	quart heavy cream
4	ounces plus 1 teaspoon confectioners' sugar
1	piece vanilla bean (about 2 inches long)
1	piece lemon peel
2	packages (2 tablespoons) unflavored gelatin
8	tablespoons cold milk
6	tablespoons light rum
1	cup plus 1 tablespoon granulated sugar
½	cup cold water
1	teaspoon freshly squeezed lemon juice

281

*I*ce cream molds may be quite elaborate, but often freshly made ice cream is simply served with a liqueur, as in this preparation. The liqueur is *nocino,* which I make from the unripe green walnuts growing in the Casentino area where the great painter Giotto grew up.

According to folklore, the green walnuts must be picked on only one special day of the year, always falling toward the middle of May, which is determined by the moon or, in some localities, by a particular saint's day. Taking no chances that my *nocino* will not be a good one, I always follow this advice and pick my walnuts toward the middle of May.

Sometimes *nocino* is served together with macerated walnuts as a dessert. The unripe walnuts have a green covering over the shell that opens and falls off when the nuts ripen. This layer, called *mallo,* is edible when the unripe nuts are macerated.

Gelato di crema con nocino
"CREAM-FLAVORED" ICE CREAM WITH GREEN WALNUT LIQUEUR

FOR THE *NOCINO*

3 pounds fresh green walnuts

2 quarts pure grain alcohol or unflavored vodka

1 whole clove

1 small cinnamon stick (about 1 inch long)

1½ quarts dry red wine

4 cups granulated sugar

FOR THE CUSTARD CREAM

3 extra large egg yolks

7 tablespoons granulated sugar

½ cup cold milk

FOR THE *GELATO*

1 tablespoon confectioners' sugar

2 cups heavy cream

¼ cup milk

2 pounds rocksalt for the ice-cream maker

Prepare the liqueur at least 2½ months before using it.

Wash the walnuts carefully and pat them dry with paper towels. Put the nuts in a large mason jar and pour in the alcohol. Add the clove and cinnamon. Close the jar tightly and let it stand in a dark place for 2 months.

After this time, prepare a syrup to mix with the contents of the jar: Heat the red wine with the sugar in a small saucepan over medium heat. Stir very well and simmer until it reduces to a light syrup (about 1 hour). The liquid should be reduced to half its original volume. Remove from the heat and let stand until cool.

Combine the cooled wine syrup with the contents of the jar in a large bowl. Mix very well and then drain everything through a colander into a second bowl, pressing the walnut rinds against the side of the colander.

Line a second colander with several layers of paper towels or with a coffee filter and pass the contents of the bowl into 1 or 2 bottles. Cork the bottles and let them stand for 15 days before serving.

Prepare the custard cream: Bring some water to a boil in the bottom of a double boiler.

Put the egg yolks into a crockery or glass bowl and add the sugar. Stir with a wooden spoon, always in the same direction, until the sugar is completely incorporated and the egg yolks turn a lighter color.

Meanwhile, heat the milk in a small saucepan over low heat and, when the milk is lukewarm, add it to the egg yolks. Stir very well; then transfer the contents of the bowl to the top part of the double boiler and insert it over the boiling water. Stir constantly with a wooden spoon. Just before it boils, the *crema* should be thick enough to coat the wooden spoon. Absolutely do not allow the *crema* to boil. Immediately remove the top part of the double boiler from the heat and stir the contents for 1 minute longer. Then transfer the sauce to a crockery or glass bowl to cool completely (about ½ hour).

Transfer the cooled *crema* to a larger bowl. Add the confectioners' sugar, cream, and milk and mix very well. Then transfer the contents of the bowl to the insert of an ice-cream maker. Run the machine for 45 minutes for the older, classical type of machine with a motor, or for 20 minutes for the newer type of ice-cream maker that does not use salt.

Remove the ice cream from the insert to a tin mold, being careful to pack the ice cream down very well. Close the mold and place it in the freezer for at least 1 hour before unmolding onto a serving dish.

Pour some of the walnut liqueur over the ice cream and serve immediately.

SERVES 8.

Left: Nocino (*Green Walnut Liqueur*) *is poured over the ice-cream mold. A walnut tree is in the background.*

Overleaf: An immense "courtyard" of almonds dries in front of a mas-seria, or villa, in Puglia. The almond trees blossom in February and March and the nuts are harvested in October, when they are spread out to dry in the sun. The almond shells are removed one by one with a hammer by the elderly people of the village. Since nothing is wasted in small-scale agriculture, the almond shells are gathered into small balls, held together with soaked leftover paper, dried in the sun, and later used as kindling for the fire, where they give off a pleasant almond perfume.

*A*nother popular molded dessert is the light, *budino*-like Genoese Chocolate Torte. (A *budino* is closer to a soufflé than to a pudding.) Aside from the chocolate flavoring, the most significant part of the dessert is the special "cooked" *zabaione* made with the addition of caramelized sugar, the taste of which blends so well with that of the Marsala in the *zabaione*.

Torta al cioccolato alla genovese con zabaione "cotto"
GENOESE CHOCOLATE TORTE WITH "COOKED" ZABAIONE

4   heaping tablespoons unsweetened cocoa powder

4   heaping tablespoons granulated sugar

2⅓ cups cold milk

6   tablespoons (3 ounces) sweet butter

½   cup unbleached all-purpose flour

½   cup finely crushed amaretti cookies

3   extra large eggs

1   tablespoon confectioners' sugar

½   cup dry Marsala wine

FOR THE *ZABAIONE "COTTO"*

5   extra large egg yolks

Put the cocoa powder and the granulated sugar in a small bowl. Add ⅓ cup of the milk and mix very well with a wooden spoon, until the cocoa powder and sugar are dissolved. Let stand until needed.

Melt the butter in a heavy saucepan over low heat. When the butter reaches the frothing point, add the flour all at once. Mix very well with a wooden spoon and cook until the flour is completely incorporated (about 2 minutes). Remove the pan from the heat and let stand for 15 minutes.

While the butter-flour mixture is standing, heat the remaining milk in another pan until it is very close to the boiling point.

Put the saucepan with the flour-butter mixture over low heat and add the hot milk all at once. Stir over low heat until the sauce is smooth. When the sauce reaches a boil, add the milk with the cocoa powder and sugar and continue to stir gently while the sauce cooks for about 10 minutes longer. Remove the pan from the heat and transfer the sauce to a crockery or glass bowl, pressing a piece of buttered wax paper down over the sauce to prevent a skin from forming. Let the sauce cool completely (about 1 hour).

Butter a nonstick loaf pan and preheat the oven to 375 degrees. Make a *bagnomaria* for the mold by half-filling a large overproof baking pan with lukewarm water.

Add the amaretti, eggs, confectioners' sugar, and ¼ cup of the Marsala to the cooled sauce and mix very well with a wooden spoon until all the ingredients are well amalgamated. Pour the contents of the bowl into the prepared loaf pan and put the loaf pan in the *bagnomaria*. Bake for 1 hour and 40 minutes, placing a piece of aluminum foil over the loaf pan

Torta al cioccolato alla genovese con zabaione "cotto" *nearly floats in* zabaione *and whipped cream sauce.*

after 1 hour. Remove the pan from the oven and cool completely before unmolding onto a serving platter (about 1 hour).

Prepare the *zabaione "cotto"*: Bring some water to a boil in the bottom of a double boiler.

Put the egg yolks in a crockery or glass bowl and add 3 tablespoons of the sugar. Stir with a wooden spoon, always in the same direction, until the sugar is completely incorporated and the egg yolks turn a lighter color. Then add the Marsala and mix very well. Transfer the contents of the bowl to the top part of a double boiler.

Put the remaining 4 tablespoons of the sugar and the water in a small saucepan, preferably of unlined copper, over medium heat and, when the sugar is completely dissolved and the water starts boiling, add the lemon juice and cook until the sugar turns light golden brown. At that moment, insert the top part of the double boiler over the boiling water in the bottom part of the double boiler and stir continuously with a wooden spoon. When the sugar has turned golden brown, pour it into the mixture in the top of the double boiler and cook, stirring constantly, until the *zabaione* coats the spoon. That is the moment it is ready. Absolutely do not allow the sauce to boil. Immediately remove the top part of the double boiler from the heat and stir the contents for 2 minutes longer.

Transfer the *zabaione* to a crockery or glass bowl to cool (about ½ hour). Cover the bowl with aluminum foil and refrigerate until completely cool.

Slowly pour the remaining Marsala over the cooled torte and let the wine be completely absorbed. Then unmold the torte onto a large platter.

Using a chilled metal bowl and a wire whisk, whip the cream, adding the granulated sugar and confectioners' sugar. Then whisk in the cooled *zabaione*. Arrange the *zabaione "cotto"* all around and on top of the torte and serve.

SERVES 8.

Sformato di arancia, Orange *Sformato*, is a molded pastry that survives from pre-Renaissance times. No flour or shortening is used in the pastry itself, only ground walnuts and almonds and oranges. Whipped cream is generally served on top today, but otherwise the recipe is unchanged.

7	tablespoons granulated sugar
¾	cup dry Marsala wine
¼	cup cold water
1	teaspoon lemon juice

PLUS

1	cup heavy cream
2	tablespoons granulated sugar
1	teaspoon confectioners' sugar

Sformato di arancia is centered on a circle of thin orange slices.

Sformato di arancia
ORANGE SFORMATO

3   large oranges

1   teaspoon coarse-grained salt

5   cups cold water

1   cup blanched almonds

¼   cup shelled walnuts

6   extra large eggs, separated

1   cup granulated sugar

1   teaspoon orange extract

FOR THE SYRUP

1   cup cold water

½   cup granulated sugar

1   teaspoon freshly squeezed lemon juice

PLUS

10   ounces blanched and toasted almonds

¾   cup heavy cream

2   tablespoons granulated sugar

1   teaspoon confectioners' sugar

¼   cup light rum

    Peel of 1 orange, white part removed, cut into thin strips

Put the whole oranges in a bowl of cold water with the salt, and let them soak for 1 hour. Wash the oranges carefully; then put them in a small saucepan with the 5 cups of cold water. The oranges should be covered completely by the water. Put the pan over medium heat and, when the water reaches a boil, cover the pan and cook for 45 minutes.

Drain the oranges and cool them under cold running water. Then put the oranges in a bowl, cut them into quarters, and remove the seeds if there are any. Transfer the orange quarters and any juice in the bowl to a blender or food processor and finely grind them. Transfer the ground oranges to a large crockery or glass bowl and let them stand until needed.

Finely chop the almonds and walnuts together on a board and add them to the ground oranges.

Put the egg yolks and sugar in a crockery or glass bowl and stir very well with a wooden spoon, always in the same direction, until the sugar is completely incorporated and the egg yolks turn a lighter color. Then add the orange extract and mix very well.

Preheat the oven to 400 degrees. Butter and lightly flour a 4-inch high, 8½-inch diameter (2-quart) soufflé dish.

Put the egg whites in a copper bowl and beat them until stiff with a wire whisk.

Pour the egg yolk mixture into the bowl with the oranges and nuts and mix very well with a wooden spoon, until all the ingredients are well amalgamated. Gently fold in the beaten egg whites, always in a rotating motion. Transfer the contents of the bowl to the prepared dish and bake for 65 minutes.

Remove from the oven, transfer the dish to a rack and let it stand until the cake is cool (about 1 hour).

Make the syrup: Put the cup of water and the sugar in a small saucepan. Put the pan over medium heat until the water reaches a boil; then add the lemon juice and simmer until a fairly thick syrup is formed (about 15 minutes).

Meanwhile, line a cake stand with parchment paper or wax paper; then unmold the cake onto it.

Coarsely chop the toasted almonds on a board.

Using a chilled metal bowl and a wire whisk, whip the cream until stiff, adding the granulated sugar and the confectioners' sugar.

When the syrup is ready, use a brush to moisten the sides of the cake all around with the syrup, and cover the sides of the cake with the toasted almonds. Let the cake stand for 5 minutes so the almonds become attached to the cake; then transfer the cake to a serving platter and pour the rum over it. Arrange the whipped cream on top of the cake and the orange strips on top.

SERVES 6 TO 8.

CAFÉS AND PASTRY SHOPS

The institution of the café was brought to Italy, specifically to Venice, in the seventeenth century from Cairo and Constantinople, where the inhabitants drank the "black water" to keep alert. Coffee itself arrived in Italy in 1640 as a medicine and was sold in pharmacies; by 1683, when the first café opened, coffee-drinking had already become a pastime.

Cafés immediately became important as the places for secret meetings of lovers and of revolutionaries, and open encounters

Opposite: Caffè Antico del Moro in Florence with its gleaming turn-of-the-century espresso machine, top; and bottom, coffee and pastries for patrons who will help themselves while standing at the marble counter.

Top: Each cup of espresso is made individually. The creamy foam on top, called crema di caffè, *contains the concentrated essence of the flavor.*

Above: An old iron hand-turned coffee roaster. The green coffee beans were placed inside the roller while burning charcoals rested on the bottom. The roller had to be continuously turned for the beans to be properly roasted.

of artists and of socialites. Since an invitation to a home in Italy has never been a casual matter, it was more convenient to invite acquaintances to meet in a café, and often a man would be "at home" at his favorite café during certain hours.

The eighteenth-century café became a locus of witty, stimulating discussion as well as the place to enjoy the new institution of the newspaper. For two centuries it was possible to go into any café to read all the current newspapers, each attached to its long stick. Unfortunately, this practice survives in only a few places today.

By the nineteenth century, it was common to find political issues being discussed and argued in cafés. Caffè Michelangelo in Florence, Caffè Pedrocchi in Padua, and Caffè Greco in Rome (the last two still exist) became important centers for partisans of the *Risorgimento,* the movement for the unification of Italy, as well as for the arts.

The café was still a central institution at the turn of the century. Caffè Giubbe Rosse and Caffè Il Bottegone were the artistic and intellectual meeting places in Florence, and welcomed patrons such as D'Annunzio, the *Macchiaioli* painters, the Futurists, and the artists and art historians of the pre-Raphaelite movement.

Until very recently, several Florentine cafés were still resplendent with their art-nouveau designs and frescoes. While some have been turned into fast food outlets or have been closed, two, Rivoire and Gilli, have recently been very well restored. One other small jewel of a café remains—the Antico Caffè del Moro, also known as "Cafè des Artistes"—in the narrow street Via del Moro.

A few years ago I used to enjoy going to watch the survivors of the last great café generation still holding court at their favorite places. The painter Rosai met the other painters every day at 5 P.M., while youngsters from the art academy watched from a respectful distance and art dealers came by to get a good deal on a painting in a moment of relaxation for the artist. Palazzeschi, Sem Benelli, and other writers of the generation born in the 1880s and 1890s, then in their eighties, were still very observant and argued unsentimentally.

Coffee is the focal point of the café, but other specialties include pastries and elegant little sandwiches, such as the ones made with truffle paste. It is here rather than in the restaurants that one finds a wide range of pastries. Of the many possibilities, tartlets with fresh fruit, which are prepared throughout Italy and according to what is in season, are among the most popular pastries.

Crostatine di frutta fresca
FRESH FRUIT TARTLETS

Sift the 12 ounces of flour onto a pastry board and arrange it in a mound. Cut the butter into pieces and lay them over the mound. Let stand for ½ hour, or until the butter softens.

Start mixing the butter into the flour with your fingers, until all of it is incorporated into the flour.

Make a well and put in the grated orange rind, sugar, rum, and salt. Mix together all the ingredients in the well with a fork; then start adding the flour-butter mixture a little at a time. When all of the ingredients have been incorporated, start forming a ball of dough, using your hands. Knead gently until all the ingredients are well amalgamated. Wrap the dough in a dampened cotton dish towel and let it rest in a cool place or on the bottom shelf of the refrigerator for 1 hour.

Meanwhile, prepare the pastry cream with the ingredients and quantities listed above, following the technique for preparing *zabaione "cotto"* on page 287. (For further details, see *Giuliano Bugialli's Classic Techniques of Italian Cooking*, pages 489–491). Let the cream stand until needed.

When the dough is ready, heavily flour a pastry board with the remaining 4 tablespoons of flour. Unwrap the dough and knead it for 1 minute, absorbing some of the flour.

Lightly butter twelve 4-inch-diameter molds with removable bottoms.

Using a rolling pin, roll out the dough into a large sheet, about ⅛ inch thick. Cut the dough into 12 pieces, then gently line each individual mold with its piece. Fit the dough onto the bottom and sides of each mold and press it down. Then move the rolling pin over the top to cut off the overhanging pastry. Use a fork to make several punctures in each pastry.

Cut aluminum foil into pieces that fit into each mold. Fit the foil pieces over each mold and put weights or dried beans on the foil to keep the shells from rising while they bake. Put the molds on a baking sheet and refrigerate for 15 minutes.

Preheat the oven to 375 degrees.

Bake the molds for 25 minutes; then remove them from the oven and lift out the weighted foil from each mold. Return the molds to the oven and bake for 10 minutes longer. Then remove and place the tarts on a rack to cool completely (about ½ hour).

Meanwhile, prepare the fruit: If using larger fruit, such as pears, apricots, peaches, or figs, cut the fruit into 1-inch pieces. Remove the stems from the berries if you are using them, but leave them whole. Put the fruit in a bowl and squeeze the juice of the lemon over it to keep it from darkening.

Prepare the glaze: Put the 4 ounces of confectioners' sugar, the water, and the rum into a small saucepan. Stir very well with a wooden spoon to incorporate all of the ingredients; then put the pan over low heat, stirring constantly until the glaze is slighty warm. Remove from the heat and keep stirring for 30 seconds longer. The glaze is now ready to be used.

When the shells are ready, use a sifter to sprinkle them with the additional confectioners' sugar. Spoon some of the prepared pastry cream into the individual molds; then place the fruit over the cream and brush it with the prepared glaze. The *crostatine* may be eaten immediately or kept for later use.

SERVES 12.

FOR THE CRUST

12 ounces plus 4 tablespoons unbleached all-purpose flour

6 ounces sweet butter

Grated rind of 1 orange

6 tablespoons granulated sugar

8 tablespoons light rum

Pinch of salt

FOR THE PASTRY CREAM

3 extra large egg yolks

4 tablespoons granulated sugar

1½ cups heavy cream

1 small piece vanilla bean

THE FRUIT

Fresh whole strawberries, raspberries, blackberries, pears, apricots, peaches, figs, etc.

1 lemon

FOR THE GLAZE

4 ounces confectioners' sugar

3 tablespoons cold water

1 tablespoon light rum

PLUS

4 teaspoons confectioners' sugar

*T*he thin wafers, *cialdoni*, were such a favorite of Lorenzo the Magnificent in the fifteenth century that he wrote a poem about them:

Giovani siam maestri molto buoni
Donne, com'udirete a far cialdoni

Ladies, we are young masters, as you shall hear,
Of the art of making *cialdoni*

Cialdoni are still very popular in Florence, where they are eaten with whipped cream. Most *cialdoni* are now made commercially with large machines, and the home *cialdoni* iron is becoming increasingly hard to find. The iron used for making the Norwegian Christmas wafer *krumkake* may still be found and works well for making *cialdoni*, using the traditional Florentine batter. (This iron may be obtained directly from the Norwegian manufacturer, Jøtul, or from H. Roth, 1577 First Avenue, New York, New York 10028.)

Cialdoni con panna
ROLLED FLORENTINE WAFERS WITH WHIPPED CREAM

Paper-thin, ultra-light wafers called cialdoni *are used to scoop up freshly made whipped cream.*

FOR THE *CIALDONI*

3 ounces lard

3 ounces granulated sugar

8 tablespoons cold water

¾ cup unbleached all-purpose flour

Pinch of salt

1 tablespoon sweet butter

FOR THE WHIPPED CREAM

2 cups heavy cream

4 tablespoons granulated sugar

2 teaspoons confectioners' sugar

Prepare the *cialdoni:* Bring some water to a boil in the bottom of a double boiler. Put the lard, sugar, and cold water in the top part of the double boiler and insert it over the boiling water. Stir with a wooden spoon until the sugar is completely dissolved and the lard melted and integrated with the other ingredients. Remove the top of the double boiler from the heat and keep stirring for 1 minute longer.

Put the flour in a crockery or glass bowl and make a well in it. Add the salt and then start pouring the contents of the top of the double boiler into the well. Add a small quantity at a time and mix very well with a wooden spoon, incorporating flour from the rim of the well. Keep mixing, until all the flour is incorporated. At that point a quite loose batter should have formed.

Use a Norwegian *krumkake* iron (see introduction) to make the wafers. Put the iron over medium heat and, when it is hot, open it over a metal bowl. Butter the iron lightly and put about 1½ tablespoons of the batter in the bottom part. Close the iron and use a knife to remove the batter dripping around the sides. Put the iron on the heat and cook for about 40 seconds on each side. Remove from the heat, open the iron, and use a paring knife to detach the first *cialdone*, which, while still soft, resembles a paper-thin pancake or waffle. Immediately roll it up into the shape of a large cigar and place it on paper towels to stand until cool (about 15 minutes). Repeat the procedure until all the *cialdoni* (about 12) are prepared. Remember to butter the iron lightly each time. When the *cialdoni* are cool, transfer them to a basket.

When the *cialdoni* are ready to be served, use a chilled metal bowl and a wire whisk to whip the cream with the granulated sugar and the confectioners' sugar until stiff. Prepare each serving by placing some of the whipped cream in a glass cup and standing 2 *cialdoni* up in the cream.

SERVES 6.

*I*n *Torta al Marsala con fragole*, Marsala wine is the principal flavoring, appearing not only in the *zabaione* filling, but also in the crust itself. Various types of fortified wine or alcohol are commonly used in Italian crusts, in order to make them crisp and flaky and to help them retain their crispiness if they are to last a day or so after baking (though before filling). The particular spirit used in the crust varies according to the filling employed for the tart.

Torta al Marsala con fragole *is richly flavored with Marsala wine in both the crust and in the* zabaione *filling.*

293

Torta al Marsala con fragole
MARSALA TART WITH STRAWBERRIES

FOR THE CRUST

4   ounces plus 2 tablespoons
    unbleached all-purpose flour

2   ounces sweet butter

4   tablespoons dry Marsala wine

    Pinch of salt

FOR THE *ZABAIONE* FILLING

5   extra large egg yolks

5   tablespoons granulated sugar

¼   cup light rum

¼   cup dry Marsala wine

PLUS

1   pint heavy cream

2   heaping tablespoons
    granulated sugar

1   teaspoon confectioners' sugar

2   pints strawberries, hulled

Prepare the crust: Sift the flour onto a pastry board and arrange it in a mound. Cut the butter into pieces and lay them over the mound. Let the butter stand for ½ hour to soften. When ready, start mixing the butter into the flour with your fingers. Then rub the flour and butter between your palms until they are well amalgamated.

Make a well in the butter-flour mixture and put the Marsala and salt into the well. Start mixing with a fork, pushing the butter-flour mixture from the rim of the well, until all the Marsala is incorporated. Remove the paste that has stuck to the fork and begin to form a ball with your hands. Knead gently until a very smooth and elastic ball of dough is formed (2 minutes). Dampen a cotton dish towel and wrap the ball of dough in it. Let rest in a cool place for 1 hour.

Butter a 9½-inch tart pan with a removable bottom.

Dust a pastry board with a little flour. Unwrap the dough and knead it for a few seconds. Then, using a rolling pin, roll out the dough into a round sheet about 16 inches in diameter. Then roll up the layer of dough onto the rolling pin and unroll it over the buttered pan. Gently press the layer of dough down onto the bottom of the pan. Cut off the overhanging pastry by moving the rolling pin over the pan. Use a fork to make several punctures in the pastry to keep it from puffing up. Fit a sheet of aluminum foil loosely over the pastry and put weights or dried beans on the foil to keep the shell from rising while it bakes. Cut off the excess aluminum foil all around. Refrigerate the prepared pastry for 15 minutes.

Preheat the oven to 375 degrees. Bake the pastry for 30 minutes. Remove it from the oven, lift out the foil containing the beans, and return the shell to the oven for 10 minutes longer. Remove from the oven and let the crust cool in the pan for 1 hour.

Prepare the *zabaione* with the ingredients and quantities listed above, following the directions on page 287. Transfer the *zabaione* to a crockery or glass bowl and let stand until cool; then cover and refrigerate until cold (about ½ hour).

Pour the cold *zabaione* into the cooled pastry shell and spread it out evenly. Place the shell in a 375-degree oven for 5 minutes. Remove the shell from the oven and transfer it to a rack. Let stand until completely cool (½ hour).

Using a chilled metal bowl and a wire whisk, whip the cream until stiff, adding the granulated sugar and the confectioners' sugar.

Remove the shell from the tart pan and transfer it to a serving dish. Arrange the strawberries all around the edge of the tart. Use a pastry bag to mound the whipped cream in the center of the tart, leaving a space between the cream and the ring of strawberries. Serve, slicing like a pie.

SERVES 6 TO 8.

*V*enetian cafés offer their own special cookies. Here one is likely to find almond cookies, often flavored with chocolate, raisins, or glacéed fruit and meant to be eaten dipped in a favorite liqueur.

One of the most popular—and certainly the oldest—cafés in Venice in which to enjoy *biscotti* and liqueur is Florian. Founded in 1725, Florian's famous patrons have included the great Venetian playwright Goldoni, who even wrote a comedy called *La bot-*

tega di caffè (The Coffee Shop), Goethe, Canova, George Sand, de Musset, Dumas père, Wagner, Henry James, Dickens, Proust, and Pirandello. Many of these writers have left us descriptions of sitting at Florian, listening to the band and watching the passing carnival. Wagner wrote the second act of *Tristan and Isolde* in Venice and went to Florian daily. He was flattered when the band in the piazza on seeing him started playing some of his music. Several of Henry James' greatest works are set in Venice, and Florian is mentioned more than once.

Biscotti di mandorle con cioccolato
ALMOND COOKIES WITH CHOCOLATE

Preheat the oven to 375 degrees.

Put the almonds on a baking sheet and bake in the oven until the nuts are golden (about 20 minutes). Finely grind one third of the toasted almonds and coarsely grind the remaining almonds.

Put the flour on a pastry board in a mound and make a well in the flour. Put the finely and coarsely ground almonds, sugar, eggs, salt, and baking soda in the well and mix all of these ingredients together with a wooden spoon. Then start incorporating the flour, little by little, until all but 2 tablespoons of the flour has been incorporated. Knead the dough for 2 minutes; then add the chocolate pieces, gently incorporating them into the dough while kneading it on the leftover flour.

Preheat the oven to 375 degrees. Lightly butter and flour a baking sheet.

Divide the dough into 4 pieces. With your hands, shape each piece into a long thin roll about ½ inch in diameter. Place the rolls on the prepared baking sheet. Beat the egg white slightly in a small bowl and brush the tops of the 4 rolls with it. Bake for 20 minutes.

Remove the rolls from the oven and, with a long knife, cut at a 45-degree angle (diagonally) every ½ inch to get the shape required for this type of *biscotti*. Return the *biscotti* to the oven, lower the oven temperature to 225 degrees, and bake for 30 minutes. Remove from the oven and let cool completely before serving.

4	ounces blanched almonds
2½	cups unbleached all-purpose flour
¾	cup granulated sugar
2	extra large eggs
	Pinch of salt
1	teaspoon baking soda
3	ounces semisweet chocolate chips or "morsels"
1	extra large egg white

*V*enice expresses its nature most fully in Carnival season. The week-long celebration before Lent gives Venetians an opportunity to revive the traditional carnival practices of wearing costumes and masks and to indulge in all-night revels. This Chocolate Carnival Cake, with its handmade chocolate roses, is special enough for this once-a-year occasion.

Dolce di Carnevale
CHOCOLATE CARNIVAL CAKE

Prepare the *pasta Genovese*: Preheat the oven to 350 degrees. Butter a 10-inch cake pan and fit a piece of wax paper over the bottom of the pan. Butter the wax paper.

Melt the 6 tablespoons of butter in the top of a double boiler over barely simmering water. Remove the top of the double boiler from the heat and let the butter cool.

Sift the cake flour and the cocoa powder together onto a board.

Put 5 cups of cold water into a deep stockpot and put the pot over medium heat. The water should be just hot enough to steam a little, but no hotter. There should be enough space between the top of the water and the top of the pot so that the water will not touch the insert when it is put into the pot.

Put the eggs and granulated sugar into an unlined copper bowl and fit the bowl into the stockpot. Start beating the eggs and sugar together with a wire whisk until the sugar is completely dissolved and a long ribbon is formed when the whisk is lifted from the mixture. Remove the bowl from the pot and gently fold in the cooled melted butter and the sifted flour mixture. Then add the orange extract and salt. Pour the batter into the prepared cake pan and bake for about 35 minutes. Remove the cake from the oven, let it rest for 5 minutes, and unmold it onto a rack. Remove the wax paper and let the cake stand until it is completely cool (about 1 hour).

Prepare the filling, using the ingredients and quantities listed above, following the instructions for *Zabaione secco* on page 58, mixing the sugars with the egg yolks at the beginning and continuing to mix until the yolks turn a lighter color. Transfer the prepared *zabaione* to a crockery or glass bowl. Let it stand until cool (about 1 hour).

Prepare the chocolate strip and roses: Pour some water into the bottom part of a double boiler and bring it to a boil over medium heat.

Chop the chocolate coarsely and transfer it to the top part of a double boiler. When the water in the bottom part of the double boiler comes to a boil, lower the heat, insert the top of the double boiler over the water, and stir the chocolate with a wooden spoon until it is completely melted; then stir in the butter until it is completely amalgamated with the chocolate. Remove the top of the double boiler from the heat and stir the corn syrup into the chocolate mixture; then stir in the brandy and continue to stir until the chocolate mixture is very smooth and rather thick. Spread the cooled chocolate on half of a long sheet of plastic wrap and fold the other half of the plastic wrap over the layer of chocolate to completely cover it. Transfer the plastic-wrapped chocolate to a baking sheet and refrigerate it for at least 1 hour.

Slice the cake horizontally into 2 layers. Spread the cooled *zabaione* filling on top of the bottom layer and cover it with the top cake layer. Transfer the filled cake layers to a cake stand.

Remove the cooled chocolate from the refrigerator and use a hand pasta machine to roll out half of the layer of chocolate, passing it through the widest roller setting, until it is very smooth and easy to work with (see pages 86–87). Then begin stretching the layer of chocolate until you have a very long strip of chocolate no more than ⅛ inch thick and long enough to

FOR THE *PASTA GENOVESE*

6 tablespoons (3 ounces) sweet butter

1 cup cake flour

¼ cup unsweetened cocoa powder, preferably Dutch

8 whole extra large eggs

1 cup granulated sugar

1 teaspoon orange extract

Pinch of salt

FOR THE FILLING

3 extra large egg yolks

4 tablespoons granulated sugar

1 teaspoon confectioners' sugar

½ cup dry Marsala wine

¼ cup light rum

FOR THE CHOCOLATE STRIP AND ROSES

20 ounces semisweet chocolate

2 tablespoons (1 ounce) sweet butter at room temperature

10 ounces heavy corn syrup

2 tablespoons brandy

PLUS

1 cup heavy cream

2 tablespoons granulated sugar

3 tablespoons confectioners' sugar

encircle the cake completely. Do not be concerned if the edges of the chocolate strip are irregular. Use the chocolate strip to completely encircle the side of the cake. The chocolate strip will extend above the top of the cake. Fold it in over the top of the cake slightly (see photo on previous page). Refrigerate the cake until needed.

To prepare the roses, divide the remaining chocolate into 10 pieces. Cut each piece into 5 smaller pieces. Use 4 of the pieces to make the rose petals by placing the pieces on a marble slab and pressing them in a circular motion with an average-sized light bulb until they are very thin. Shape the fifth piece into a small cone by hand.

Use a knife to remove each thin rose petal from the marble. Wrap the petals one over the other around the narrow end of the cone, folding the petals outward to form full-blown roses. As each rose is shaped, put it on a wax-paper lined plate in the refrigerator to harden.

While the roses are hardening, whip the heavy cream with the granulated sugar and 1 teaspoon of the confectioners' sugar in a chilled metal bowl with a wire whisk until stiff.

Remove the cake from the refrigerator and place one rose in the center of the cake. Arrange the remaining roses around the edge of the cake. Arrange the whipped cream around the rose in the center. Use a small sieve to sift the remaining sugar all over the top of the cake.

Acknowledgments

A book of this scope requires the help of many people and I am grateful for the graciousness of so many, but especially the following: Andy Stewart, whose initial enthusiasm for the project infected us all; designer Nai Chang; and my sympathetic and skillful editors, Leslie Stoker and Marya Dalrymple, for literary and visual help, respectively.

Thanks to Laurie Goldrich, for her help in coordinating the photography in Italy; David Ross for writing the captions; Mr. Dominis's assistants, Neri Fadigati and Paolo Castaldi; my cooking assistants in Italy and New York, Wendy Bridgman, Arlene Battifarano, Yocheved Hirsch, and Florence Polizzi.

I am grateful to Audrey and Bernie Berman for introducing me to Marina and Simone Di Cagno, who acquainted me with the beauty and richness of Puglia and helped me with so many of the arrangements. My thanks to so many helpful people in Italy: Nicola Bulgari; Giovanni Ramunni; Dott. Giorgio Orlandini of Parma; the Martini family, Cheesemakers of Parma; Dott. Enrico Citterio and his associates; the administration of Villa d'Este, its chef, Luciano Parolari, and personally to Jean and Luca Salvadore; Conte Neri Capponi; Sig. Sergio Manetti; Fattoria Castellare in Castellina in Chianti; Principe Fabio Romacelli Filomarino, Castello Marchione, Conversano; the Urbani family of Scheggino; Avv. Fabrizio Vitaletti, the bakery in Sesto Fiorentino; the people of the beautiful medieval village of San Gusmè, their mayor and their priest; the Pedone family, cheesemakers in Putignano; Antico Caffè del Moro in Florence; Bagno Bruno in Forte dei Marmi; Caffè Florian in Venice; Ditta Alfredo Raffaelli, terra-cotta makers in Sinalunga; Hotel Augustus, Hotel Continental, and Hotel Lungarno in Florence; Hotel dei Duchi in Spoleto; Hotel Stendahl and Hotel Toscanini in Parma; Il Salumaio in Milan; Ristorante Arnaldo, Rubiera di Modena; Ristorante "Carmagnini del '500'," Pontenuovo di Calenzano, not only for the help of the restaurant, but for the considerable personal help of Saverio Carmagnini, himself; Ristorante La Vecchia Cucina in Florence; Ristorante Il Ponte in Scheggino; Ristorante La Delfina in Artimino; Trattoria La Vecchia Bettola in Florence; Sbigoli Terra Cotta Shop in Florence; the Administration of Villa La Ferdinanda in Artimino; the Monuments Office of Parma; the Monuments Office of Mantua; Mario Conti, my fruit and vegetable supplier in San Lorenzo Market in Florence, and all the other suppliers in Florence and all over Italy; our very special driver, Marcello Tiberi; and my sister, Lella, in Florence.

Thank you to my warm and helpful friends in the United States: Lydia Fischler and Sarah Malone; Gérard Choisnet, pastry chef at Delices La Côte Basque in New York; and Akron Meats, my supplier in New York.

Special thanks go to Mario Buccellati in New York, for the silver, flatware, and table decoration pieces; Ginori, in Florence and New York, for the china table settings; Tognana in Treviso, for china; Cristallo di Censo Colle Val d'Elsa for the crystal ware and glasses; Tessilarte, in Florence, for all the tablecloths and napkins; Sig. Cecchi for dishes from his showroom in New York.

And, finally, my thanks to Henry Weinberg, without whose help this book could never have been done.

Appendix

Solid Measures Conversion Chart

U.S. and Imperial measures		Metric measures	
ounces	pounds	grams	kilos
1		28	
2		56	
3½		100	
4	¼	112	
5		140	
6		168	
8	½	225	
9		250	¼
12	¾	340	
16	1	450	
18		500	½
20	1¼	560	
24	1½	675	
27		750	¾
28	1¾	780	
32	2	900	
36	2¼	1000	1
40	2½	1100	
48	3	1350	
54		1500	1½
64	4	1800	
72	4½	2000	2
80	5	2250	2¼
90		2500	2½
100	6	2800	2¾

Oven Temperature Equivalents

Fahrenheit	Gas mark	Celsius	Heat of oven
225	¼	105	very cool
250	½	120	very cool
275	1	135	cool
300	2	150	cool
325	3	160	moderate
350	4	175	moderate
375	5	190	fairly hot
400	6	200	fairly hot
425	7	222	hot
450	8	230	very hot
475	9	245	very hot

Note: Oven temperatures are given as degrees Fahrenheit throughout the text.

Liquid Measures Conversion Chart

Fluid ounces	U.S. measures	Imperial measures	Milliliters
	1 tsp	1 tsp	5
¼	2 tsp	1 dessert-spoon	7
½	1 tbs	1 tbs	15
1	2 tbs	2 tbs	28
2	¼ cup	4 tbs	56
4	½ cup or ¼ pint		110
5		¼ pint or 1 gill	140
6	¾ cup		170
8	1 cup or ½ pint		225
9			250, ¼ liter
10	1¼ cups	½ pint	280
12	1½ cups or ¾ pint		340
15		¾ pint	420
16	2 cups or 1 pint		450
18	2¼ cups		500, ½ liter
20	2½ cups	1 pint	560
24	3 cups or 1½ pints		675
25		1¼ pints	700
27	3½ cups		750
30	3¾ cups	1½ pints	840
32	4 cups or 2 pints or 1 quart		900
35		1¾ pints	980
36	4½ cups		1000, 1 liter
40	5 cups or 2½ pints	2 pints or 1 quart	1120
48	6 cups or 3 pints		1350
50		2½ pints	1400
60	7½ cups	3 pints	1680
64	8 cups or 4 pints or 2 quarts		1800
72	9 cups		2000, 2 liters
80	10 cups or 5 pints	4 pints	2250
96	12 cups or 3 quarts		2700
100		5 pints	2800

Note: All conversions are approximate. They have been rounded off to the nearest convenient measure.

English and American Terminology Equivalents

arugola	rocket lettuce	eggplants	aubergines	semisweet chocolate	baking chocolate
Boston lettuce	lettuce	fava beans	broad beans	shrimp	large prawns
broiler	grill	grind	mince	sweet butter	unsalted butter
broth	stock	guinea hen	guinea fowl	variety meats	offal (liver, kidneys,
confectioners' sugar	icing sugar	heavy cream	double cream		sweetbreads, etc.)
cornmeal	polenta	jelly roll pan	baking tray	zucchini	courgettes

Index

Italic numbers indicate photographs.